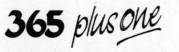

VEGETARIAN MAIN MEALS

Wholesome and appetizing vegetarian dishes to see you through the whole year.

D0783993

365 plus one
VEGETARIAN
MAIN MEALS

A Year of Ideas for Delicious Wholefood Dishes

JANET HUNT

Thorsons

An Imprint of HarperCollinsPublishers

Thorsons
An Imprint of HarperCollins*Publishers*
77–85 Fulham Palace Road,
Hammersmith, London W6 8JB

Published by Thorsons 1987
11   13   15   14   12   10

A catalogue record for this book is available from the British Library

ISBN 0 7225 0895 6

Printed in Great Britain at The Bath Press, Avon

Contents

Introduction

'What's for dinner?' is a question that can strike chill into the heart of the most enthusiastic cook. Day after day, week after week, summer and winter, it isn't easy to keep coming up with meals that taste good, are nutritionally sound, and not too difficult to prepare. Especially after a hectic day, or during a heatwave, or when you're already dipped into the last of the housekeeping — and even more so if you're vegetarian.

At least, it wasn't until now.

This book has been written to help anyone who has ever been stuck for an idea. Using a range of familiar wholefoods (many now available from supermarkets as well as speciality shops), it shows how you can ring enough changes to serve up something different every day of the year. The secret is to use a variety of cooking techniques, to add zip and interest with spices and herbs, to change the taste completely by trying unusual combinations of ingredients, by adding sauces. In short: by being adventurous.

Using this Book

The recipes are divided into four sections, one for each of the seasons, with thirteen weeks of recipes within each section. They have been carefully chosen to take into account the vegetables and fruits you are most likely to find in your local shops and garden, as well as considering the kind of meals you and your family will enjoy most. For example, you may fancy nothing more than a large, crisp salad on a hot summer's evening; or a chilled soup with fresh muffins. In winter you'll probably prefer your meals to be heavier, more filling. There are also recipes for dishes that require more exotic ingredients, and more preparation time — just the thing for when you're entertaining. These are usually given as weekend suggestions.

And just in case you can't think what to serve with your main course, you'll find ideas for accompaniments, too.

How closely you follow the book is entirely up to you. You can work straight through from the 1st January to Christmas Day (there's a special recipe for that feast too). Or you can dip into it, try any recipe that catches your eye — whatever the time of year, whatever the occasion. Use frozen vegetables if the ones you need are out of season, though don't make a habit of it — all food items are best when fresh.

And if you think this book contains enough recipes to get you through one year, you're wrong. Use it as a starting point and it will keep you going much, much longer. Try adapting the recipes you particularly enjoy. Fill a flan base with a favourite vegetable or bean dish (reducing the liquid content if necessary); do the same with pancakes. Vary the ingredients according to what's in your fridge or cupboard — use a different cheese from the one specified, different nuts, tofu or dry roasted beans instead of either. Try chilling a soup you usually serve hot, making left-over pasta or grains into a salad. The ideas are endless once you stop thinking along conventional lines and see the kitchen as a place to be imaginative, creative — and to have fun.

Eating for Health

As well as tasting good, the recipes in this book are nutritionally balanced to supply you and your family with the basic requirements for good health. Though there is disagreement, even amongst nutritionists, about exactly how and what we should eat, there are a number of points about which most of them seem to agree. We should eat less of the saturated fats found in meat and dairy produce, use less salt, restrict or eliminate completely our intake of white sugar and other refined, processed foods. These should be replaced with more whole grains, fresh vegetables and fruits.

Even so, we are all individuals with varying needs. Protein, for example, is certainly necessary for health, but the amount we can efficiently use will vary enormously, some of us actually functioning better on a very low amount. Whereas one person may need lots of carbohydrate to keep his or her energy level high, someone else may put on weight as soon as he or she looks at bread. Then, of course, there are taste preferences — and although the main purpose of eating is to take in

Introduction

nourishment, it is also important to enjoy our food and our mealtimes.

With individual choice in mind, most recipes in this book do not specify butter or margarine (on the few occasions butter alone is recommended, this is because of its flavour advantage). Butter is rich in saturated fats, but it is a natural food — if you do decide to use it, stick to the un-dyed, salt-free kind (and still keep it to a minimum). Soft vegetable margarines, while low in cholesterol and high in polyunsaturated fats, are a processed food. It's up to you. Use, too, the cheeses you prefer if those suggested do not appeal. Edam is one of the lowest-fat hard cheeses, and can replace Cheddar in any recipe. There are now a variety of medium- and low-fat cream cheeses that work well in most recipes except where full-fat cream cheese is needed to obtain a thicker texture.

A Vegan Diet

A growing number of people want to eliminate dairy produce as well as flesh food from their diets, for reasons of compassion, health, concern about world food resources (and the wastefulness of producing these foods on a large scale) — or for all three reasons! For such people, there are already a large number of recipes in this book that can be used as they stand. Many more can easily be adapted by the substitution of vegan products for dairy. For example, use soya milk instead of cow's, soya flour instead of eggs when a binding ingredient is needed. Where grated cheese tops a dish, try using chopped or flaked nuts instead, or sprinkle the dish with breadcrumbs or crushed potato crisps for a different texture. An excellent white sauce can be made using vegetable oil, flour, water or stock, and then a spoonful or two of tahini to give the traditional creamy taste. Coarsely mashed tofu makes a good alternative to chopped, hard-boiled egg in any dish; there is now available a completely vegan yogurt that can replace the dairy variety in dishes or with desserts; a non-dairy mayonnaise just as smooth and tasty as the more conventional egg-based variety; smooth peanut butter stirred into soups or casseroles makes a different but delicious alternative to soured cream. And in many cases you can just leave out the offending ingredient without substantially changing the dish — though you may like to add extra herbs and seasoning to boost the flavour.

All recipes are for 4 average servings. For easy reference, basic recipes referred to have been grouped together at the end of the book.

SPRING

Week 1:
Monday
Creamy Onion and Pepper Casserole

2 large onions
2 large green peppers
½ pint (285ml) white
  sauce (see page 153)
6 oz (170g) curd cheese
2 small packets of potato
  crisps
2 oz (55g) flaked almonds
Seasoning to taste
2 oz (55g) wholemeal
  breadcrumbs

1 Slice the onions and peppers and steam or cook in the minimum amount of water for 10 minutes to soften. Drain well.
2 Make the white sauce and stir in the mashed cheese, so that it melts. If the sauce seems too thick, add a drop more liquid.
3 Arrange half the crisps in the bottom of an ovenproof dish, top with half the vegetables, half the nuts, and half of the sauce. Season as you do so.
4 Repeat the layering as above to use up the rest of the ingredients. Top with the breadcrumbs.
5 Bake at 350°F/180°C (Gas Mark 4) for 30 minutes.

Serve with: Jacket potatoes, plus a red cabbage, orange and raisin salad.

Tuesday
Dutch Cheese Slices

½ lb (225g) shortcrust
  pastry (see page 151)
For the topping
½ lb (225g) Gouda cheese,
  sliced
1 green pepper, cut into
  strips
4 oz (115g) mushrooms,
  sliced
½-1 teaspoon marjoram
Seasoning to taste
Vegetable oil

1 Roll out the prepared pastry and use to line a Swiss-roll tin.
2 Place the sliced cheese evenly over the pastry base.
3 Arrange the pepper and mushrooms in a decorative pattern over the cheese.
4 Sprinkle with marjoram and seasoning. Trickle a little oil over the top of the vegetables.
5 Bake at 400°F/200°C (Gas Mark 6) for 20-30 minutes, or until cooked. Cut into slices and serve hot.

Serve with: Broccoli or green beans, and new potatoes lightly steamed and topped with a knob of butter.

Wednesday
Millet Patties

½ lb (225g) millet
1 pint (570ml) vegetable
    stock or water
2 tablespoons vegetable oil
1 stick celery, sliced
½ small onion, sliced
½ small red pepper, sliced
Marjoram
Seasoning to taste
6 oz (170g) grated Cheddar
    cheese

1 Cook the millet in the vegetable stock until all the liquid has been absorbed, and the millet is thick.
2 Heat the vegetable oil in a pan and sauté the celery, onion and pepper until soft.
3 Mix together the millet, vegetables, majoram, seasoning and grated cheese, then set aside to cool.
4 When ready shape pieces of the mixture into round patties. Cook under a medium grill for a few minutes each side, until lightly browned.

Serve with: A cucumber and yogurt salad, plus wholemeal rolls.

Thursday
Celery and Soured Cream Macaroni

½ lb (225g) wholemeal
    macaroni
2 sticks celery, chopped
1 oz (30g) margarine or
    butter
Seasoning to taste
⅓ pint (200ml) soured cream
1 oz (30g) wholemeal
    breadcrumbs
1 oz (30g) salted peanuts,
    coarsely chopped

1 Bring a pan of water to the boil and add the macaroni and celery. Cook for 10 minutes, or until both pasta and celery are just tender. Drain well.
2 Stir in the fat so that it melts, add seasoning, then quickly stir in the cream. Turn into an ovenproof dish and top with the breadcrumbs and nuts.
3 Bake at 400°F/200°C (Gas Mark 6) for 15 minutes, or until crisp and golden.

Serve with: Hot grilled tomatoes, and maybe some French bread.

Friday
'Sausage' and 'Bacon' Pancakes

½ pint (285ml) pancake
    batter (see page 152)
Vegetable oil for frying

For the filling:
1 oz (30g) margarine or
    butter
1 onion, finely chopped
4 oz (115g) mushrooms,
    sliced
2 large tomatoes, chopped
Seasoning to taste
Soya 'bacon' bits
Small tin soya 'sausages',
    sliced
Parsley to garnish
Tomato sauce to serve (see
    page 153)

1 Make up the batter and set aside in a cool place.
2 Heat the fat in a saucepan and, when melted, add the onion, mushrooms and tomatoes.
3 Cook gently, stirring occasionally, until all the vegetables are cooked. Stir in seasoning and a generous amount of soya 'bacon' bits. Add the 'sausages'. Keep the mixture warm.
4 Heat a little oil in a heavy-based pan. Whisk the batter and pour in just enough to cover the base. Cook gently until lightly browned underneath, tipping the pan occasionally to spread the mixture evenly.
5 Flip the pancake, or use a spatula to turn it. Cook the other side briefly. Transfer to a dish and keep warm while making the rest of the pancakes.
6 Fill each pancake with some of the mixture, roll up, and garnish with fresh parsley. Serve with tomato sauce.

Serve with: A crisp green salad and, if liked, lightly steamed new potatoes.

Saturday
Felaffels

*1 lb (455g) chick-peas,
  soaked overnight
1 onion, finely chopped
1-2 cloves garlic, crushed
2 tablespoons olive oil
1 tablespoon chopped
  parsley
1 teaspoon ground
  coriander
½ teaspoon ground cumin
½ teaspoon turmeric
½ teaspoon cayenne
  pepper
Seasoning to taste
Juice of 1 lemon
1 egg (optional)
Wholemeal breadcrumbs
  (if needed)
Wholemeal flour to coat
Vegetable oil for frying*

1 Rinse the chick-peas, place in a saucepan, add fresh water and bring to the boil. Fast boil for 10 minutes, then lower the heat, cover, and cook for about an hour, or until tender.
2 Drain the chick-peas and grate, grind or blend them together with the onion and garlic.
3 In a bowl combine the paste with the oil, parsley, spices, seasoning, lemon juice and egg. The mixture should be thick and fairly firm; add a few wholemeal breadcrumbs or extra lemon juice to adjust the consistency if necessary.
4 Shape into balls about the size of walnuts and coat with flour.
5 Deep fry, a few at a time, in hot oil until golden and crisp on the outside. Drain on paper towels and keep the felaffels warm whilst cooking the rest of the mixture in the same way.

Serve with: Wholemeal pitta bread, a cucumber and mint salad, and a sauce — either hummus (made with chick-peas, tahini and parsley) or yogurt.

Sunday
Tofu and Tomato Flan

*½ lb (225g) shortcrust
  pastry (see page 151)*

For the filling:
*6 oz (170g) cooked
  sweetcorn
1 tablespoon chopped
  chives
1 tablespoon chopped
  parsley
10 oz (285g) silken tofu
Seasoning to taste
2 large tomatoes, sliced
  into rings
½ teaspoon paprika
Watercress to garnish*

1 Make up the pastry, and set aside in a cool place.
2 Drain the sweetcorn kernels and mix together with the herbs and well-mashed tofu. Add seasoning to taste.
3 Roll out the pastry on a floured board, and use to line a medium-sized flan dish.
4 Pour in the tofu and sweetcorn mixture. Arrange tomato rings to cover the top. Sprinkle with paprika.
5 Bake at 400°F/200°C (Gas Mark 6) for 20-30 minutes, or until the pastry is cooked. Garnish with watercress.

Serve with: A potato salad, plus a green salad of lettuce, cucumber, a little extra watercress.

Spring

Week 2:
Monday
Rice and Split Pea Soup

4 oz (115g) split peas,
soaked overnight
2 spring onions, finely
chopped
2 carrots, finely chopped
2 sticks celery, finely
chopped
Approx. 1¾ pints (1 litre)
vegetable stock
Seasoning to taste
Soya sauce
6 oz (170g) cooked brown
rice
2 chopped, hard-boiled eggs
to garnish
Parsley to garnish

1 Drain the peas and put into a clean pan. Add the onions, carrots and celery.
2 Add the stock, bring to the boil, then cover and simmer for 50-60 minutes, or until tender.
3 Stir in the seasoning, soya sauce and rice, cook for just a few minutes more so that all the ingredients are hot. Add a drop more stock if the soup is too thick.
4 Garnish with the eggs and parsley.

Serve with: A coleslaw with nuts or cubes of cheese added, plus fresh wholemeal bread.

Note: If you have any left-over, or any other pre-cooked, beans handy, you can prepare this soup in 10 minutes.

Tuesday
Turnip and Carrot au Gratin

1 lb (455g) turnips, peeled
and sliced
1 lb (455g) carrots, peeled
and sliced
½ pint (285ml) white
sauce (see page 00)
3 tablespoons cream or
plain yogurt
Seasoning to taste
3 oz (85g) wholemeal
breadcrumbs
3 oz (85g) grated Cheddar
cheese
Parsley to garnish

1 Place the turnips and carrots in a pan, cover with water and bring to the boil. Lower the heat and cook for 20 minutes, or until tender. Drain.

2 Make the sauce and add the cream or yogurt and seasoning. Stir in the prepared vegetables and turn into a shallow ovenproof dish. Smooth the top.
3 Mix together the crumbs and cheese, and sprinkle over the top. Pop under a moderate grill for just a few minutes, until the top is crisp and brown. Garnish with chopped parsley.

Serve with: French-fried potatoes, and a green vegetable such as spring greens or young spinach.

Wednesday
Apple and 'Ham' Omelette

6 eggs
2 tablespoons water
Seasoning to taste
2 tablespoons vegetable oil
1 small onion, sliced
3 oz (85g) soya 'ham'
chunks, hydrated in
water
1 large apple
1½ oz (45g) butter or
margarine

1 Beat the eggs lightly with the water and seasoning.
2 Heat the oil in a pan and fry the onion to soften. Add the drained 'ham' chunks and cook a few minutes more, stirring, until they begin to colour.
3 Finely slice the apple and add to the pan. Cook just long enough to heat through. Season to taste.
4 Melt most of the fat in a clean pan and, when hot, pour in half the egg mixture. Cook gently, lifting the sides and tilting the pan to allow uncooked egg to run underneath.
5 Continue cooking until the omelette begins to set. Spoon in half the 'ham' and apple mixture, fold the omelette, and divide in two. Serve at once, or keep it warm.
6 Use up the rest of the ingredients in the same way to make two more servings.

Serve with: Jacket potatoes, grilled tomatoes and mushrooms.

Thursday
Cauliflower Lentil Stew

3 tablespoons vegetable oil
1 onion, sliced
1 green pepper, sliced
1 carrot, sliced
1 small cauliflower
1 oz (30g) wholemeal flour
4 oz (115g) split red lentils
½ pint (285ml) vegetable
   stock or water
Seasoning to taste
1 teaspoon marjoram
2 oz (55g) walnuts,
   coarsely chopped
Parsley to garnish

1 Heat the vegetable oil in a pan and fry the onion, pepper and carrot for a few minutes. Break the cauliflower into florets and add to the pan.
2 Sprinkle in the flour and cook briefly.
3 Add the lentils, stock, seasoning and marjoram. Stir well. Bring gently to the boil, then lower the heat and simmer for about 20 minutes, or until all the ingredients are cooked. Stir occasionally, and add more liquid if necessary.
4 Stir in the nuts and cook a minute more. Serve garnished with parsley.

Serve with: Potato crisps and a tomato, cucumber and red pepper salad.

Friday
Nut Meat Bake

½ lb (225g) brown rice
1 pint (570ml) vegetable
   stock or water
1 small onion, finely
   chopped
1 small green pepper,
   finely chopped
2 sticks celery, finely
   chopped
½-1 teaspoon marjoram
Seasoning to taste
Medium tin nut meat,
   sliced
2 large tomatoes, sliced
Parsley to garnish

1 Put the rice in a pan and cook in the liquid for 30-40 minutes, or until just tender.
2 Stir the onion, pepper and celery into the rice with the marjoram and seasoning.
3 Transfer to a shallow ovenproof dish.

4 Arrange overlapping slices of the tinned nut meat and tomatoes on top of the rice mixture to make a decorative pattern.
5 Bake, covered, at 375°F/190°C (Gas Mark 5) for 20 minutes, or until heated through.

Serve with: A salad of chicory, celery and orange slices.

Saturday
Curried Parsnip Flan

For the pastry:
½ lb (225g) wholemeal
   flour
Pinch of sea salt
5 oz (140g) margarine
Approx. 2 tablespoons cold
   water

For the filling:
2 medium parsnips, peeled
   and cubed
2 tablespoons vegetable oil
1 onion, chopped
1-2 teaspoons curry
   powder
Seasoning to taste
2 eggs, lightly beaten
4 tablespoons cooked peas
Tomato to garnish

1 Sift together the flour and salt.
2 Use a fork to mix together the margarine and water, then gradually add the flour, mixing well, to make a firm dough. Knead until smooth. Set aside in a cool place for at least 30 minutes.
3 Steam the parsnips until very soft. Drain well.
4 Heat the oil in a clean pan. Fry the onion until it begins to soften, then stir in the curry powder and cook a few minutes more.
5 Off the heat, mash the drained parsnips into the curry mixture to make a thick purée. Season to taste. Stir in the beaten eggs and the peas.
6 Roll out the pastry and use to line a medium-sized flan dish. Spoon in the parsnip mixture and smooth the top.
7 Bake at 375°F/190°C (Gas Mark 5) for 30 minutes, or until set.

Serve with: Wholemeal chapatis, plus a beetroot salad in yogurt dressing.

Sunday
Persian-Style Rice

¾ lb (340g) brown rice
1½ pints (850ml) water
2 potatoes, peeled and
   thinly sliced
2 oz (55g) cashew nuts
2 oz (55g) dried apricots,
   soaked in water
¼ teaspoon saffron
   threads
⅛ pint (70ml) hot water
2 oz (55g) margarine or
   butter
Seasoning to taste
½ pint (285ml) natural
   yogurt
1-2 spring onions, finely
   chopped

1 Rinse the rice, then put in a pan and cook in the water for 30-40 minutes, or until just tender (add more liquid during cooking if necessary). Drain well.
2 In a greased ovenproof dish arrange very thin slices of potato. Cover with half the rice, half the nuts, and half the chopped apricots.
3 Dissolve the saffron threads in the hot water, and dribble a little of the saffron water over the rice. Add a few knobs of fat and seasoning.
4 Repeat this process to use up all the remaining ingredients.
5 Bake, covered, at 350°F/180°C (Gas Mark 4) for about 30 minutes, or until the potatoes are cooked.
6 Mix together the yogurt and spring onions, and hand round at the table to be spooned over the rice.

Serve with: A lettuce, green and red pepper salad with watercress sprigs.

Week 3:
Monday
Macaroni Mushroom Bake

4 oz (115g) wholemeal
   macaroni
2 eggs, beaten
⅓ pint (200ml) milk
2 oz (55g) wholemeal
   breadcrumbs
2 tablespoons vegetable oil
1 small onion, sliced
1 small red pepper, sliced
6 oz (170g) mushrooms,
   sliced
6 oz (170g) grated Cheddar
   cheese
Seasoning to taste
1 oz (30g) sunflower seeds

1 Cook the macaroni in a saucepan of boiling water for 10 minutes, or until just tender, then drain well.
2 Mix with the beaten eggs, milk and breadcrumbs.
3 Heat most of the vegetable oil in a pan and gently fry the onion and pepper until they begin to soften.
4 Add the rest of the oil and the mushrooms. Cook for just a few minutes more.
5 Stir the well-drained vegetables into the macaroni mixture, adding the grated cheese and seasoning.
6 Turn into a greased ovenproof dish, smooth the top and sprinkle with seeds. Bake at 375°F/190°C (Gas Mark 5) for 30 minutes, or until set.

Serve with: Hot steamed Brussels sprouts and, if liked, a tomato and spring onion salad.

Tuesday
'Ham' Charlotte

3 oz (85g) soya 'ham'
   chunks, hydrated in
   water
4 slices wholemeal bread
2 oz (55g) margarine or
   butter
⅓ pint (200ml) white
   sauce
4 oz (115g) grated Cheddar
   cheese
Seasoning to taste
Parsley sprigs

1 Cook the 'ham' chunks in a pan of water for 5-10 minutes, or until just tender. Drain well and then chop or shred the chunks coarsely.

2 Cut the bread into fingers.

3 Melt the fat and fry the bread, on both sides, until crisp. Arrange half the bread across the base of a shallow ovenproof dish.

4 Make the white sauce, add the cheese, seasoning, and the 'ham' chunks. Spread this mixture over the bread, then cover with the rest of the bread.

5 Bake at 375°F/190°C (Gas Mark 5) for 15-20 minutes.

6 Garnish with parsley sprigs.

Serve with: Small new potatoes, steamed and sprinkled with parsley. A salad of raw Brussels sprouts, finely shredded, mixed with beansprouts, tomato and sweetcorn would make a good accompaniment.

Wednesday
Potato, Bean and Fennel Salad

1 lb (455g) new potatoes
½ lb (225g) broad beans,
  shelled
1 small fennel bulb, finely
  chopped
Seasoning to taste
Chopped parsley
Mayonnaise
Soya 'bacon' bits to
  garnish

1 Scrub and then cook the potatoes in a pan of water until just tender. When cool enough to handle cut into cubes.

2 If the broad beans are young and tender they can be left raw; otherwise, cook them lightly in water, then drain well and cool.

3 Mix together the potatoes, beans and fennel; season generously and add chopped parsley to taste. Stir in just enough mayonnaise to moisten, handing round extra at the table. Garnish with soya 'bacon' bits.

Serve with: A cucumber and tomato salad with blue cheese dressing. If something hot is preferred, try grilled tomatoes sprinkled with grated cheese or sesame seeds.

Thursday
Quick Rice Ring

½ lb (225g) brown rice
1 pint (570ml) water
1 oz (30g) margarine or
  butter
2 eggs, lightly beaten
Seasoning to taste
¾ lb (340g) frozen mixed
  vegetables
6 oz (170g) cream, curd or
  Ricotta cheese
1 oz (30g) pumpkin seeds

1 Rinse the rice, then put in a saucepan, cover with water and cook for 30-40 minutes, or until tender, adding more liquid as necessary.

2 Mix the fat and beaten eggs into the rice, and cook briefly until the mixture starts to set. Season to taste.

3 Meanwhile, cook the frozen vegetables in boiling water for as long as directed on the packet. Drain well.

4 Stir the cheese into the vegetables until it melts to form a sauce. Season well.

5 Press the rice mixture firmly into a lightly greased ring mould, then cover with a serving plate. Turn so that the plate is underneath, and carefully remove the ring.

6 Fill with the vegetable mixture. Sprinkle with the pumpkin seeds.

Serve with: A red cabbage and apple salad, topped with sprigs of watercress.

Friday
Alsatian Onion Tart

10 oz (285g) shortcrust
    pastry (see page 151)

For the filling:
2 oz (55g) margarine or
    butter
1¼ lb (565g) onions, sliced
1 oz (30g) wholemeal flour
3 eggs
3 tablespoons single cream
Seasoning to taste

1 Make the pastry and set aside in a cool place.
2 Melt the fat in a pan and gently fry most of the sliced onion until soft. Sprinkle with flour and cook a minute longer.
3 Beat the eggs, add the cream and seasoning, and stir into the onions.
4 Roll out the pastry, and use it to line a medium to large flan dish. Spoon in the onion mixture and smooth the top. Decorate with a few finely sliced onion rings, arranged in a circle. Bake at 400°F/200°C (Gas Mark 6) for 30 minutes, or until cooked.

Serve with: A salad of tomatoes, raw mushrooms, and olives, plus wholemeal French bread.

Saturday
Aubergine Lasagne with Pine Nuts

6 oz (170g) wholemeal
    lasagne
1 medium aubergine
2 tablespoons vegetable oil
1 onion, sliced
3 tomatoes, chopped
Marjoram
Seasoning to taste
4 oz (115g) Mozzarella
    cheese
1 oz (30g) margarine or
    butter
1 oz (30g) wholemeal flour
¼ pint (140ml) milk
¼ pint (140ml) natural
    yogurt
2 oz (55g) grated
    Parmesan cheese
1 oz (30g) pine nuts

1 Bring a large pan of water to the boil. Add the lasagne one sheet at a time and cook for 8 minutes, or until just tender. Drain, rinse in cold water, and lay out on a clean tea towel.
2 Peel the aubergine and cut into cubes. Heat the oil in a pan and sauté the aubergine with the onion. Stir frequently. Add the tomatoes, marjoram and seasoning, and cook a few minutes more, or until the vegetables are tender.
3 Arrange some of the lasagne in a lightly greased ovenproof dish. Top with some of the aubergine and a few thin slices of the cheese, and repeat to use up all the ingredients.
4 Melt the fat in a clean pan and add the flour. Sauté briefly. Add the milk and then the yogurt, cooking gently and stirring continually to make a smooth sauce. Season to taste.
5 Pour the sauce over the ingredients in the casserole. Top with the grated cheese.
6 Bake at 375°F/190°C (Gas Mark 5) for 30 minutes. Add the nuts halfway through the cooking time.

Serve with: A coleslaw of shredded cabbage and carrots mixed with chopped dried apricots.

Sunday
Cauliflower Wheatgerm Soufflettes

1 small cauliflower
2 oz (55g) margarine or
    butter
1 oz (30g) wholemeal flour
1 oz (30g) wheatgerm
⅓ pint (200ml) milk
Seasoning to taste
Good pinch of nutmeg
3 large eggs, separated

1 Wash and trim the cauliflower, then break into small florets. Melt ½ oz (15g) of the fat in a pan and cook the cauliflower gently, stirring frequently, until soft (add a spoonful or two of water if necessary). Drain well.
2 Melt the rest of the fat in a clean saucepan and stir in the flour, cooking briefly. Add the wheatgerm, stir to mix, then pour in the milk. Bring the mixture to the boil gently to make a thick sauce.
3 Add seasoning, nutmeg and the egg yolks. When well blended, stir in the cauliflower.
4 Whisk the egg whites until stiff and use a metal spoon to fold them carefully into the cauliflower mixture.
5 Spoon into 4 lightly greased ramekins. Bake at once in an oven preheated to 375°F/190°C (Gas Mark 5) for 20 minutes, or until puffed up and golden.

Serve with: A ratatouille salad sprinkled with walnuts. Hot or cold bulgur would also go well.

Week 4:
Monday
Tagliatelle with Broccoli

1 lb (455g) fresh broccoli
  or frozen equivalent
10 oz (285g) wholemeal
  tagliatelle
6 tablespoons vegetable
  oil, preferably olive
2 cloves garlic, (or to
  taste), chopped
Seasoning to taste
2 oz (55g) walnuts

1 Wash the broccoli, trim off coarse leaves and any thick stems, and cut remaining broccoli into small florets. Cook in a pan of boiling water for 3-4 minutes only, then drain well.
2 In a second pan of boiling water, cook the tagliatelle for 8 minutes or until just tender.
3 Meanwhile, heat the vegetable oil in a pan and add the finely chopped garlic, cooking gently to colour. Stir in the broccoli and heat through for a minute or two only.
4 Drain the tagliatelle, tip into a warmed serving dish, and top with the broccoli. Season to taste. Top with walnuts.

Serve with: Green pepper, tomato and onion salad, sprinkled with a few cooked beans or soya 'bacon' bits.

Tuesday
Cornish Vegetable Pasties

¾ lb (225g) shortcrust
  pastry (see page 151)

For the filling:
2 oz (55g) margarine or
  butter
1 onion, sliced
1 carrot, peeled and diced
1 parsnip, peeled and
  diced
1 potato, peeled and diced
4 tablespoons cooked peas
1 oz (30g) wholemeal flour
¼ pint (140ml) vegetable
  stock
Seasoning to taste
½ teaspoon marjoram
4 oz (115g) grated Cheddar
  cheese — optional
Milk to glaze

1 Make up the pastry, divide into four pieces, and roll each one into a circle.
2 Melt the fat in a pan and fry the sliced onion gently until it is soft but not browned.
3 Add the diced carrot, parsnip and potato to the onion. Stir well, then cook briefly before adding a spoonful or two of water and covering the pan. Simmer gently for 10 minutes or until the vegetables are tender.
4 Stir in the peas. Sprinkle the flour over the mixture, cook for a minute, then pour in the stock. Continue cooking until the sauce thickens.
5 Add seasoning, marjoram and cheese, if using it. Cool the mixture slightly.
6 Divide the vegetables between the pastry circles. Brush the edges with water and fold in half, pressing the edges together to seal. Brush lightly with milk. Transfer to an oiled baking sheet and cook in the oven at 400°F/200°C (Gas Mark 6) for 30 minutes.

Serve with: French-fried potatoes and a tomato and chicory salad.

Wednesday
Baked Vegetable Omelette

1 pepper, sliced
1 onion, sliced
2 tomatoes, coarsely
  chopped
2 tablespoons cooked sweetcorn
1 oz (30g) butter or
  margarine
6 eggs
2 oz (55g) grated Cheddar
  cheese
Seasoning to taste
Parsley to garnish

1 Cook the pepper and onion very briefly in a pan of boiling water. Drain well.
2 Add the tomatoes and sweetcorn, and mix lightly together.
3 Melt the fat in the base of a shallow ovenproof dish, and tip so that it is evenly distributed.
4 Arrange all the vegetables in the dish. Beat together the eggs, cheese and seasoning, and pour over the vegetables.
5 Bake at 400°F/200°C (Gas Mark 6) for about 10 minutes, or until just set — do not overcook. Cut into wedges, and garnish with plenty of fresh parsley.

Serve with: Potato slices in white sauce, plus a salad such as cucumber, endive and chicory.

Spring

Thursday
Creamy Mushroom Pancakes

½ pint (285ml) pancake
   batter (see page 152)
Vegetable oil for frying

For the filling:
½ lb (225g) mushrooms
1 oz (30g) margarine or
   butter
⅓ pint (200ml) soured
   cream
Squeeze of lemon juice
Seasoning to taste
1 teaspoon chopped fresh
   chives
A few knobs of butter
More chives, or parsley, to
   garnish

1 Whisk the batter. Heat the minimum amount of oil in a heavy-based pan and pour in a little of the batter. Cook the pancake gently, tipping the pan frequently, and when it begins to colour, flip or turn with a spatula. Cook a few minutes more, then keep it warm whilst making the rest of the pancakes.
2 Clean and trim the mushrooms and cut them into fairly thick, even slices. Melt the fat in a pan and sauté the mushrooms for about 5 minutes, stirring frequently.
3 Pour in the soured cream and lemon juice, add seasoning to taste and the chopped chives. Continue cooking very gently for a few minutes more, so that the cream is heated through, taking care that the mixture does not boil.
4 Divide the filling between the prepared pancakes, roll them up, and serve dabbed with a little extra butter, and garnished with herbs.

Serve with: A large mixed salad that includes strips of red and green peppers.

Friday
Millet Pilau

½ lb (225g) millet
2 tablespoons vegetable oil
½-1 clove garlic, crushed
2-3 spring onions, chopped
1¼ pints (700ml) water
4 oz (115g) mushrooms,
   sliced
2 oz (55g) cooked peas
2 oz (55g) sultanas
2 oz (55g) pine nuts
Seasoning to taste
Fresh mint to garnish
Natural yogurt to serve

1 Wash the millet, then drain well.
2 Heat the oil in a pan and lightly fry the crushed garlic and spring onions for a few minutes.
3 Add the millet, stir, and cook until it begins to colour.
4 Pour in the water, bring to the boil, then lower the heat and continue cooking until most of the water has been absorbed.
5 Stir in the mushrooms, peas, sultanas and nuts. Cook a few minutes more to heat through. Season to taste. Garnish with chopped mint.
6 Hand round yogurt at the table.

Serve with: A lettuce, mushroom and tomato salad with a creamy dressing.

Saturday
Swiss Chard Nut Loaf

½ lb (225g) Swiss chard
2 tablespoons vegetable oil
1 onion, finely sliced
1 clove garlic, crushed
½ lb (225g) walnuts,
   coarsely ground
4 oz (115g) dry wholemeal
   breadcrumbs
1 large egg, lightly beaten
2 oz (55g) bran
1 teaspoon tarragon, or to
   taste
Seasoning to taste
Vegetable stock as
   necessary

1 Trim the Swiss chard and wash well. Steam for 20 minutes or until tender. Drain, then chop and set aside.
2 Heat the oil in a pan and sauté the onion with the garlic. When soft mix with the chopped chard.
3 Add the nuts to the vegetables, together with the breadcrumbs, lightly beaten egg, bran, tarragon and seasoning.
4 Moisten with a little vegetable stock (or the water left from steaming the Swiss chard).
5 Lightly grease a medium-sized loaf tin, spoon in the mixture and smooth the top.
6 Bake at 350°F/180°C (Gas Mark 4) for 30 minutes, or until firm.

Serve with: Jacket potatoes, and a carrot and raisin salad.

Sunday
Leek and Aduki Crumble

For the base:
1 lb (455g) leeks
½ pint (285ml) white
sauce (see page 153)
3 oz (85g) grated Cheddar
cheese
6 oz (170g) cooked aduki
beans

For the crumble:
2 oz (55g) margarine or
butter
4 oz (115g) wholemeal
flour
Good pinch sage
Seasoning to taste

1 Trim, clean and chop the leeks into segments. Boil or steam them until just tender, then drain well.
2 Heat the white sauce gently and stir in the grated cheese until it melts completely.
3 Drain the beans and mix into the leeks and cheese; transfer to an ovenproof dish.
4 Rub the fat into the flour to make a crumb-like mixture; add the sage and seasoning.
5 Sprinkle the crumble topping over the base ingredients. Bake at 375°F/190°C (Gas Mark 5) for approximately 30 minutes, or until the crumble is cooked.

Serve with: A freshly made coleslaw sprinkled with a handful of roasted peanuts, plus lightly steamed new potatoes.

Week 5:
Monday
Egg Croquettes

4 hard-boiled eggs
1 egg, beaten
½ oz (15g) margarine or
butter
3 oz (85g) wholemeal
breadcrumbs
Good pinch thyme
Seasoning to taste
1 oz (30g) mung
beansprouts
Wheatgerm to coat
Vegetable oil for frying

1 Mash the hard-boiled eggs and mix with the raw egg and fat.
2 Add the crumbs, thyme, seasoning and beansprouts. The mixture should be moist but hold its shape, so add extra breadcrumbs if necessary.
3 Divide into small pieces and shape them into croquettes, rolling each one in wheatgerm.
4 Fry gently in hot oil, turning them occasionally so that they brown evenly. Drain on paper towel.

Serve with: A purée of potatoes, plus Brussels sprouts, steamed first then fried with chopped onion and mushrooms.

Tuesday
Spinach and Soya Bean Soup

2 tablespoons vegetable oil
1 large onion, sliced
2 pints (1 litre) vegetable
stock
2 large potatoes, diced
1 lb (455g) fresh spinach
or frozen equivalent
3 oz (85g) soya bean
flakes
Seasoning to taste
Soya sauce
Natural yogurt to serve
(optional)

1 Heat the vegetable oil in a saucepan. Lightly sauté the onion for a few minutes until it begins to soften.
2 Pour in the vegetable stock and add the potatoes. Cook for 10 minutes.
3 Add the washed and shredded spinach and the soya bean flakes. Continue cooking until all the ingredients are tender. Season to taste.
4 Blend very briefly to make a thick, coarse purée. Return to pan and heat through gently. Flavour to taste with soya sauce.
5 If liked, stir a spoonful or two of plain yogurt into each bowl of soup just before serving.

Serve with: Rye or pumpernickel bread, and a Waldorf salad of lettuce, celery, apple and walnuts.

Wednesday
Tofu Curry

3 tablespoons vegetable oil
1 lb (455g) tofu
*1 pint (570ml) curry
  sauce (see page 154)
1 apple
Squeeze of lemon juice
2 oz (55g) sunflower seeds

1 Heat the oil in a pan. Press the tofu so that it is as dry as possible, then cut into cubes and lightly fry in the oil, turning frequently.
2 Stir the tofu into the curry sauce and cook gently to heat through.
3 Slice the apple and toss it in the lemon juice. Scatter the slices over the top of the curry, together with the sunflower seeds.

Serve with: Brown rice and lightly fried shredded cabbage.

* Make a day in advance and leave overnight for the flavour to develop. Reheat gently.

Thursday
Lasagne with 'Meat' Sauce

1 tablespoon vegetable oil
½ small onion, finely
  chopped
½ clove garlic, crushed
3 oz (85g) soya 'minced
  beef', hydrated in water
Seasoning to taste
½ lb (225g) tomatoes,
  chopped
2 tablespoons tomato
  purée
A little water
6 oz (170g) wholemeal
  spinach lasagne
½ lb (225g) cottage cheese
1 small egg, lightly beaten
2 oz (55g) grated
  Parmesan cheese

1 Heat the oil in a pan and sauté the finely chopped onion for a few minutes. Add the garlic and cook a few minutes longer.
2 Stir in the drained 'meat', seasoning, tomatoes and tomato purée. Add a few spoonfuls of water and cook the mixture gently for 10 minutes, adding more water if necessary.
3 Bring a pan of water to the boil and drop in the lasagne sheets, one at a time. Cook for 8 minutes, or as long as directed on the packet. When tender, rinse in cold water and lay on a clean tea towel.

4 Sieve the cottage cheese, then mix with the beaten egg, half the grated Parmesan and seasoning to taste.
5 Grease a small, ovenproof dish. Arrange a third of the lasagne in the base, add half the cottage cheese, then half the 'meat'. Repeat this process, and top with the remainder of the lasagne. Sprinkle with Parmesan cheese.
6 Bake at 350°F/180°C (Gas Mark 4) for about 30 minutes or until heated through.

Serve with: A crisp green salad sprinkled with fresh, finely chopped basil.

Friday
Courgette Pizza

8 oz (225g) pizza dough of
  your choice

For the topping:
¼ pint (140ml) thick
  tomato sauce (see page
  153)
2 courgettes, thinly sliced
1 red pepper, thinly sliced
14 oz (395g) tin artichoke
  hearts or fresh
  equivalent
12 black olives, sliced
Seasoning to taste
2 teaspoons oregano
6 oz (170g) grated Cheddar
  cheese

1 Make up the pizza dough according to instructions.
2 Divide and roll out the dough to make two medium-sized circles. Spread each one with tomato sauce, taking it right to the edge.
3 Arrange the courgettes and red pepper over the top of the pizzas with the drained and quartered artichoke hearts. Sprinkle with sliced olives, seasoning and oregano. Top with grated cheese.
4 Bake the pizzas at 400°F/200°C (Gas Mark 6) for 20-30 minutes, or until the base is cooked and the cheese melted. Cut into wedges.

Serve with: A tomato and parsley salad, maybe sprinkled with soya 'bacon' bits.

Saturday
Tomato Soufflé with Pasta

*3 oz (85g) wholemeal
    noodles
1 oz (30g) margarine or
    butter
1 oz (30g) wholemeal flour
Scant ½ pint (285ml) milk
¼ pint (140ml) tomato
    purée
Seasoning to taste
1 oz (30g) grated Cheddar
    cheese
4 eggs, separated*

1 Break the noodles into small pieces and cook in boiling salted water until just tender. Drain and set aside.
2 Melt the fat in a saucepan and add the flour. Cook briefly. Off the heat, stir in the milk, then the tomato purée and seasoning, and mix well. Return pan to heat and cook, stirring, until the sauce thickens.
3 Add the grated cheese to the sauce. Leave to cool slightly, then stir in the egg yolks and prepared pasta.
4 Whisk the egg whites until stiff; fold into the other ingredients using a metal spoon.
5 Turn the mixture into a greased, 2-pint soufflé dish, and bake at once in an oven pre-heated to 375°F/190°C (Gas Mark 5) for 35-40 minutes, or until well risen.

Serve with: Hot buttered fennel, a green salad, and maybe some fresh wholemeal bread.

Sunday
Celery and Walnut Quiche

For the case:
*4 oz (115g) wholemeal
    flour
1½ oz (45g) rolled oats
3 oz (85g) margarine or
    butter
Cold water to mix*

For the filling:
*1 head of celery, cleaned
    and chopped
2 oz (55g) walnuts,
    coarsely chopped
2 eggs
6 oz (170g) low-fat cream
    cheese
½ pint (285ml) milk
Good pinch marjoram
Seasoning to taste*

1 Mix together the flour and oats, then rub in the fat to make a crumb-like mixture. Blend in just enough water to make a dough, and knead briefly. Set aside in a cool place.
2 Steam the celery until tender but not overcooked.
3 Roll out the pastry and use to line a medium-sized flan dish. Bake blind at 400°F/200°C (Gas Mark 6) for 10 minutes.
4 Arrange the celery in the flan case and sprinkle with most of the nuts.
5 Beat the eggs together with the well-beaten cream cheese and milk (or use a blender). Add marjoram and seasoning. Pour over the celery and sprinkle with the remaining nuts.
6 Bake at 375°F/190°C (Gas Mark 5) for 30-35 minutes, or until set.

Serve with: A cold rice salad, with tomato and nuts added.

Week 6:
Monday
Spaghetti 'Bolognese'

*2 oz (55g) margarine or
    butter
½-1 clove garlic, crushed
1 onion, sliced
1 pepper, sliced
4 oz (115g) mushrooms,
    chopped
5 oz (140g) soya 'minced
    beef', hydrated in water
14 oz (395g) tin tomatoes,
    coarsely chopped
Seasoning to taste
Marjoram
⅓ pint (200ml) vegetable
    stock
⅛ pint (70ml) red wine
    optional
10 oz (285g) wholemeal
    spaghetti*

1 Melt the fat in a pan and gently fry the garlic, onion and pepper for 5 minutes. Add the chopped mushrooms and cook until the vegetables begin to soften.
2 Add the drained soya 'meat', cook briefly, then stir in the tomatoes, seasoning, marjoram, vegetable stock and wine. Simmer until the sauce thickens.
3 Drop the spaghetti into a large pan of boiling water and cook for 10 minutes, or until just tender. Drain well.
4 Serve the spaghetti topped with the sauce.

Serve with: A large mixed green salad with a few nuts or cooked beans added for contrast.

Tuesday
Aubergine Yogurt Flan

*½ lb (225g) pastry of your
 choice*

For the filling:
1 large aubergine
*Approx. 3 tablespoons
 vegetable oil*
1 onion, sliced
1 clove garlic, crushed
*14 oz (395g) tin tomatoes,
 chopped*
*1 tablespoon tomato
 purée*
Good pinch of basil
Seasoning to taste
*¼ pint (140ml) natural
 yogurt*
*½ oz (15g) wholemeal
 flour*
½ oz (15g) pine nuts

1 Make up the pastry mix and set aside in a cool place.
2 Cut the aubergine into thin slices and arrange on a plate. Sprinkle with salt and leave for 30 minutes, then rinse and pat dry.
3 Heat 2 tablespoons of the oil in a pan and gently fry the aubergine, turning once, until tender. Drain and set aside.
4 Add the rest of the oil, if necessary, and fry the onion and garlic for 5 minutes.
5 Stir in the tomatoes, tomato purée, basil and seasoning. Cook until the sauce thickens.
6 Roll out the pastry and use to line a medium-sized flan dish. Bake blind at 400°F/200°C (Gas Mark 6) for 10 minutes.
7 Arrange some of the aubergine slices over the base of the flan, cover with some of the tomato mixture, then repeat these layers to use up the rest of the ingredients.
8 Beat together the yogurt and flour and pour over the flan. Sprinkle with nuts. Bake at 375°F/190°C (Gas Mark 5) for 30 minutes.

Serve with: A salad made with bulgur, parsley, mint and tomatoes, plus oil and vinegar dressing, and a sprinkling of soya 'bacon bits' or extra pine nuts.

Wednesday
Artichoke Omelette

3 globe artichokes
*Approx. 2 oz (55g)
 wholemeal flour*
3 tablespoons vegetable oil
*2 oz (55g) margarine or
 butter*
6 eggs
Pinch of dill
Seasoning to taste

1 Wash the artichokes well, then trim off and discard the outer leaves and the chokes. Cut in half, and then into slivers, coating each one lightly with flour.
2 Heat the oil in a saucepan and gently fry the artichokes, turning them once, until lightly browned. Drain on paper towels.
3 Melt the fat in a large frying pan and spread it evenly over the base. Lay the artichokes in the pan, then pour in the well-beaten eggs flavoured with the dill and seasoning.
4 Cook slowly, tilting the pan frequently, until the omelette sets. (If liked, you can speed up the process by putting it under the grill when the bottom of the omelette begins to colour.) Serve cut in wedges.

Serve with: French bread and a chicory and orange salad.

Thursday
Pepper and Mushroom Lasagne

*Approx. 3 tablespoons
  vegetable oil
1 large red pepper,
  coarsely chopped
1 large green pepper,
  coarsely chopped
1 large yellow pepper,
  coarsely chopped
1 large onion, chopped
4 oz (115g) mushrooms,
  sliced
2 large tomatoes, peeled
  and chopped
1 tablespoon tomato purée
1-2 teaspoons oregano
Seasoning to taste
6 oz (170g) wholemeal
  spinach lasagne
½ pint (285ml) white
  sauce (see page 153)
6 oz (170g) grated Cheddar
  cheese
Wholemeal breadcrumbs*

1 Heat the oil in a pan and gently cook the peppers and onion until they begin to soften.
2 Add the mushrooms and cook a few minutes more.
3 Add the tomatoes, the tomato purée, oregano and seasoning and cook gently, stirring occasionally, until the mixture thickens.
4 Bring a large pan of water to the boil and drop in the sheets of lasagne one at a time. Cook for 8 minutes or as long as directed on the packet. Rinse with cold water and arrange a third of the lasagne in a small oblong tin.
5 Top with half the vegetable mixture, then more lasagne, and the rest of the vegetables. Add a final layer of lasagne.
6 Heat the sauce, stir in 4 oz (115g) of the cheese and pour over the prepared ingredients, smoothing the top. Sprinkle with the remaining cheese and breadcrumbs.
7 Bake at 375°F/190°C (Gas Mark 5) for 30 minutes.

Serve with: A celery, beetroot and apple salad sprinkled with chopped, roasted hazelnuts.

Friday
Potato Galette with Cheese

*1½ lb (680g) potatoes
1 tablespoon vegetable oil
2 spring onions, finely
  chopped
2 eggs, lightly beaten
4 oz (115g) Lancashire
  cheese, grated
Seasoning to taste
Pinch of dry mustard
2 oz (55g) beansprouts
2 tomatoes, sliced
Parsley to garnish*

1 Peel and cube the potatoes. Steam them for 10 minutes, or until soft. Drain well.
2 Mash the potatoes to make a thick purée.
3 Heat the oil in a pan and fry the spring onions for a few minutes to soften, then stir them into the potato purée.
4 Add the beaten eggs, cheese, seasoning and mustard, mixing well. Stir in the beansprouts.
5 Spoon the mixture into a lightly greased sandwich tin, smooth the top and cover with slices of tomato.
6 Bake at 350°F/180°C (Gas Mark 4) for 40-50 minutes, or until cooked. Turn out, cut in wedges, and garnish with parsley.

Serve with: A coleslaw with watercress and chopped brazil nuts, plus wholemeal baps.

Saturday
Kidney Beans Creole

*2 tablespoons vegetable oil
1 onion, sliced
1 green pepper, sliced
Small tin (½lb/225g)
  tomatoes, chopped
1 teaspoon raw cane sugar
Seasoning to taste
½ lb (225g) cooked kidney
  beans
Soya 'bacon' bits*

1 Heat the oil in a pan and lightly fry the onion and pepper. When they begin to soften, stir in the tomatoes and juice, sugar and seasoning.
2 Simmer for 10 minutes to thicken slightly.
3 Add the drained beans and transfer to an ovenproof dish. Cover, and bake at 350°F/180°C (Gas Mark 4) for 20-30 minutes.
4 Stir in a generous amount of soya 'bacon' bits.

Serve with: A mixed green salad and fresh-from-the-oven corn muffins spread with cream or curd cheese.

Sunday
African 'Beef' Stew

5 oz (140g) soya 'beef'
  chunks, hydrated in
  water
3 tablespoons vegetable oil
1 large onion, sliced
1 large red pepper, sliced
3 sticks celery, sliced
1 clove garlic, crushed
2 tablespoons tomato
  purée
¼ teaspoon ground ginger
¼ teaspoon ground cloves
1 bay leaf
Squeeze of lemon juice
½ pint (285ml) vegetable
  stock
Seasoning to taste
1 oz (30g) wholemeal flour
2 tablespoons peanut
  butter
A little water
2 oz (55g) peanuts

1 Drain the soya chunks.
2 Heat the oil in a pan and add the 'beef' and prepared vegetables with the garlic. Stir well, and cook for 5 minutes.
3 Add the tomato purée, spices, bay leaf, lemon juice, vegetable stock and seasoning. Bring to the boil, then cover and simmer for 30 minutes, or until all the ingredients are tender. Remove the bay leaf.
4 Mix the flour and peanut butter into a drop of water, then stir into the stew, together with the nuts. Continue cooking gently until it thickens.

Serve with: Mashed potatoes and lightly steamed broccoli.

Week 7:
Monday
Beansprout Omelette

2 oz (55g) margarine or
  butter
4 spring onions, chopped
8 eggs
Seasoning to taste
4 oz (115g) beansprouts

1 Heat a small amount of the fat in a pan and fry the onions until just cooked. Remove from the pan.
2 Add a little more fat and heat to melt.

3 Beat the eggs lightly with seasoning to taste. Add the onion and beansprouts.
4 Pour half the egg mixture into the pan, reduce the heat, and cook gently until it begins to set underneath. Lift the sides and tip the pan to allow the uncooked liquid to run underneath.
5 When the top of the omelette begins to set, fold it in half at once and slide onto a warmed plate. Divide and serve, or put aside to keep warm.
6 Use up the remaining ingredients in the same way, making two more servings.

Serve with: French bread plus a watercress, red pepper and tomato salad.

Tuesday
Coleslaw with Pasta

4 oz (115g) wholemeal
  pasta shells
½ lb (225g) white cabbage
2 large carrots
½ small onion
½ green pepper
2 tablespoons natural
  yogurt
2 tablespoons mayonnaise
Squeeze lemon juice
Seasoning to taste
2 oz (55g) roasted peanuts

1 Cook the pasta in boiling water for 8-10 minutes, or until just tender. Rinse in cold water at once, then drain well.
2 Finely grate the cabbage, carrots, onion and pepper, and stir together. Add the pasta shells.
3 Mix the yogurt, mayonnaise, lemon juice and seasoning, and stir into the other ingredients. Sprinkle with nuts.

Serve with: Bread or a wholegrain crispbread, lightly spread with butter or peanut butter. Start with a soup if you like.

Wednesday
Vegetable Paella

10 oz (285g) brown rice
1½ pints (850ml) water
3 tablespoons olive oil
2 onions, sliced
2 cloves garlic, crushed
2 sticks celery, sliced
4 tomatoes, coarsely
  chopped
16 stuffed olives
1 bay leaf, crushed
1 teaspoon powdered
  saffron
Seasoning to taste
½ small tin pimentos,
  chopped
4 hard-boiled eggs, sliced

1 Rinse the rice, put in a pan and cook in the water for 30 minutes.
2 Meanwhile, heat the oil in a clean pan and add the onions, garlic, and celery. Cook gently, stirring frequently, until the vegetables begin to soften.
3 Stir the rice and any remaining liquid into the vegetables — if the mixture is dry, add a drop more water. Add the tomatoes, olives, bay leaf, saffron and seasoning.
4 Cover and cook for 15 minutes, or until the rice and vegetables are tender, taking care the paella does not dry out. Stir in the pimentos.
5 Turn into a warmed serving dish and top with the sliced eggs.

Serve with: A simple green salad with a sprinkling of soya 'bacon' bits or roasted soya beans.

Thursday
Nutty Courgette Lasagne

6 oz (170g) wholemeal
  lasagne
2 tablespoons vegetable oil
1 clove garlic, crushed
1 small onion, sliced
1 small red pepper, sliced
¾ lb (340g) courgettes,
  sliced
3 tomatoes, chopped
4 tablespoons dry white
  wine
2 oz (55g) blanched
  almonds
Seasoning to taste
Thyme to taste
1 oz (30g) margarine or
  butter
1 oz (30g) wholemeal flour
¼ pint (140ml) milk
¼ pint (140ml) natural
  yogurt

1 Cook the lasagne in a pan of boiling salted water, dropping it in a sheet at a time. Simmer for 8 minutes, or until just tender, then drain well and rinse in cold water. Arrange the lasagne on a clean tea towel and set aside.
2 Heat the vegetable oil in a clean pan and sauté the garlic, onion and pepper. When they begin to colour, add the courgettes and tomatoes. Stir in the wine. Continue cooking until the vegetables are tender.
3 Stir in most of the almonds, the seasoning and thyme, and cook a minute or two more.
4 In another pan, melt the fat and sprinkle in the flour. Cook until it begins to colour, then add the milk and simmer, stirring, until the sauce thickens. Add the yogurt.
5 Arrange a layer of the lasagne in the base of a greased ovenproof dish, top with some of the courgette and nut mixture. Repeat the layers to use up all the ingredients.
6 Pour the sauce over the lasagne. Top with the remaining nuts, coarsely chopped. Bake at 375°F/190°C (Gas Mark 5) for 30 minutes.

Serve with: A coleslaw with beansprouts added.

Friday
Bulgur with Cottage Cheese

2 tablespoons vegetable oil
1 large onion, sliced
½ lb (225g) bulgur
¾ pint (425ml) vegetable
*   stock*
Small tin pimentos,
*   chopped*
1 teaspoon marjoram
Seasoning to taste
2 oz (55g) sunflower seeds
½ lb (225g) cottage cheese
Watercress to garnish

1 Heat the oil in a pan and lightly fry the onion until it begins to soften.
2 Sprinkle in the bulgur, stirring so that it is coated with the oil. Add the vegetable stock, bring to the boil, then cover the pan and simmer for 20 minutes.
3 Stir in the pimentos, marjoram, seasoning and sunflower seeds. Remove from heat but leave to stand for 5 minutes.
4 Transfer to a serving dish, top with the cheese, garnish with watercress.

Serve with: A cooked vegetable such as spring greens would go well.

Saturday
Curried Butter Bean Loaf

½ lb (225g) butter beans,
*   soaked overnight*
4 oz (115g) wholemeal
*   breadcrumbs*
1 tablespoon vegetable oil
1 large onion, sliced
1-2 tablespoons curry
*   paste*
2 tomatoes, coarsely
*   chopped*
1 oz (30g) soya flour
Marjoram
Seasoning to taste
1 oz (30g) margarine
Parsley to garnish

1 Drain the beans, put in a pan, cover with fresh water and bring to a fast boil. Continue boiling for 10 minutes, then lower the heat and simmer them until tender.
2 Drain the beans and mash to a purée, then stir in the crumbs.
3 Heat the oil in another pan and lightly fry the onion. Stir in the curry paste, then add the contents of the pan to the bean mixture.

4 Combine the tomatoes with the beans, then stir in the flour, marjoram and seasoning to taste. Mix thoroughly.
5 Turn into a small, greased loaf tin and dot the top with knobs of margarine.
6 Bake at 375°F/190°C (Gas Mark 5) for 30 minutes. Garnish generously with fresh, chopped parsley.

Serve with: Hot buckwheat, plus a lettuce and tomato salad with raisins and peanuts in a French dressing.

Sunday
Spinach Pancakes with Peanuts

½ pint (285ml) pancake
*   batter (see page 152)*

For the filling:
2 tablespoons vegetable oil
1 clove of garlic
2 oz (55g) raw peanuts
1½ lb (680g) fresh
*   spinach, finely chopped*
Seasoning to taste
Vegetable oil for frying
Butter or margarine
Coarsely crushed crisps to
*   garnish*

1 Make up the batter, and leave covered in a cool place for at least half an hour.
2 Meanwhile, heat the oil in a saucepan and add the skinned garlic and peanuts. Cook gently for 5-10 minutes, shaking the pan frequently, until the nuts begin to colour. Remove the nuts from the pan and set aside; discard the garlic.
3 Add the spinach to the pan and cook until soft. Mix the peanuts into the spinach, season to taste, and leave over a very low heat whilst cooking the pancakes.
4 To do this, heat a little oil in a frying pan and add a few spoonfuls of the whisked batter. Cook gently, tipping the pan frequently. When the pancake begins to colour underneath, flip or turn it with a spatula. Cook the second side.
5 Use the remaining batter in the same way and keep cooked pancakes warm.
6 Fill each of the pancakes with some of the spinach and peanut mixture, roll them up, top with knobs of butter or margarine and garnish with crushed crisps.

Serve with: A rice salad with banana slices and raisins added.

Week 8:
Monday
Polenta with 'Sausage'

1½ pints (850ml) water
Seasoning to taste
½ lb (225g) fine polenta
(cornmeal)
2 tablespoons vegetable oil
4 oz (115g) mushrooms,
chopped
14 oz (395g) tin tomatoes,
coarsely chopped
2 tablespoons tomato
purée
1 small tin soya 'sausages',
sliced
Oregano to taste
Seasoning to taste
2 oz (55g) margarine or
butter

1 Bring the water to the boil in a pan, season, and sprinkle in the polenta. Cook, stirring occasionally, for 20-30 minutes, or until the polenta is thick.
2 Meanwhile, heat the vegetable oil in another pan and fry the mushrooms for a few minutes only. Add the tomatoes and the tomato purée, bring to the boil, then simmer until the sauce thickens.
3 Stir the 'sausages' gently into the tomato sauce, add oregano and seasoning to taste. Cook gently to heat through.
4 When ready to serve, stir the fat into the polenta. Transfer to a warmed serving dish and top with the 'sausage' mixture.

Serve with: A green vegetable such as cabbage with sunflower or caraway seeds, and granary bread.

Tuesday
Broccoli Onion Crumble

For the base:
1 lb (455g) broccoli
2 large onions
½ pint (285ml) white
sauce (see page 153)
2 oz (55g) curd or low-fat
cream cheese
Good pinch of nutmeg
Seasoning to taste

For the crumble:
2 oz (55g) margarine
4 oz (115g) wholemeal
flour
2 oz (55g) grated Cheddar
cheese

1 Trim the broccoli and divide into florets. Peel the onions and cut into chunks. Steam the vegetables together until just tender, then drain well.
2 Heat the sauce and add the cheese, stirring with a wooden spoon until it melts. Add the nutmeg and seasoning. Mix the vegetables into the sauce and spoon into an ovenproof dish.
3 Rub the margarine into the flour to make a crumb-like mixture. Stir in the finely grated cheese. Spread over the vegetables.
4 Bake at 375°F/190°C (Gas Mark 5) for 20-30 minutes, or until crumble is cooked.

Serve with: A celery, apple and walnut salad.

Wednesday
Globe Artichokes with Mushroom Tofu Filling

4 large globe artichokes
½ oz (15g) margarine or
butter
1 small onion, sliced
4 oz (115g) mushrooms,
sliced
4 oz (115g) tofu
2 oz (55g) wholemeal
breadcrumbs
Parsley
Seasoning to taste

1 Remove any tough or bruised outer leaves from the artichokes, then cook the heads in boiling salted water for 30 minutes, or until a leaf comes out easily.
2 Drain well, then carefully open the artichokes and pull out the inner leaves and chokes. Arrange the shells in a greased ovenproof dish.
3 Melt the fat in a pan and sauté the onion for a few minutes, then add the mushrooms. Continue cooking until they begin to soften.
4 Drain the tofu well, mash coarsely, and add to the pan. Cook a few minutes more. Stir in the breadcrumbs, parsley and seasoning.
5 Divide the mixture between the artichokes, cover the dish, and bake at 375°F/190°C (Gas Mark 5) for about 20 minutes, or until cooked.

Serve with: Hot crisps and a cooked green vegetable such as spinach sprinkled with almonds.

Thursday
Wholewheat and Vegetable Casserole

½ lb (225g) wholewheat
 berries
3 tablespoons vegetable oil
4 tomatoes, chopped
1 large onion, sliced
1 large green pepper,
 sliced
2 large sticks celery, sliced
2 oz (55g) mushrooms,
 sliced
2 oz (55g) frozen
 sweetcorn
2 teaspoons mixed herbs
Seasoning to taste

For the sauce:
4 tablespoons tahini
Cold water
Good squeeze lemon juice

1 Wash the wholewheat berries, place them in enough water to cover, and leave them to soak overnight. Drain well, then put in a pan with fresh water, bring to the boil, and simmer for about 1 hour or until tender. Drain and set aside.
2 Heat the oil in a large pan, and add the vegetables and herbs. Cover and simmer for about 20 minutes, or until the vegetables are cooked. You may need to add a drop of water.
3 Add the cooked wholewheat berries to the pan, mix well, and season to taste.
4 Combine the tahini with enough water to make a pouring consistency. Add lemon juice and seasoning to taste. Hand round at the table for those who want it.

Serve with: A salad of grated raw courgette in a vinaigrette dressing, with parsley and chopped hazelnuts sprinkled over the top.

Friday
Stroganoff

2 oz (55g) margarine or
 butter
1 onion, sliced
½ lb (225g) mushrooms,
 sliced
5 oz (140g) soya 'beef'
 chunks, hydrated in
 water and briefly cooked
½ oz (15g) wholemeal
 flour
¼ pint (140ml) natural
 yogurt
Seasoning to taste

1 Melt half the fat in a saucepan and sauté the onion until it begins to brown; add the mushrooms and cook a few minutes longer until tender. Remove from the pan.
2 Coat the 'meat' chunks lightly with flour. Melt the rest of the fat, and gently fry the chunks. Stir well, so that they are evenly coloured.
3 Return the vegetables to the pan along with the yogurt. Cook very gently for a minute only. Season to taste and serve at once.

Serve with: Brown rice and a side salad of red cabbage and sweetcorn on a lettuce base.

Saturday
Aduki Bean Pasties

½ lb (225g) shortcrust
 pastry (see page 151)

For the filling:
4 oz (115g) aduki beans,
 soaked overnight
2 tablespoons vegetable oil
1 clove garlic, crushed
1 large onion, sliced
1 tablespoon tomato purée
½ teaspoon basil
1 tablespoon chopped
 parsley
1 oz (30g) walnuts,
 chopped
Soya sauce

1 Make up the pastry and set aside in a cool place.
2 Drain the beans, and put them in a pan. Cover with fresh water, bring to the boil, and continue boiling for 10 minutes. Lower the heat and simmer for 30 minutes or until the beans are tender. Drain well.

3 Heat the oil and fry the garlic and onion until soft.

4 Mash the beans and add to the pan with the tomato purée, herbs, nuts and soya sauce to taste.

5 Roll out the pastry and cut into four circles about the size of small plates.

6 Put a spoonful or two of the mixture onto each of the dough circles. Dampen the edges, fold and press down to seal. Prick with a fork. Bake at 400°F/200°C (Gas Mark 6) for 20-30 minutes, or until pastry is crisp and brown.

Serve with: A cold bulgur salad, and watercress with celery and orange.

Sunday
Creamy Spaghetti with Peas

10 oz (285g) wholemeal
* spaghetti*
6 oz (170g) curd or Ricotta
* cheese*
2 oz (55g) grated
* Parmesan cheese*
Good pinch of nutmeg
Seasoning to taste
4 oz (115g) cooked peas
Soya 'bacon' bits, to
* garnish (optional)*

1 Cook the spaghetti in a saucepan of boiling water for 10 minutes, or until just tender.

2 Meanwhile, blend together the Ricotta cheese, Parmesan cheese, nutmeg and seasoning.

3 Add the cooked peas to the spaghetti pan for the last minute or two, to heat through, then drain well.

4 Stir the cheese into the spaghetti gently, so that a thick sauce forms. Tip into a serving dish and sprinkle with soya 'bacon' bits.

Serve with: A raw spinach, tomato and spring onion salad.

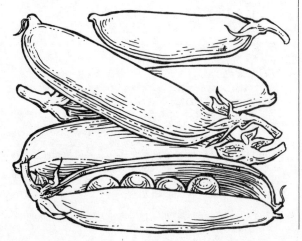

Week 9:
Monday
Turnip Soup

¾ lb (340g) young turnips
2 oz (55g) margarine or
* butter*
1 teaspoon curry powder
1 large carrot, finely
* chopped*
1 onion, finely chopped
2 pints (1.15 litres)
* vegetable stock*
Seasoning to taste
5 oz (140g) cooked brown
* rice*
Parsley, chopped
4 tablespoons tahini

1 Peel and slice the turnips. Melt half the fat in a pan and fry the turnips for a few minutes, stirring frequently.

2 Cover them with boiling water, and then simmer for 15-20 minutes, or until tender. Drain well.

3 In a clean pan melt the remaining fat. Add the curry powder with the carrot and onion, and cook until the vegetables begin to soften.

4 Add the vegetable stock and seasoning, bring to the boil. Cook for a few minutes, then stir in the rice and turnips, plus a generous amount of fresh parsley. Simmer to heat through.

5 Stir in the tahini just before serving.

Serve with: Fresh-from-the-oven wholemeal scones, and a large salad of grated root vegetables on a lettuce base, sprinkled with pumpkin seeds.

Tuesday
Italian-Style Broccoli

1½ lb (680g) broccoli
2 tablespoons vegetable oil
1 onion, thinly sliced
1 clove garlic, thinly sliced
½ oz (15g) wholemeal
flour
Seasoning to taste
⅓ pint (200ml) vegetable
stock
12 black olives, stoned and
chopped
6 oz (170g) cubed Fontina
or Cheddar cheese
Roasted sunflower seeds to
garnish

1 Trim the broccoli and break into large florets. Cook in boiling water for 10-15 minutes, or until just tender. Drain and keep warm.
2 Heat the vegetable oil in a clean pan and add the onion and garlic. Cook until the onion is soft.
3 Sprinkle in the flour and seasoning and cook a minute or two, then stir in the stock. Cook gently to make a sauce.
4 Add the olives to the sauce along with the cheese.
5 Arrange the broccoli in a shallow serving dish. Pour on the sauce, distributing it evenly. Sprinkle with the sunflower seeds.

Serve with: Jacket potatoes and a salad of apple chunks, celery and sweetcorn with lemon dressing.

Wednesday
'Pork' with Beans

3 oz (85g) soya 'pork'
chunks, hydrated in
water
3 tablespoons vegetable oil
1 large onion, sliced
3 sticks celery, chopped
14 oz (395g) tin baked
beans
1 oz (30g) margarine or
butter, melted
2 oz (55g) wholemeal
breadcrumbs
Seasoning to taste
Parsley

1 Drain the soya chunks well.
2 Heat the oil in a pan and fry the onion until it softens. Stir in the soya chunks and cook a few minutes more, stirring frequently. Add the celery and mix well.

3 Tip the mixture into an ovenproof dish and cover with the beans.
4 Stir together the melted fat, breadcrumbs, seasoning and parsley, and sprinkle over the other ingredients.
5 Bake at 350°F/180°C (Gas Mark 4) for 30-40 minutes, or until heated through.

Serve with: Potatoes or crisps, and a hot green vegetable — spring greens would go well.

Thursday
Greek Salad

½ small cauliflower
2 carrots, finely chopped
2 sticks celery, chopped
1 green pepper, chopped
4 tomatoes, chopped
10 radishes
2 oz (55g) cooked butter
beans, drained
Seasoning to taste

For the dressing:
4 tablespoons olive oil
2 tablespoons cider
vinegar
Seasoning to taste
4 oz (115g) Féta cheese
10 black olives

1 Trim the cauliflower and break into small florets.
2 Mix together all the vegetables and beans. Season to taste.
3 Make up the salad dressing by combining the oil, vinegar and seasoning in a screw-top jar and shaking well.
4 Pour a little of the dressing over the salad ingredients and toss lightly. Leave to stand for a while.
5 Sprinkle crumbled cheese and olives over the top, and hand round any extra dressing at table.

Serve with: Wholemeal pitta bread, and maybe some hummus (chick-pea dip) to spread onto it.

Friday
Rice and Tofu Bake

½ lb (225g) brown rice
1 pint (570ml) water
2 tablespoons vegetable oil
1 onion, sliced
1 carrot, sliced
4 oz (115g) mushrooms,
* sliced*
10 oz (285g) tofu
Seasoning to taste
2 oz (55g) grated Cheddar
* cheese*
1 tablespoon bran
½ oz (15g) margarine or
* butter*

1 Rinse the rice, then put into a pan with the water and cook for 30-40 minutes, or until tender. Add more water if necessary. Drain well.
2 Heat the oil in a pan and fry the onion and carrot for 5 minutes, or until beginning to colour.
3 Add the mushrooms and cook a few minutes more.
4 Press any excess moisture from the tofu, crumble it coarsely, and stir into the pan. Cook briefly. Season to taste.
5 Carefully mix together the vegetable tofu mixture and the rice, and transfer to a lightly greased ovenproof dish.
6 Combine the grated cheese and bran and sprinkle over the top. Dot with the fat. Bake at 350°F/180°C (Gas Mark 4) for 20 minutes.

Serve with: A salad of lettuce, tomato, cucumber and olives.

Saturday
Spinach Ravioli

½ lb (225g) wholemeal
* pasta dough (see page*
* 152)*

For the filling:
1 oz (30g) margarine or
* butter*
½ small onion, chopped
2 oz (55g) soya 'minced
* meat', hydrated in water*
¾ lb (340g) spinach
2 oz (55g) grated
* Parmesan cheese*
2 eggs, beaten
Seasoning to taste
2 oz (55g) butter, melted, to
* serve*

1 Divide the dough into two and roll into oblongs, making the dough as thin as possible. Mark one half into squares about 2″ (5cm) across.
2 Melt the fat in a saucepan and fry the onion and drained 'meat' together for a few minutes.
3 Cook the spinach until soft, then chop and add to the 'meat' mixture, together with the cheese, beaten eggs and seasoning, stirring for a few minutes to combine thoroughly.
4 Use a teaspoon to drop small amounts of the filling in the centre of each of the marked squares then brush the lines with water. Lay the second sheet of dough on top, pressing gently to remove any air pockets.
5 Use a pastry cutter, preferably with a serrated edge, to cut into squares, pressing the edges to seal. Leave the ravioli on a lightly floured surface and covered with a damp cloth for at least 30 minutes.
6 Bring a large pan of salted water to the boil and drop in the ravioli a few at a time. Cook for 5-8 minutes, or until tender, stirring occasionally to prevent them sticking together. Remove with a perforated spoon and keep warm whilst cooking the rest in the same way. Top with the melted butter.

Serve with: A sweetcorn and beansprout salad sprinkled with chopped hazelnuts, garnished with watercress.

Sunday
Sukiyaki

*Approx. 3 tablespoons
  vegetable oil
1 onion, sliced
4 oz (115g) mushrooms,
  sliced
¼ pint (140ml) water
½ teaspoon raw brown
  sugar
Soya sauce
1 lb (455g) Swiss chard,
  sliced
1 small head Chinese
  leaves, sliced
A few water chestnuts,
  sliced
2 oz (55g) mung
  beansprouts
¾ lb (340g) tofu*

1 Heat the oil in a pan or wok, and cook the onion and mushrooms for literally a few minutes.
2 Mix together the water, sugar, and enough soya sauce to give a good colour, and stir into the pan.
3 Add the Swiss chard, Chinese leaves and water chestnuts to the pan. Cook gently, stirring frequently, for 5 minutes, or until the vegetables are cooked but still quite crisp. Add more water and soya sauce if necessary.
4 Add the beansprouts and crumbled tofu, and leave over the heat for only a minute or two more. Hand round more soya sauce for those who want it.

Serve with: Brown rice, plus a pepper, cucumber and celery salad with roasted sunflower seeds added.

Week 10:
Monday
Butter Bean Croquettes

*6 oz (170g) butter beans,
  soaked and cooked
2 tablespoons vegetable oil
½ small onion, finely
  sliced
1 stick celery, finely sliced
1 carrot, grated
Seasoning to taste
Crushed rosemary
1 egg, beaten (optional)
Wholemeal breadcrumbs
Rolled oats to coat
Vegetable oil for frying
Tomato or cheese sauce
  to serve (see page 153)*

1 Drain the beans and mash well to make a thick purée.
2 Heat the oil in a pan and fry the onion and celery with the grated carrot. When soft, add the seasoning and rosemary, also the bean purée.
3 Stir in the beaten egg and just enough breadcrumbs to make the mixture hold its shape. Leave to cool, then divide into small pieces and roll into croquettes.
4 Coat each croquette lightly with oats, then shallow fry in hot oil until crisp and brown. Drain on paper towels. Hand round cheese sauce at the table for those who want it.

Serve with: Cauliflower cheese and jacket potatoes.

Tuesday
Spanish Soufflé

*1½ oz (45g) margarine or
  butter
3 oz (85g) wholemeal flour
1 pint (570ml) milk
4 eggs, separated
Seasoning to taste
Pinch of nutmeg
1 tablespoon vegetable oil
1 small pepper, finely
  chopped
1 small onion, finely
  chopped
1 tomato, finely chopped
Paprika*

1 Melt the fat in a pan and sprinkle in the flour; cook gently for 2 minutes. Remove from the heat and stir in the milk, then return to heat and continue cooking until sauce thickens. Cool briefly.
2 Add the egg yolks to the sauce with the seasoning and nutmeg.
3 Heat the oil in a clean pan and cook the chopped vegetables until soft. Drain well and stir into the sauce.
4 Whisk the egg whites and fold carefully into the other ingredients, using a metal spoon.
5 Pour into a greased, 2-pint soufflé dish and sprinkle lightly with paprika. Bake at once in an oven pre-heated to 375°F/190°C (Gas Mark 5) for 35-40 minutes, or until well risen.

Serve with: Garlic bread and a green salad.

Wednesday
Spaghetti with Mushroom Walnut Topping

For the sauce:
1½ oz (45g) margarine or
   butter
1 onion, finely chopped
4 oz (115g) mushrooms,
   sliced
2 oz (55g) walnuts,
   chopped
2 egg yolks
¼ pint (140ml) single
   cream
Seasoning to taste

½ lb (225g) wholemeal
   spaghetti
Parsley to garnish

1 Melt the fat in a pan and add the prepared vegetables, cooking them gently for 5-10 minutes, until tender. Add the nuts and cook a few minutes more.
2 Lightly whip together the egg yolks and cream.
3 Bring a saucepan of water to the boil and add the spaghetti, cooking it for 8-10 minutes, so that it is just softening. Drain well.
4 Return the spaghetti to the saucepan and pour on the egg and cream mixture, stirring so it is well combined. Heat very gently for a minute or two only.
5 Tip the spaghetti into a serving dish and top with the prepared mushroom walnut mixture. Garnish with parsley and take to the table at once.

Serve with: A salad of chopped fennel, onion and radishes, with Italian dressing.

Thursday
Mixed Vegetable Loaf

1 oz (30g) margarine or
   butter
1 onion, sliced
1 leek, sliced
1 large carrot, sliced
4 oz (115g) wholemeal
   breadcrumbs
4 oz (115g) peanuts,
   coarsely chopped
Seasoning to taste
1 teaspoon sage, chopped
2 eggs, lightly beaten
Approx. ⅓ pint (200ml)
   milk
Brown gravy to serve (see
   page 153)

1 Melt the fat and gently fry the sliced onion, leek and carrot for a few minutes, or until they begin to soften.
2 Stir in the breadcrumbs, chopped peanuts, seasoning and sage.
3 Add the beaten eggs and enough milk to make the mixture hold together without being too moist.
4 Spoon into a lightly greased loaf tin. Bake at 350°F/180°C (Gas Mark 4) for 40 minutes, or until set. Hand round brown gravy at the table for those who want it.

Serve with: A salad of chicory, pepper, celery, tomatoes and watercress, plus French-fried potatoes.

Friday
Bulgur and Tomato Salad

½ lb (225g) bulgur
4 spring onions
2 tablespoons chopped
*   parsley*
2 tablespoons chopped
*   mint*
2 tablespoons vegetable oil
2 tablespoons lemon juice
Seasoning to taste
2 oz (55g) roasted
*   hazelnuts*
4 oz (115g) smoked tofu
6 tomatoes

1 Wash the bulgur in cold water, drain, then soak in fresh water for 1 hour. Drain well again, and then wring out in a clean tea towel so that it is completely dry.
2 Trim and chop the onions.
3 Stir together the bulgur, onions, herbs, oil, lemon and seasoning. Leave to chill for as long as possible.
4 Coarsely chop the nuts and cut the smoked tofu into cubes. Quarter the tomatoes. Add these to the bulgur just before eating.

Serve with: A salad of shredded raw spinach leaves (the younger and fresher, the better they'll taste).

Saturday
Asparagus Quiche

For the pastry:
6 oz (170g) wholemeal
*   flour*
Pinch of salt
3 oz (85g) margarine
1 egg, beaten
Cold water to mix

For the filling:
½ lb (225g) asparagus,
*   fresh or frozen*
2 eggs
¼ pint (140ml) milk
¼ pint (140ml) single
*   cream*
4 oz (115g) grated Swiss
*   cheese*
Seasoning to taste

1 Sift together the flour and salt; rub in the fat to make a crumb-like mixture.
2 Use a knife to stir in the beaten egg, adding just enough water to form a dough. Knead for a few minutes, then set aside in a cool place.
3 If the asparagus is frozen, cook in the usual way. If fresh, trim the stalks then cook in boiling water for 10 minutes. Drain well. Chop most of the asparagus into short lengths, reserving the best.
4 Beat together the eggs, milk, cream, cheese and seasoning.
5 Roll out the pastry and use to line a medium-sized flan dish. Bake blind at 400°F/200°C (Gas Mark 6) for 10 minutes.
6 Arrange the cut asparagus in the flan, and cover with the egg mixture. Make a wheel pattern on top of the flan with the remaining asparagus spears.
7 Bake at 375°F/190°C (Gas Mark 5) for 30-40 minutes, until set.

Serve with: Tiny new potatoes, and a cucumber and green bean salad with olives.

Sunday
Aubergine Yogurt Curry

2 aubergines

*For the sauce:
2 tablespoons ghee
1 onion, chopped
1 clove garlic, crushed
2-3 teaspoons curry
*   powder*
Good pinch of ground
*   ginger*
½ oz (15g) wholemeal
*   flour*
½ pint (285ml) vegetable
*   stock*
½ pint (285ml) natural
*   yogurt*
Seasoning to taste
Chopped chives for
*   garnish*

1 Boil the aubergines until tender, then cut them into small pieces and mash coarsely.
2 Meanwhile, melt the ghee in a clean pan and fry the onion and garlic until beginning to soften.
3 Add the spices and flour, stir well and cook a few minutes more. Pour in the vegetable stock, bring to the boil, stirring continually, then simmer for 10 minutes.
4 Mix in the yogurt and seasoning, and simmer very gently until heated through. Add the hot aubergine purée. Serve garnished with fresh chopped chives.

Serve with: Wholemeal chapatis. A banana and coconut salad would make a good contrast.

*Make a day in advance and leave overnight for the flavour to develop. Reheat gently.

Week 11:
Monday
Onion and Olive Pizza

½ lb (225g) pizza dough
 of your choice

For the topping:
2-3 tablespoons vegetable
 oil
1½ lb (680g) onions,
 sliced
1 oz (30g) wholemeal flour
⅓ pint (200ml) milk
Seasoning to taste
Black olives, sliced

1 Make up the pizza dough according to instructions.
2 Heat the oil in a pan and cook the onions gently until they soften. Sprinkle in the flour and cook a minute or two more.
3 Remove the pan from the heat and stir in the milk, then return to heat and continue cooking until the onions are coated in a thick sauce. Season to taste.
4 Divide the dough into four and roll out to make four small circles. Top with the onion mixture and sprinkle generously with olives.
5 Bake at 400°F/200°C (Gas Mark 6) for 20-30 minutes or until cooked.

Serve with: As these traditionally Italian pizzas are low in protein, serve them with an Italian salad of sliced Mozzarella cheese, avocado and tomatoes sprinkled with fresh basil or parsley.

Tuesday
Beetroot in Yogurt Sauce

1 lb (455g) beetroot
2 tablespoons vegetable oil
1 onion, finely chopped
½ pint (285ml) natural
 yogurt
½-1 clove garlic, finely
 crushed
Seasoning to taste
Watercress to garnish

1 Twist the stems of the beetroot until they come away. Place in a pan, cover with water and bring to the boil. Simmer gently for an hour or until tender. Drain, slip off the skins, and dice the beetroot.
2 Heat the oil in a pan and fry the onion until soft, then add the beetroot and stir well.
3 Beat the yogurt lightly, and add the garlic and seasoning.

4 Stir the yogurt sauce in with the beetroot and heat through very gently. Garnish with watercress.

Serve with: Jacket potatoes, plus a freshly made coleslaw salad with grapes, celery and walnuts.

Wednesday
Onions with Almond Rice Stuffing

4 large onions
2 tablespoons vegetable oil
1 small green pepper,
 chopped
1-2 teaspoons curry
 powder
½-1 teaspoon ground
 cardamom
6 oz (170g) cooked brown
 rice
2 oz (55g) almonds,
 chopped
2 oz (55g) raisins
Parsley
Seasoning to taste
Tomato or cheese sauce to
 serve (see page 153)

1 Cut a slice from the top of each onion and scoop out the centre to leave a fairly thick shell.
2 Heat the vegetable oil in a pan and lightly fry some of the chopped, scooped-out onion (reserve the rest for use in another recipe) with the chopped pepper.
3 When the vegetables begin to soften, add the spices and cook a few minutes more, then stir the mixture into the cooked rice.
4 Add the almonds to the rice mixture with the raisins, parsley and seasoning, stirring well. Divide between the prepared onion shells.
5 Wrap individually in silver foil, folding so that each package is completely sealed. Bake at 350°F/180°C (Gas Mark 4) for about 30 minutes, or until tender. Hand round sauce at the table.

Serve with: An endive, chicory, cress and cheese salad, plus fresh French bread.

Thursday
'Sausage' and Bean Hot-Pot

½ lb (225g) haricot beans,
  soaked overnight
2 onions, coarsely chopped
14 oz (395g) tin tomatoes,
  chopped
Medium tin of soya
  'sausages', sliced
½ pint (285ml) vegetable
  stock
⅓ pint (200ml) dry cider
2 tablespoons tomato
  purée
Seasoning to taste
½ oz (15g) wholemeal
  flour

1 Drain the beans and place in a pan. Cover with fresh water, and cook for 30 minutes.
2 In a casserole mix together the drained beans, onions and tomatoes, and the sliced 'sausages'.
3 Mix the vegetable stock and cider with the tomato purée, seasoning and flour and heat gently, stirring until the sauce thickens. Pour over the ingredients and mix well.
4 Cover the casserole and bake at 350°F/180°C (Gas Mark 4) for 30 minutes, or until all the ingredients are cooked. Adjust seasoning.

Serve with: Roast potatoes and a green salad.

Note: Use tinned baked beans if you prefer.

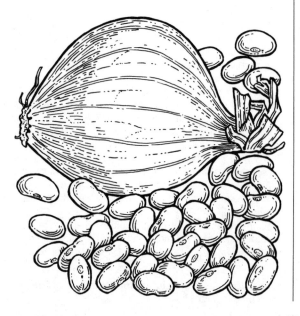

Friday
Samosas

For the pastry:
½ lb (225g) self-raising
  wholemeal flour
1 oz (30g) butter
Cold water to mix

For the filling:
1 large potato, sliced
1 large carrot, sliced
¼ small cauliflower
2 tablespoons vegetable oil
¼ teaspoon ground cumin
¼ teaspoon ground
  turmeric
¼ teaspoon ground
  coriander
¼ teaspoon ground ginger
1 onion, finely chopped
Pinch of sea salt
2 oz (55g) salted peanuts,
  coarsely chopped
1 teaspoon finely chopped
  coriander leaves
Vegetable oil for frying

1 Put the flour into a bowl and rub in the butter. Add enough water to make a smooth dough, knead well, then cover and set aside in a cool place.
2 Boil the potato and carrot until they begin to soften, then drain well and cut into small cubes. Break the cauliflower into florets.
3 Heat the oil in a pan and stir in the spices and onion. Cook gently for a few minutes.
4 Add the vegetables and continue cooking, stirring often, until they soften. If liked you can mash them coarsely.
5 Add salt, the prepared nuts and coriander leaves. Set aside to cool slightly.
6 Knead the dough again, then break off small pieces, shape into balls, and roll out thinly into circles about 4 inches (10cm) in diameter.
7 Cut these into even halves and form into cones. Fill each with some of the mixture, then fold the dampened top twice, pressing firmly to seal.
8 Deep fry the samosas a few at a time in hot oil until crisp and golden. Drain on paper towels and keep hot whilst cooking the rest in the same way.

Serve with: A dish of hot rice and a tomato, onion and yogurt salad. Coconut chutney goes well with samosas.

Saturday
Spinach Leaf Rolls

16 large spinach leaves
1 oz (30g) margarine or
  butter
4 oz (115g) mushrooms,
  sliced
4 tomatoes, chopped
4 oz (115g) wholemeal
  breadcrumbs
3 tablespoons cooked
  sweetcorn
Seasoning to taste
Good pinch of marjoram
Good pinch of garlic salt
2 oz (55g) walnut pieces
1 pint (570ml) white sauce
  (see page 153)
4 oz (115g) grated Cheddar
  cheese

1 Cook the trimmed leaves in boiling water for literally a minute or two.
2 Melt the fat in a clean pan and fry the mushrooms and tomatoes until just tender. Stir in the breadcrumbs, sweetcorn, seasoning, herbs, garlic salt and walnut pieces.
3 Lay one of the spinach leaves flat and top it with a spoonful or two of the mixture. Make it into a roll, carefully turning in the ends to keep the filling in place, and lay it in a greased, shallow ovenproof dish.
4 Use up the rest of the ingredients in the same way, packing the rolls fairly close together.
5 Heat the sauce and add most of the cheese, stirring until it melts. Pour over the spinach rolls and sprinkle with the remaining cheese.
6 Bake at 375°F/190°C (Gas Mark 5) for 20 minutes or until heated through.

Serve with: A celery, carrot and chopped prune salad, plus wholemeal baps.

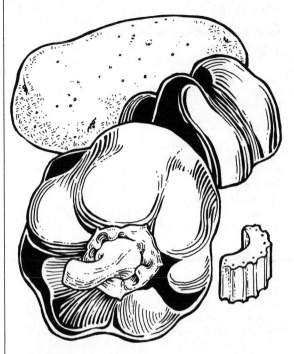

Sunday
Jacket Potatoes with 'Chicken' and Pepper

4 large potatoes
4 oz (115g) soya 'chicken'
  pieces, hydrated in water
2 tablespoons vegetable oil
1 red pepper, sliced
2 sticks celery, sliced
Soya sauce to taste
Seasoning to taste

1 Scrub the potatoes and place in a large saucepan. Cover them with water, bring to the boil, then simmer for about 20 minutes.
2 Drain the potatoes, pat dry, and bake at 375°F/190°C (Gas Mark 5) for about 15 minutes more.
3 Meanwhile, bring the soya 'chicken' to a boil, simmer for a few minutes, then drain well.
4 Heat the vegetable oil in a pan and fry the pepper and celery until they begin to soften. Add the soya 'chicken', stir, and cook a minute longer. Add soya sauce and seasoning to taste.
5 When the potatoes are crisp and completely cooked, cut a cross in the top of each one and open the potato out. Top with a generous serving of the filling mixture.

Serve with: A hot vegetable such as buttered carrots, and a watercress salad.

Week 12:
Monday
Oven-Baked Asparagus Pancakes

½ pint (285ml). pancake
batter (see page 152)
Vegetable oil for frying

For the filling:
¾ lb (340g) asparagus
(fresh, frozen or tinned)

For the sauce:
½ pint (285ml) milk
2 eggs
1 teaspoon wholemeal
flour
Seasoning to taste
Tarragon

1 Make the batter according to instructions.
2 When ready to use, heat a little oil in a heavy-based frying pan and pour in a small amount of the batter.
3 Cook until lightly browned underneath, then flip or turn the pancake with a spatula, and cook the second side. Use the rest of the batter in the same way.
4 If using fresh asparagus, rinse and trim, then tie in a bundle and stand in a tall pan of boiling salted water (with the tips at the top), and cook for about 10 minutes, or until tender. (Use silver foil to make a lid if you do not have a suitable pan.) If using frozen asparagus, cook in the usual way; or drain tinned asparagus.
5 Wrap each pancake round a few of the asparagus spears and arrange them side by side in a shallow ovenproof dish.
6 Whisk together the milk, eggs, flour, seasoning and tarragon. Pour over the pancakes. Bake at 375°F/190°C (Gas Mark 5) for about 30 minutes or until set.

Serve with: Lightly steamed new potatoes, and a red pepper and tomato salad.

Tuesday
Gnocchi Cheese Fritters

1 pint (570ml) milk
4 oz (115g) wholemeal
semolina
2 large eggs, beaten
Seasoning to taste
Pinch of nutmeg
2 oz (55g) grated
Parmesan cheese
2 oz (55g) grated
Emmental cheese
Wholemeal breadcrumbs
Vegetable oil for frying
Tomato sauce to serve (see
page 153)

1 Heat the milk and, when it boils, sprinkle in the semolina, and continue cooking over a low heat, stirring continually. When the mixture thickens, remove from heat and cool slightly.
2 Stir in most of the beaten eggs, seasoning and nutmeg, and the two cheeses. Blend thoroughly.
3 Turn the mixture onto an oiled or wetted plate or dish, smooth the top, and leave to get completely cold.
4 Use a cutter or small glass to cut the mixture into rounds. Dip in the remaining beaten egg, and then the breadcrumbs, coating them well.
5 When ready, drop the fritters into hot, deep fat and fry for a few minutes only, until crisp and brown. Drain well on paper towels and keep warm whilst using the rest of the mixture in the same way. Serve with a hot tomato sauce.

Serve with: Creamy mashed potatoes plus a French bean salad, with garlic dressing and sesame seeds.

Wednesday
Courgette Flan

For the case:
8 oz (225g) pastry of your
  choice

For the filling
4 small courgettes
2 oz (55g) wholemeal
  breadcrumbs
2 tablespoons milk
6 oz (170g) Ricotta cheese,
  mashed
1 egg, lightly beaten
Seasoning to taste
Garlic salt
½-1 teaspoon oregano
2 oz (55g) grated
  Parmesan cheese
1 teaspoon capers

1 Make up the pastry mix, and set aside in a cool place.
2 Trim and steam the courgettes. Drain well and chop coarsely,
  including the skin.
3 Soak 1½ oz (45g) of the crumbs in the milk for a few minutes,
  then squeeze dry.
4 Mix together the courgettes, breadcrumbs, Ricotta cheese,
  egg, seasoning and oregano.
5 Roll out the pastry and line a medium-sized flan dish. Spoon
  in the courgette mixture, spreading it evenly, and smoothing
  the top. Sprinkle with the remaining breadcrumbs and the
  capers.
6 Bake at 400°F/200°C (Gas Mark 6) for 10 minutes, then
  reduce the oven temperature to 375°F/190°C (Gas Mark 5)
  for 25-30 minutes more, or until the pastry is cooked, and
  the filling fairly firm.

Serve with: Carrots and mushrooms sautéd in butter, and a
cucumber salad. For the extra-hungry, add wholemeal rolls.

Thursday
Mushroom Goulash

2 oz (55g) margarine
1 onion, chopped
1 lb (455g) mushrooms,
  sliced
2 sticks celery, sliced
1 green pepper, sliced
1 teaspoon paprika
Seasoning to taste
⅓ pint (200ml) soured cream
1 tablespoon wholemeal
  flour
2 oz (55g) walnuts,
  coarsely chopped
Parsley to garnish

1 Melt the fat and fry the onion until it begins to soften.
2 Add the mushrooms, celery and green pepper. Cook until
  the mushrooms are tender, then add the paprika and
  seasoning and cook a few minutes more.
3 Add a drop of water and continue simmering until all the
  vegetables are cooked.
4 Mix the soured cream with the flour and then stir into the
  vegetables. Cook over a low heat until heated through. Add
  the nuts.
5 Transfer to a serving dish and garnish with parsley.

Serve with: Parsley potatoes and a beetroot and raw onion
salad.

Friday
Sunflower Soya Fritters

1 green pepper
2 sticks celery
1 onion
¼ small cabbage
1 teaspoon mixed herbs
3 oz (85g) soya flour
1 oz (30g) ground
  sunflower seeds
Seasoning to taste
Vegetable stock to mix
Vegetable oil for frying
Brown gravy to serve (see
  page 153)

1 Chop the pepper, celery, onion and cabbage as finely as possible.
2 Mix together with the herbs, soya flour and sunflower seeds, and season generously. If necessary, moisten with a little vegetable stock.
3 Divide the mixture into small pieces and shape into fritters.
4 Heat some vegetable oil in a pan and shallow fry the fritters gently, turning once, until browned. Drain well on paper towels. Hand round brown gravy for those who want it.

Serve with: Red and white cabbage salad with caraway seeds added for extra flavour. A hot grain dish could also be served.

Saturday
Greek-Style Aubergine Crumble

For the base:
1 medium aubergine
3 tablespoons vegetable oil
1 oz (30g) margarine or
  butter
1 onion, sliced
1 clove garlic, crushed
14 oz (395g) tin tomatoes,
  drained and chopped
Squeeze of lemon juice
Chopped parsley
Seasoning to taste

For the crumble:
3 oz (85g) wholemeal flour
3 oz (85g) margarine
Chopped parsley
1-2 oz (30-55g) pine nuts
  or chopped walnuts
Seasoning to taste

1 Peel and cube the aubergine. Heat the oil and butter together in a pan and sauté the aubergine, stirring occasionally, until it begins to colour. Remove from the pan and set aside.
2 Add the onion and garlic to the pan and cook to soften. Stir in the aubergine, tomatoes, lemon juice, parsley and seasoning.
3 Bring to the boil, cover, and simmer for 10 minutes. Transfer the vegetable mixture to an ovenproof dish.
4 Put the flour in a bowl and rub in the margarine. Add parsley and nuts; season well.
5 Sprinkle mixture over the vegetables, and bake at 375°F/190°C (Gas Mark 5) for 20-30 minutes, or until crumble is crisp and brown.

Serve with: Warm pitta bread; raw broad bean salad with yogurt or tofu dressing.

Sunday
Two-Cheese Soufflé

1 oz (30g) margarine or
  butter
1 oz (30g) wholemeal flour
⅔ pint (340ml) milk
4 egg yolks
2 oz (55g) Gouda cheese,
  grated
3 oz (85g) Lancashire
  cheese, grated
Seasoning to taste
5 egg whites

1 Melt the fat in a saucepan and add the flour; cook gently for a few minutes.
2 Remove pan from the heat and stir in the milk, then return to cooker and simmer, stirring, until the sauce thickens. Set aside to cool slightly.
3 Stir in the egg yolks; add the grated cheeses and seasoning, and mix thoroughly.
4 Whisk the egg whites until stiff, then fold carefully into the cheese mixture, using a metal spoon.
5 Turn into a greased 2-pint soufflé dish. Bake at once in an oven pre-heated to 375°F/190°C (Gas Mark 5) for 35-40 minutes, until risen and golden.

Serve with: Fennel cooked in an onion, tomato and red wine sauce. New potatoes.

Week 13:
Monday
Vichyssoise

*1 oz (30g) margarine or
    butter*
2 onions, finely chopped
2 leeks, finely chopped
2 parsnips, diced
2 potatoes, diced
*1½ pints (850ml) vegetable
    stock*
*1 tablespoon parsley,
    chopped*
2 egg yolks
*¼ pint (140ml) single
    cream*
Seasoning to taste
Parsley to garnish
*Chopped roasted hazelnuts
    to garnish*

1 Melt the fat, and gently fry the onions and leeks for 5 minutes, or until they begin to soften.
2 Add the parsnips and potatoes and cook briefly, then stir in the stock and parsley.
3 Bring to the boil, then simmer for 20 minutes, or until the vegetables are tender.
4 Purée in a blender, or push through a sieve, and return the mixture to the pan.
5 Whisk the egg yolks lightly with the cream, and stir into the soup. Cook gently for a few minutes more, taking care not to let it boil. Season and chill well.
6 Serve garnished with parsley and the chopped nuts.

Serve with: Salad sandwiches with yeast extract, or a salad plus wholemeal muffins. Finish with fresh fruit.

Tuesday
Macaroni and Blue Cheese Bake

*10 oz (285g) wholemeal
    macaroni*
*2 oz (55g) margarine or
    butter*
2 oz (55g) wholemeal flour
1 pint (570ml) milk
*4 oz (115g) blue cheese,
    coarsely crumbled*
Seasoning to taste
*1 oz (30g) wholemeal
    breadcrumbs*
Parsley to garnish

1 Cook the macaroni in a pan of boiling water for 10 minutes or until just tender, then drain well.
2 Meanwhile, melt the fat in a clean pan and sprinkle in the flour. Cook briefly, then add the milk, stirring well as you heat it, to make a smooth thick sauce. Add the crumbled cheese.
3 Mix together the sauce and macaroni, season to taste, and turn into an ovenproof dish. Top with breadcrumbs.
4 Bake at 350°F/180°C (Gas Mark 4) for 15-20 minutes to heat through. Garnish with fresh parsley.

Serve with: A salad of raw courgettes in a light herb dressing, sprinkled with peanuts.

Wednesday
Wholewheat and Egg Loaf

2 tablespoons vegetable oil
1 large onion, chopped
*1 large red pepper,
    chopped*
*½ lb (225g) wholewheat
    berries, soaked overnight*
4 oz (115g) soya flour
Seasoning to taste
1-2 teaspoons mixed herbs
4 hard-boiled eggs
*½ oz (15g) margarine or
    butter*
Watercress to garnish

1 Heat the oil in a saucepan and fry the chopped onion and pepper to soften.
2 Drain the wholewheat berries and mix with the vegetable. the soya flour, seasoning and herbs.
3 Spoon half the mixture into a greased loaf tin. Halve the eggs and arrange on top of the wholewheat berries, cut side down Top with the rest of the mixture and smooth the top. Dot with knobs of fat.
4 Bake at 400°F/200°C (Gas Mark 6) for 40-50 minutes, or until set. Garnish generously with watercress.

Serve with: A red cabbage and orange salad in soured cream dressing. Tiny steamed new potatoes would go well, too.

Thursday
Mushroom and Cauliflower Quiche

*½ lb (225g) pastry of your
  choice*

For the filling:
*1 small cauliflower
½ oz (15g) margarine
4 oz (115g) mushrooms,
  sliced
2 eggs
¼ pint (140ml) milk
4 tablespoons single cream
2 oz (55g) grated
  Parmesan cheese
Seasoning to taste
Pinch of nutmeg*

1 Make up the pastry mix and set aside in a cool place.
2 Trim the cauliflower, break into florets, and steam gently for 3-5 minutes, or until just cooked.
3 Melt the margarine and fry the mushrooms to soften.
4 Roll out the pastry and use to line a medium-sized flan dish. Bake blind at 400°F/200°C (Gas Mark 6) for 10 minutes.
5 Put the well-drained vegetables into the flan case.
6 Beat together the eggs, milk, cream, cheese, seasoning and nutmeg; pour over the vegetables. Bake at 375°F/190°C (Gas Mark 5) for 30 minutes, or until set.

Serve with: Fresh baps and a crisp green salad.

Friday
Aubergine Pizza

*½ lb (225g) pizza dough
  of your choice*

For the topping:
*3 tablespoons vegetable oil
1 onion, chopped
1 clove garlic, crushed
1 large aubergine
14 oz (395g) tin tomatoes
1 tablespoon tomato purée
1 teaspoon marjoram
Seasoning to taste
4 oz (115g) Féta cheese,
  crumbled or 2 oz (55g)
  pine nuts*

1 Make up the dough according to instructions.
2 Heat the vegetable oil in a large pan and sauté the onion and garlic for a few minutes.

3 Peel and cube the aubergine and add to the pan, stirring well.
4 Add the contents of the tin of tomatoes, the tomato purée, marjoram and seasoning. Continue cooking, stirring occasionally, until the sauce thickens and the aubergine is cooked.
5 Divide the pizza dough into four and roll out into small circles. Spread each one with some of the aubergine mixture (if it is too moist, drain off the excess liquid first). Scatter with crumbled cheese or pine nuts.
6 Bake at 400°F/200°C (Gas Mark 6) for 20-30 minutes, until cooked.

Serve with: A salad of raw mushrooms, celery and pepper, plus chopped black olives.

Saturday
Spinach Curry with Chick-Peas

**1 pint (570ml) curry
  sauce (see page 154)
1 lb (455g) spinach
4 oz (115g) cooked chick
  peas, coarsely chopped
4 oz (115g) tofu, sliced
Chopped spring onions to
  garnish*

1 Bring the sauce gently to the boil.
2 Wash, trim and shred the spinach and add to the sauce. Stir well, lower the heat, and simmer for 10 minutes, or until the spinach is well cooked.
3 Stir the drained chick-peas into the spinach mixture. Heat a minute or two more.
4 Top the curry with coarsely chopped tofu, and sprinkle with the chopped spring onions.

Serve with: Wholemeal chapatis. Mango chutney, and cucumber in yogurt would go well with the flavours, too.

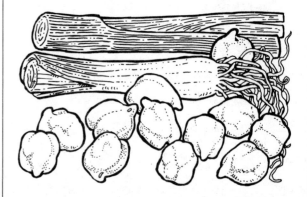

*Make a day in advance and leave overnight for the flavour to develop. Reheat gently.

Sunday
Russian Blinis (Savoury)

For the blinis:
4 oz (115g) buckwheat
   flour
4 oz (115g) wholemeal
   flour
½ pint (285ml) warm milk
   and water, mixed
½ oz (15g) fresh yeast
Good pinch of raw brown
   sugar
1 large egg, separated
½ oz (15g) butter, melted
Pinch of sea salt
Vegetable oil for frying

For the filling:
4 hard-boiled eggs
2 sticks celery
1 small red pepper
Seasoning to taste
½ pint (285ml) soured cream
Poppy seeds (optional)

1 Mix the sifted flours together in a bowl.
2 Add a little of the liquid to the yeast and mix well, then stir
   into the rest of the liquid together with the sugar.
3 Add to the flours and leave in a warm spot for about 30
   minutes, or until the mixture is frothy and about twice its
   original volume.
4 Knock back the dough and lightly whisk in the egg yolk,
   melted butter and salt. Set aside again to rise.
5 Beat the egg white until just able to hold its shape, then fold
   into the batter. If time allows, leave in the warm a little longer.

6 Heat the oil in a pan, spoon in a little of the mixture, and
   cook gently until lightly browned underneath. Turn and cook
   the other side. Keep the cooked blinis warm whilst using all
   the batter in the same way.
7 Chop the eggs, celery and pepper, season to taste, and moisten
   with a little of the soured cream.
8 Put a spoonful onto each of the blinis, fold in half, and serve
   at once. Hand round extra soured cream at the table to be
   spooned over the blinis as required. A light sprinkling of
   poppy seeds adds an interesting flavour.

Serve with: A dark bread, such as rye, and a lettuce, beetroot
and spring onion salad with chopped walnuts.

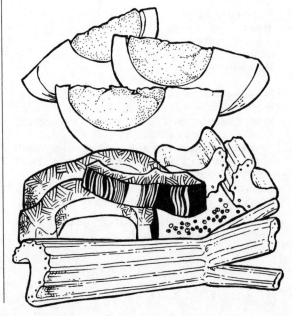

2.

SUMMER

Week 1:
Monday
Cashew Fritters

½ lb (225g) cashew nuts
4 Weetabix
1 egg, lightly beaten
2 tablespoons vegetable oil
1 onion, finely sliced
1 stick celery, finely sliced
1 carrot, finely sliced
2 tomatoes, chopped
1 teaspoon marjoram, or
*   to taste*
Seasoning to taste
Approx. ½ pint (285ml)
*   vegetable stock or milk*
Rolled oats to coat
Vegetable oil for frying

1 Grind the nuts and mix with the crumbled Weetabix and egg.
2 Heat the oil in a pan and sauté the onion, celery and carrot for five minutes to soften. Add the tomatoes, marjoram and seasoning and cook a few minutes more.
3 Stir together the nut mixture and vegetables, adding enough liquid to make a thick but moist-textured dough. Divide and shape into fritters.
4 Coat each one in some of the oats and deep or shallow fry the fritters until crisp and brown. Drain on paper towels.

Serve with: Apple, beetroot and red cabbage plus a dish of wholewheat berries, hot or cold.

Tuesday
Mixed Grain Pilau

2 tablespoons vegetable oil
1 clove garlic, crushed
1 red pepper, sliced
1 onion, sliced
1 teaspoon mixed spice
2 courgettes, chopped
½ lb (225g) mixed cooked
*   grains e.g. rice, millet,*
*   wholewheat berries)*
Seasoning to taste
1 oz (30g) raisins
2 oz (55g) brazil nuts,
*   coarsely chopped*
Chives, to garnish

1 Heat the vegetable oil in a pan, and gently fry the crushed garlic with the sliced pepper and onion for 5-10 minutes to soften. Add the spice and cook one minute more.
2 Stir in the courgettes and continue cooking 5 minutes more.
3 Add the cooked grains (with just a tiny drop of water if very dry). Heat through over a low heat, taking care not to burn. Season to taste. Add raisins.
4 Sprinkle the pilau with chopped nuts and garnish with chopped chives.

Serve with: A spinach salad sprinkled with chopped, hard-boiled eggs or cubes of tofu for extra protein.

Note: This is an ideal recipe for when you have a variety of left-over grains to use up.

Wednesday
Swiss Cheese Fondue

1 oz (30g) unsalted butter
½ lb (225g) Gruyère
  cheese, grated
½ lb (225g) Emmental
  cheese, grated
½ pint (285ml) dry white
  wine
Seasoning to taste
Drop of brandy (optional)

To serve:
Wholemeal bread or toast
  cubes
Cucumber sticks
Celery sticks
Carrot sticks
Strips of pepper
Raw cauliflower florets
Potato crisps
Corn chips

1 Grease the base and sides of a heavy casserole or saucepan (a fondue dish is ideal).
2 Put the cheeses into the casserole with the wine. Heat very gently, stirring continually, until the sauce thickens. Add seasoning and, if liked, a little brandy.
3 Stand the fondue over a warming tray in the centre of the table, and allow people to dip into it with their choice of bread, vegetables, crisps or chips.

Serve with: A simple lettuce salad is all that is needed to complete your fondue.

Note: This is a very rich fondue. For a milder version, substitute Cheddar cheese for half of the Swiss cheese — or use Cheddar cheese only.

Thursday
Pizza with Tofu

½ lb (225g) pizza dough
  of your choice

For the topping:
½ lb (225g) fresh spinach
  or frozen equivalent
2 tablespoons vegetable oil
1 onion, sliced
6 oz (170g) tofu
Seasoning to taste
Soya sauce to taste
2 oz (55g) roasted
  sunflower seeds

1 Prepare the pizza dough according to instructions.
2 Wash the spinach, put it wet into a pan, cover, and steam for 10-15 minutes or until just cooked. Drain well and chop coarsely, then set aside.
3 Heat the oil in a pan and sauté the onion until it begins to colour. Drain the tofu and add to the onion, mashing it well with a fork or wooden spoon. Cook a few minutes more.
4 Add the spinach, seasoning and soya sauce, stir, and cook a little longer.
5 Divide the dough and roll out to make four small circles. Share the topping between them, spreading it to the edge of each one. Sprinkle with seeds.
6 Bake at 400°F/200°C (Gas Mark 6) for 20 minutes or until dough is cooked.

Serve with: Fresh wholemeal bread and a tomato and onion salad.

Friday
Spanish Omelette

3 tablespoons vegetable oil
1 large onion, sliced
1 green pepper, sliced
1 large potato, cubed
3 tomatoes, coarsely
  chopped
6 eggs
Seasoning to taste
Parsley to garnish

1 Heat most of the oil in a large pan. Add the onion and pepper, then the potato.
2 Sauté the vegetables briefly, then cover the pan and cook gently for 10 minutes more.
3 Add the tomatoes to the pan, cooking just long enough to heat through. Remove the vegetables from the pan and set aside somewhere warm.
4 Wipe the pan clean, or use a fresh one. Heat the remaining oil.
5 Beat the eggs, add the seasoning, and blend with the vegetables. Pour into the pan.
6 Allow to set lightly on the bottom, then loosen the sides of the omelette and tilt the pan so that the mixture flows underneath. You can, if liked, put the omelette under the grill for a minute or two to set the top. Serve flat, cut into wedges. Sprinkle with parsley.

Serve with: Steamed green beans, plus crisps or new potatoes.

Saturday
Avocado Risotto

2 tablespoons vegetable oil
2 spring onions, chopped
4 oz (115g) mushrooms,
*   sliced*
10 oz (285g) brown rice
1½ pints (850ml) vegetable
*   stock*
10 black olives
2 avocados
3 hard-boiled eggs or 2 oz
*   (55g) walnuts*
Seasoning to taste
Soya 'bacon' bits to
*   garnish*

1 Heat the vegetable oil and lightly sauté the chopped onions for 5 minutes, stirring frequently.
2 Add the sliced mushrooms and cook gently for 5 minutes more.
3 Stir in the rice until coated with the oil, then add the stock. Bring to the boil, then cover the pan and simmer for 30-40 minutes, or until the rice is cooked.
4 Chop the stoned olives; slice the avocados, also the eggs if using them. Stir into the rice and cook briefly. Season to taste.
5 Garnish with soya 'bacon' bits.

Serve with: A cucumber and radish salad, maybe with a yogurt dressing.

Sunday
Peanut Balls with Spaghetti

4 oz (115g) soya 'minced
*   beef', cooked*
1 onion, finely chopped
2 oz (55g) smooth peanut
*   butter*
1 tablespoon tomato purée
Seasoning to taste
1 tablespoon parsley,
*   chopped*
1 egg, beaten
Approx. 1 oz (30g)
*   wholemeal breadcrumbs*
Vegetable oil for frying
8 oz (225g) wholemeal
*   spaghetti*
Tomato sauce to serve (see
*   page 153)*

1 Put the drained 'minced beef' into a large bowl.
2 Add the onion, the peanut butter, tomato purée, seasoning and parsley.
3 Bind with the beaten egg and enough crumbs to stiffen the mixture. Divide and shape into small balls.
4 Fry the balls gently in hot oil so that they brown on the outside, and are heated right through.
5 At the same time, cook the spaghetti in a large pan of boiling water until just tender. Drain well.
6 Transfer the spaghetti to a heated serving dish and top with the peanut balls and then a little of the tomato sauce. Hand round extra sauce at the table for those who want it.

Serve with: A salad of coarsely grated courgettes, mixed with sliced mushrooms and green beans — all the vegetables raw.

Week 2:
Monday
Ratatouille Salad with Almonds

2 tablespoons vegetable oil
2 oz (55g) margarine or
*   butter*
2 oz (55g) almonds
2 onions, sliced
1 large green pepper,
*   sliced*
1 clove garlic, crushed
1 large aubergine, diced
4 tomatoes, coarsely
*   chopped*
Seasoning to taste
3 oz (85g) cooked peas
Lettuce to serve
Parsley to garnish

1 Heat half the oil and half the margarine together in a pan, and lightly sauté the almonds. Remove them and set aside.
2 Add the remaining oil and margarine to the pan. Cook the sliced onion and pepper with the garlic until the vegetables begin to soften.
3 Add the aubergine, tomatoes and seasoning, cover, and continue cooking for about 15 minutes, or until the vegetables are tender and the oil has been absorbed. Add the peas.
4 Adjust seasoning and chill. Serve on a bed of lettuce, and sprinkle with the almonds and a generous amount of fresh chopped parsley.

Serve with: Wholemeal bread, Melba toast or a wholegrain crispbread.

Tuesday
'Beef' Stuffed Peppers

4 large peppers
2 tablespoons vegetable oil
1 small onion, finely
  chopped
3 oz (85g) soya 'minced
  beef', hydrated in water
1 oz (30g) wholemeal
  breadcrumbs
Chopped parsley
Seasoning to taste
Good pinch of marjoram
2 teaspoons capers,
  chopped
1 tablespoon tomato purée
1 egg, beaten
2 oz (55g) grated Cheddar
  cheese

1 Cut the stalks off the peppers and remove the seeds from inside. Place under a hot grill, turning frequently, until the skins begin to blister.
2 Cool slightly, then rub off the skins. Stand the peppers upright and close together in a small ovenproof dish.
3 Heat the oil and fry the onion for a few minutes. Add the drained 'minced beef' and cook a little longer.
4 Remove from the heat and mix in the breadcrumbs, a generous amount of parsley, seasoning, marjoram, chopped capers, and the tomato purée. Add the egg. If the mixture seems very dry, moisten it with a drop of the water in which the 'minced beef' was soaked, or with extra tomato purée.
5 Stuff each of the peppers with some of the mixture. Top with the grated cheese.
6 Bake at 350°F/180°C (Gas Mark 4) for 30-45 minutes, or until the peppers are cooked.

Serve with: Hot brown rice, plus a salad of blanched, chilled courgettes mixed with tomatoes and onions, in a mint dressing.

Wednesday
Blue Cheese Lasagne

6 oz (170g) wholemeal
  lasagne
6 oz (170g) mushrooms,
  sliced
2 oz (55g) walnut pieces
1 oz (30g) margarine or
  butter
¾ pint (425ml) white
  sauce (see page 153)
Approx. 6 oz (170g) blue
  cheese, crumbled
Milk
Seasoning to taste
2 oz (55g) wholemeal
  breadcrumbs

1 Drop the lasagne into a pan of boiling water, one sheet at a time, and cook for 8 minutes, or until just tender. Drain, rinse in cold water, and lay the sheets on a clean tea towel.
2 Sauté the mushrooms and the walnut pieces in the melted fat for just a few minutes, stirring occasionally. The mushrooms should be just cooked.
3 Heat the white sauce and add enough crumbled blue cheese to flavour it to taste. Add a drop of milk to give sauce a soft consistency. Season to taste.
4 Arrange a third of the lasagne in the base of a lightly greased casserole, top with half of the mushroom and walnut mixture, then some of the blue cheese sauce. Repeat, then add the rest of the lasagne and top with sauce.
5 Sprinkle with breadcrumbs and bake at 375°F/190°C (Gas Mark 5) for 30 minutes.

Serve with: A tomato, pepper and endive salad.

Friday
Italian Vegetable Casserole

2 tablespoons vegetable oil
1 large onion, sliced
½-1 clove garlic, crushed
4 oz (115g) split peas,
*   soaked overnight*
4 oz (115g) fresh broad
*   beans*
1 small aubergine, diced
1 courgette, sliced
4 tomatoes, skinned and
*   coarsely chopped*
4 oz (115g) mushrooms,
*   sliced*
1-2 teaspoons tomato
*   purée*
1 teaspoon oregano
Seasoning to taste
½ oz (15g) margarine or
*   butter*
½ oz (15g) wholemeal
*   flour*
Parsley to garnish

1 Heat the vegetable oil in a pan, and add the onion and garlic. Cook gently for 5-10 minutes to soften.
2 Add the drained split peas and cover with fresh water. Cover the pan, and cook for 30 minutes.
3 Add the broad beans, aubergine and courgette. Stir in the tomatoes and continue to cook for 15 minutes.
4 Add the mushrooms with the tomato purée, oregano and seasoning. If necessary pour in a drop more water, but not too much. Cook 10-15 minutes more, or until the beans and vegetables are tender.
5 Soften the fat and add the flour to make a roux. Mix into the other ingredients, stir well, and cook a few minutes to thicken the stock.
6 Garnish with fresh chopped parsley.

Serve with: Lightly steamed new potatoes with parsley and butter, plus a green salad with protein-rich dressing.

Thursday
Soya Loaf

2 tablespoons vegetable oil
1 clove garlic, crushed
1 onion, chopped
2 sticks celery, chopped
½ lb (225g) cooked soya
*   beans*
2 large eggs, lightly beaten
½-1 teaspoon of thyme
½-1 teaspoon savory
Seasoning to taste
2 oz (55g) wheatgerm
2 oz (55g) chopped
*   walnuts*
2 oz (55g) grated Edam
*   cheese*

1 Heat the oil in a pan and sauté the garlic, onion and celery until they begin to soften.
2 Crush or mince the drained beans until coarsely ground.
3 Mix together the vegetables, beans, beaten eggs, herbs, seasoning and wheatgerm.
4 Spoon half the mixture into a greased loaf tin and smooth the top. Sprinkle with the nuts and grated cheese, then top with the rest of the soya bean mixture.
5 Bake at 350°F/180°C (Gas Mark 4) for 30-40 minutes, or until cooked.

Serve with: A salad with chicory, pepper and lettuce, plus a hot rice bowl.

Saturday
Beany Yogurt Pancakes

For the batter:
4 oz (115g) wholemeal
   flour
Pinch of salt
1 egg
¼ pint (140ml) cold water
¼ pint (140ml) natural
   yogurt
1 tablespoon vegetable oil

For the filling:
3 tablespoons vegetable oil
1 large onion, sliced
1 large green pepper,
   sliced
½-1 teaspoon chilli
   powder, or to taste
1 teaspoon paprika
14 oz (395g) tin tomatoes,
   chopped
10 oz (285g) cooked
   kidney beans
Seasoning to taste
Vegetable oil for frying
Natural yogurt to serve

1 Sift together the flour and salt. Make a well in the centre and
   stir in the egg, then the water. Gradually add the yogurt and
   oil; whisk the batter until smooth. Set aside in a cool place
   for half an hour.
2 Heat the oil in a large pan and gently sauté the sliced onion
   and pepper. Add the chilli powder and paprika and cook a
   few minutes more.
3 Add the chopped tomatoes with any liquid that was in the
   tin, stir well, and continue cooking over a higher heat until
   the sauce begins to thicken.
4 Add the drained kidney beans and cook long enough to heat
   through. Season to taste.
5 Meanwhile whisk the batter and, if necessary, add a drop more
   liquid to make a pouring consistency. Heat a drop of oil in
   a heavy-based frying pan and spoon in some of the batter.
6 Cook gently, tipping the pan frequently, until the pancake
   begins to brown underneath, then flip or turn with a spatula
   and cook briefly on the other side. Keep pancakes warm whilst
   using the rest of the batter in the same way.
7 Fill each pancake with some of the bean mixture, fold, and
   serve topped with a spoonful or two of yogurt.

Serve with: A salad of raw, finely chopped celeriac, apple
raisins and walnuts.

Sunday
Courgette and Sweetcorn Soufflé

1½ oz (45g) margarine or
   butter
1 oz (30g) wholemeal flour
⅓ pint (200ml) milk
Seasoning to taste
1 medium courgette
6 oz (170g) cooked
   sweetcorn
3 oz (85g) grated Cheddar
   cheese
3 egg yolks
4 egg whites

1 Melt the fat in a pan and sprinkle in the flour. Cook briefly,
   then remove from heat and add the milk. Return to heat and
   continue cooking gently, stirring continually, until the sauce
   thickens. Season to taste.
2 Wash the courgette, then grate or chop finely. Drain the
   sweetcorn. Stir the vegetables into the sauce.
3 Add the grated cheese and egg yolks, mixing well.
4 Whisk the egg whites until stiff. Fold them into the other
   ingredients, using a metal spoon, then pour the mixture into
   a greased, 2-pint soufflé dish.
5 Bake at once in an oven pre-heated to 375°F/190°C (Gas
   Mark 5) for 25-30 minutes.

Serve with: A dish of hot millet with chopped nuts sprinkled
on top, plus a carrot salad.

Summer

Week 3:
Monday
Jacket Potatoes with Stir-Fried Vegetables

4 large potatoes
3 tablespoons vegetable oil
½ small onion, sliced
1 carrot, sliced
Small chunk white
  cabbage, shredded
2 oz (55g) mushrooms,
  sliced
3 tablespoons mung
  beansprouts
2 oz (55g) cashew pieces
Soya sauce to taste
Seasoning to taste

1 Scrub the potatoes, pat dry, and prick. Rub lightly with a little of the oil, then bake at 400°F/200°C (Gas Mark 6) for about an hour, or until soft.
2 Meanwhile heat the rest of the oil in a pan and fry the onion, carrot and cabbage for a few minutes, stirring frequently.
3 Add the mushrooms and cook a minute or two more, then add the beansprouts and cashew pieces. Moisten with soya sauce and cover the pan. Cook gently for 5 minutes, taking care not to burn. The vegetables should still be crisp.
4 Halve the potatoes and top with a spoonful or two of the vegetable nut mixture.

Serve with: A mixed salad with cooked beans added for protein.

Tuesday
Curried Avocado Soup (Cold)

2 large, ripe avocados
1 teaspoon curry paste or
  to taste
1 pint (570ml) vegetable
  stock
⅓ pint (200ml) natural
  yogurt
Squeeze of lemon juice
Seasoning to taste
1 oz (30g) flaked almonds

1 Peel the avocados, remove the stones and chop the flesh coarsely.
2 In a blender, purée the avocados together with the curry paste and vegetable stock.
3 Stir in the yogurt, lemon juice and seasoning. Chill well.
4 Adjust the seasoning.

5 Lightly roast the almonds in a dry pan, cool, and then sprinkle over the soup before serving.

Serve with: A green salad with cooked flageolet beans and tomatoes added. You could also serve wholemeal bread or — for a change — wholemeal chapatis or puris.

Wednesday
'Beefburgers'

5 oz (140g) soya 'minced
  beef', hydrated in water
1 onion, finely chopped
2 oz (55g) wholemeal
  breadcrumbs
Celery salt
Freshly ground pepper
1 teaspoon mixed herbs, or
  to taste
1 teaspoon chilli powder,
  or to taste
1 egg, lightly beaten

1 Bring the 'minced beef' to a boil, simmer for 5 minutes, then drain, reserving a little of the liquid.
2 In a bowl mix together the 'minced beef', onion, breadcrumbs, seasoning, herbs, chilli powder and beaten egg. Blend thoroughly. If necessary, add a drop of the reserved liquid to help the mixture hold together.
3 Use hands to mould the mixture, then divide it into even-sized balls and shape into burgers.
4 Grill the burgers for about 10 minutes, turning once, until well cooked.

Serve with: Wholemeal baps, onion rings, tomato slices, pickles, chutney, mustard — all the usual trimmings. Finish your meal with fresh fruit.

Thursday
Greek Spinach Quiche

½ lb (225g) pastry of your
* choice*

For the filling:
½ lb (225g) cooked
* spinach*
½ oz (15g) margarine or
* butter*
1 small onion, chopped
6 oz (170g) Féta cheese,
* mashed*
3 eggs, lightly beaten
¼ pint (140ml) creamy
* milk*
Seasoning to taste
Garlic salt
Basil

1 Make up the pastry mix and set aside in a cool place.
2 Drain the spinach and chop as fine as possible.
3 Melt the fat and lightly sauté the onion. Off the heat, stir in the spinach.
4 Mix the cheese with the eggs, milk, seasoning, garlic salt and basil. Stir the spinach into the mixture.
5 Roll out the pastry and use to line a medium-sized flan dish. Bake blind at 400°F/200°C (Gas Mark 6) for 10 minutes.
6 Pour in the prepared mixture, smooth the top, and bake at the same temperature for 15 minutes, then lower the heat to 375°F/190°C (Gas Mark 5) for a further 15 minutes, or until set.

Serve with: A salad of tomatoes, cucumber, radishes, lettuce, olives and fresh mint. Pitta bread could also be served.

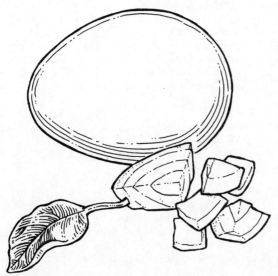

Friday
Vegetable Lentil Dhal

½ lb (225g) red lentils,
* soaked briefly*
1 pint (570ml) water
Seasoning to taste
2 tablespoons ghee
1 large onion, chopped
1 clove garlic, crushed
1-2 tablespoons curry
* powder*
2 courgettes, trimmed and
* sliced*
½ small cauliflower,
* broken into florets*
3 tomatoes, peeled and
* coarsely chopped*
2 oz (55g) cashews
Garam masala (optional)

1 Add the cleaned lentils to the water, bring to a boil and fast boil for 10 minutes, then simmer until tender.
2 Mash the lentils to a purée with seasoning to taste and half the ghee. Set the dhal aside in a warm spot.
3 Melt the remaining ghee in a clean pan, and fry the chopped onion with the garlic until they begin to colour. Add the curry powder and cook a few minutes more.
4 Add the vegetables and cook gently until all of them are tender. Stir in the nuts.
5 Mix together the dhal and the vegetables and put over a low heat just long enough to warm through. Add garam masala for a stronger flavour, if liked.

Serve with: Wholemeal puris, and a salad of lightly cooked celeriac with parsley.

Saturday
Blue Cheese Pizza

*½ lb (225g) pizza dough
of your choice*

For the topping:
*1 lb (455g) firm tomatoes
4-6 oz (115-170g)
Gorgonzola or Danish
Blue cheese
1-2 teaspoons marjoram
2 tablespoons soya 'bacon'
bits*

1 Make the pizza dough and, when ready to use, roll out to make 4 small or 2 large pizzas.
2 Arrange the dough on a baking sheet, and bake blind at 400°F/200°C (Gas Mark 6) for 20 minutes, or until just cooked.
3 Slice the tomatoes and arrange on top of the pizzas. Crumble the cheese, add marjoram and 'bacon' bits, and sprinkle over the tomato slices.
4 Either return the pizzas to the oven for 5-10 minutes to melt the cheese, or put them under the grill briefly.

Serve with: A chicory, mushroom and celery salad. Sprinkle with walnuts.

Sunday
Pea and Courgette Vol-au-Vent

For the puff pastry:
*½ lb (225g) wholemeal
flour
Pinch of salt
7 oz (200g) unsalted butter
Cold water to mix
1 egg, beaten*

For the filling:
*1 lb (455g) courgettes,
trimmed and sliced
6 oz (170g) cooked
peas
½ pint (285ml) white
sauce (see page 153)
1 teaspoon thyme
Seasoning to taste
2 oz (55g) almonds,
coarsely chopped
4 oz (115g) grated Cheddar
cheese
Fresh parsley to garnish*

1 Make up the pastry first. Sift together the flour and salt, rub in the butter to make a crumb-like mixture, then stir in enough cold water to form a fairly stiff dough.
2 Roll out to an oblong on a floured board. Fold both ends towards the middle, give the pastry a quarter turn, and roll out again. Fold in the same way, wrap in cling film, and chill for 30 minutes.
3 Repeat this rolling, folding and turning process 3 more times, allowing the dough to chill for 30 minutes in between each session.
4 Roll out the pastry and cut 2 circles about 8 inches (20cm) in diameter, then cut a large lid in one of them.
5 Brush beaten egg around the edge of the complete circle, place the ring on top. Brush the top of the ring and the lid with egg. Set aside for 30 minutes more.
6 Bake at 400°F/200°C (Gas Mark 6) for 20-30 minutes, or until cooked.
7 Meanwhile, steam the courgettes until just tender. Drain well, do the same with the peas, and stir the vegetables into the white sauce.
8 Heat the sauce gently, and add the thyme, seasoning, almonds and the cheese.
9 Spoon the mixture into the hot vol-au-vent case, garnish with parsley, and serve at once.

Serve with: A red cabbage and beetroot salad with apple added, plus a cold grain salad — rice or bulgur, for example. French bread would go well, too, if needed.

Week 4:
Monday
Pasta Shells with Potatoes

*2 tablespoons vegetable oil
1 oz (30g) margarine or
butter
1 large onion, sliced
1 lb (455g) potatoes,
peeled and diced
14 oz (395g) tin tomatoes,
coarsely chopped
Seasoning to taste
Parsley
6 oz (170g) wholemeal
pasta shells
3 oz (85g) cooked peas
Grated Parmesan cheese to
serve*

1 Heat the oil together with the fat in a large pan. Sauté the onion until it begins to soften.
2 Add the potatoes to the pan, stirring well. Cover and simmer for 10 minutes.
3 Add the tomatoes, seasoning and parsley. Bring to the boil

then lower heat and simmer until the sauce is thick.

4 Cook the pasta shells in boiling water for 10 minutes, or until tender. Drain well and stir into the vegetable mixture with the peas. Heat through briefly.

5 Serve topped with a generous helping of grated cheese.

Serve with: A salad of green beans, lettuce, peppers and chopped hard-boiled eggs.

Tuesday
Fruit and Nut Salad

4 sticks celery
½ cucumber
2 oz (55g) mushrooms
1 peach
1 orange
1 apple
1 banana
2 oz (55g) walnuts,
  chopped

For the dressing:
2 tablespoons lemon juice
2 tablespoons honey
2 tablespoons vegetable oil
Seasoning to taste
Crisp Iceberg lettuce to
  serve
6 oz (170g) cottage cheese
  to serve

1 Clean and chop the celery, cucumber and mushrooms.
2 Slice the fruit and mix with the prepared vegetables and the nuts.
3 Combine the salad dressing ingredients in a screw-top jar, then pour over the fruit mixture and toss lightly.
4 Shred the lettuce and arrange in a salad bowl. Spoon the fruit and nut mixture into the centre, top with cottage cheese and serve at once.

Serve with: Wholemeal sesame crispbread tastes good with this salad. Spread it with nut butter or a low-fat cream cheese. Wholemeal baps or bread could also be served.

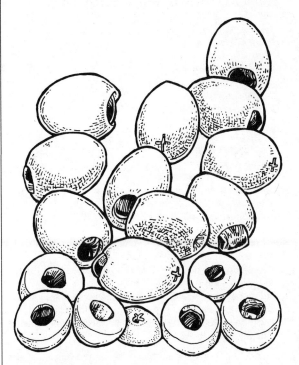

Wednesday
Quiche with Green Olives

½ lb (225g) pastry of your
  choice

For the filling:
6 oz (170g) curd cheese
2 large eggs, beaten
Seasoning to taste
Approx. 16 stuffed olives,
  sliced
2 oz (55g) grated Cheddar
  cheese

1 Make up the pastry mix and set aside in a cool place.
2 Sieve the curd cheese to make it smooth and creamy. Combine well with the beaten eggs, seasoning, and sliced olives.
3 Roll out the pastry and use to line a medium-sized flan case. Bake blind at 400°F/200°C (Gas Mark 6) for 10 minutes.
4 Pour the egg and cheese mixture into the flan case, and top with the grated cheese. Lower the oven temperature to 375°F/190°C (Gas Mark 5) and cook for 30 minutes, or until set.

Serve with: A salad of raw (or blanched) courgettes and mushrooms with red pepper, herb dressing, and roasted peanuts.

Thursday
Savoury Rice with Bananas

½ lb (225g) brown rice
1 pint (570ml) vegetable
  stock
2 oz (55g) margarine or
  butter
2 onions, sliced
1 clove garlic, crushed
2 sticks celery, chopped
4 oz (115g) cooked peas
2 oz (55g) peanuts
2 oz (55g) sultanas
Good pinch of cinnamon
Seasoning to taste
3 large bananas, sliced
Natural yogurt to serve

1 Rinse the rice, then add to the water and cook for 30-40 minutes, or until tender. Drain, and keep warm.
2 Meanwhile, melt the fat in a pan and fry the onions, garlic and celery until soft but not brown.
3 Stir in the peas, peanuts, sultanas, cinnamon and seasoning together with the rice. Mix well and heat through gently.
4 Add the sliced bananas. Remove from heat and serve at once with yogurt for those who want it.

Serve with: A chicory, endive and watercress salad.

Friday
Soufflé Omelette with Sweetcorn

6 eggs, separated
1 oz (30g) wholemeal flour
Seasoning to taste
Pinch of paprika
4 tablespoons cooked
  sweetcorn
½ oz (15g) butter or
  margarine
Chopped chives to garnish

1 Put the egg whites into a chilled bowl, and whisk until stiff.
2 Stir the flour into the egg yolks, add seasoning and paprika. Drain the sweetcorn and combine with the egg yolks.
3 Use a metal spoon to fold the egg whites carefully into the sweetcorn mixture.
4 Heat the fat in a large frying pan and pour in the mixture. Cook for a short time until the omelette begins to colour underneath.

5 Place under a moderate grill and continue cooking for a very short time, until puffed up and golden. Serve cut into slices and sprinkled with chopped chives.

Serve with: Lightly steamed new potatoes with mint, and a beetroot and celery salad.

Saturday
Fennel with Beans

2 heads of fennel
3 tablespoons vegetable oil
1 onion, sliced
⅓ pint (200ml) red wine
2 tablespoons lemon juice
2 tablespoons tomato
  purée
Good pinch raw cane
  sugar
1 teaspoon fresh basil,
  chopped
½ lb (225g) fresh broad
  beans
4 oz (115g) Haloumi cheese
  or other medium soft
  cheese
Fennel leaves to garnish

1 Trim the fennel bulbs and cut lengthways into thin slices.
2 Heat the oil in a large pan and fry the onion for a few minutes, then add the fennel and cook briefly.
3 Pour in the wine and lemon juice, stir in the tomato purée, sugar, basil and shelled beans.
4 Bring to the boil, cover, and simmer for 20-30 minutes, or until the fennel and beans are tender. You may need to add a drop more liquid during the cooking process.
5 Transfer the mixture carefully to a shallow heat-proof dish and top with slices of Haloumi cheese. Put under a grill for 5 minutes, or until the cheese begins to soften and colour. Garnish with fennel leaves.

Serve with: Tiny new potatoes and a salad of cucumber, tomatoes, radishes and olives. Add chopped, hard-boiled egg if you feel you need extra protein.

Sunday
Bazargan

½ lb (225g) bulgur
½ small onion, chopped
4 tablespoons olive oil
3 tablespoons tomato
  purée
3 tomatoes, coarsely
  chopped
Fresh oregano leaves,
  chopped
Fresh parsley, chopped
½ teaspoon of ground
  cumin
½ teaspoon of ground
  allspice
Seasoning to taste
3 oz (85g) walnut pieces

1 Pour plenty of boiling water over the bulgur, then cover and set aside for 30 minutes. Drain the bulgur very well, then transfer to a bowl.
2 Chop the onion finely and stir into the bulgur with the oil and tomato purée.
3 Add the tomatoes to the mixture with a generous amount of chopped oregano leaves and parsley, plus the spices and seasoning.
4 Add the nuts. Chill the bazargan overnight, then bring to room temperature before serving.

Serve with: A coleslaw with tofu mayonnaise, plus wheatgerm bread for those who want it.

Week 5:
Monday
Kohlrabi Casserole

1 oz (30g) margarine or
  butter
1 onion, sliced
1 lb (455g) kohlrabi
2 large carrots, chopped
2 sticks celery, sliced
4 oz (115g) peas
Small tin (7 oz/200g)
  tomatoes, chopped
½ pint (285ml) vegetable
  stock
½ teaspoon basil
Seasoning to taste
4 oz (115g) grated
  Lancashire cheese

1 Melt the fat in a pan and fry the onion until soft.
2 Add the peeled, coarsely chopped kohlrabi and carrots, plus

the celery. Stir and cook for 5 minutes.
3 Add the peas, tomatoes and their juice, the vegetable stock, basil and seasoning.
4 Transfer to an ovenproof dish, cover, and bake at 350°F/180°C (Gas Mark 4) for about an hour, or until the vegetables are cooked.
5 Top with the grated cheese and return to the oven for 10 minutes more.

Serve with: Jacket potatoes, plus a salad of sweetcorn, raisins and apple, with a sprinkling of peanuts.

Tuesday
Creamy Cauliflower Crumble

For the base:
1 large cauliflower
2 tablespoons vegetable oil
1 onion, sliced
1 red pepper, sliced
Approx. 4 tablespoons
  tahini
Squeeze of lemon juice
Seasoning to taste

For the crumble:
4 oz (115g) rolled oats
2 tablespoons vegetable oil
Water to mix
Seasoning to taste

1 Divide the cauliflower into florets and steam very briefly.
2 Heat the oil in a frying pan and gently fry the sliced onion and pepper until they begin to soften. Add the drained cauliflower florets and cook a few minutes more.
3 Stir in enough tahini to make a creamy coating. Add lemon juice and seasoning. Transfer to an ovenproof dish.
4 Put the oats into a bowl and add the oil, distributing it as evenly as possible. Then add enough water to make the mixture moist and crumbly. Season.
5 Spread the oats over the cauliflower and press down. Bake at 350°F/180°C (Gas Mark 4) for 25-30 minutes, or until top is crisp.

Serve with: A radish and onion salad. Roast potatoes would go well with this dish, too.

Summer

Wednesday
Tagliatelle with Curried Yogurt Sauce

10 oz (285g) wholemeal
tagliatelle
1 oz (30g) margarine or
butter
1 onion, finely chopped
1 clove garlic, crushed
1 tablespoon curry powder,
or to taste
1 oz (30g) wholemeal flour
½ pint (285ml) natural
yogurt
¼ pint (140ml) milk
Seasoning to taste
Chives, to garnish

1 Cook the tagliatelle in a pan of boiling water for 10 minutes, or until just tender.
2 Meanwhile, melt the fat in another pan and sauté the onion with the garlic. When they begin to soften, add the curry powder and flour and cook a few minutes more.
3 Stir in the yogurt and milk and cook gently until the sauce thickens.
4 Drain the tagliatelle and cover with the sauce. Toss gently, put into a warmed serving dish, and garnish generously with fresh chopped chives.

Serve with: A cucumber and carrot salad, with chicory as a base, and a garnish of cashew nuts.

Thursday
Cheesy Carrot Flan

For the pastry:
½ lb (225g) wholemeal
flour
2 oz (55g) cream cheese
2 oz (55g) margarine
Cold water with lemon
juice added

For the filling:
1 lb (455g) carrots
4 tablespoons cooked
brown rice
2 eggs, beaten
⅓ pint (200ml) creamy
milk
2 oz (55g) grated Gruyère
cheese
Seasoning to taste
Good pinch of savory or
thyme
2-3 carrots extra
½ oz (15g) butter, melted

1 Put the flour into a bowl, and use fingertips to rub in the cream cheese and margarine to make a crumb-like mixture. Stir in just enough water to bind to a dough.
2 Knead the dough until smooth and elastic, then wrap and leave in a cool place for at least 30 minutes.
3 Peel and grate the carrots and mix well with the rice, beaten eggs, milk, cheese, seasoning and herbs.
4 Roll out the pastry and line a medium-sized flan dish. Bake blind at 400°F/200°C (Gas Mark 6) for 10 minutes.
5 Spoon the prepared mixture into the flan and smooth the top. Steam the remaining carrots until beginning to soften, then cut carefully into thin slices, and arrange decoratively on top of flan. Brush with the melted butter.
6 Bake at 375°F/190°C (Gas Mark 5) for 20-30 minutes, or until filling is set.

Serve with: Deep fried cauliflower in batter, mashed potatoes, and a watercress and tomato salad.

Friday
Beans Provençale with Eggs

2 tablespoons vegetable oil
1 onion, sliced
1 clove garlic, crushed
14 oz (395g) tin tomatoes,
  roughly crushed
1 teaspoon fresh basil,
  chopped
Seasoning to taste
1 lb (455g) green beans
½ lb (225g) fresh broad
  beans
6 hard-boiled eggs,
  quartered

1 Heat the oil in a pan, and fry the onion and garlic until they begin to soften.
2 Add the crushed tomatoes, basil and seasoning, and simmer for 20-30 minutes to make a sauce.
3 Meanwhile, top, tail and slice the green beans, shell the broad beans, and cook in the minimum amount of water. When tender, add them to the sauce. Cook briefly to heat through.
4 Transfer to a serving dish and top with the quartered eggs.

Serve with: Hot millet as a base, and an endive, cucumber and chicory salad with olives sprinkled over it.

Saturday
Kebabs

5 oz (140g) soya 'ham'
  chunks, hydrated in
  water
1 large courgette
1 large red pepper
4 oz (115g) button
  mushrooms
Small tin pineapple chunks
Bay leaves
Seasoning to taste
Vegetable oil

1 Simmer the 'ham' chunks in water for literally a few minutes, then drain well and set aside.
2 Trim and slice the courgettes into thick pieces; cube the pepper; wash and pat dry the mushrooms.
3 Drain the juice off the pineapple chunks.
4 Carefully arrange all the ingredients on skewers, alternating them so that they look attractive, and including the occasional bay leaf. Season, and sprinkle lightly with oil.

5 Cook gently under a hot grill, turning them frequently, until everything is cooked but still holds a shape. Take care not to burn the kebabs. Add more oil as necessary.

Serve with: A dish of hot bulgur or rice, plus a mixed green salad.

Sunday
Spinach, Mushroom and Peanut Loaf

4 oz (115g) wholemeal
  bread
¼ pint (140ml) milk
1 lb (455g) spinach
4 oz (115g) peanuts
4 oz (115g) mushrooms
4 oz (115g) grated Cheddar
  cheese
2 large eggs, separated
Seasoning to taste
Good pinch of marjoram
1 oz (30g) sesame seeds
Tomato sauce to serve (see
  page 153)

1 Crumble the bread and leave to soak in the milk for a few minutes.
2 Wash, trim and chop the spinach.
3 Grate the peanuts; chop the cleaned mushrooms.
4 Squeeze any excess liquid out of the breadcrumbs, then stir them together with the spinach, peanuts, mushrooms and grated cheese.
5 Add the egg yolks, seasoning and marjoram.
6 Beat the egg whites until stiff, then fold into the other ingredients. Spoon the mixture into a greased loaf tin, level the top, and sprinkle with the sesame seeds.
7 Bake at 350°F/180°C (Gas Mark 4) for 50 minutes, or until set. Cut into slices and serve with tomato sauce for those who want it.

Serve with: Potato slices in a creamy white sauce, plus tomato and onion salad.

Week 6:
Monday
Onion Soup Gratinée

1 tablespoon vegetable oil
1 oz (30g) margarine or
butter
1½ lb (680g) onions,
thickly sliced
1¾ pints (1 litre) vegetable
stock
Seasoning to taste
1 clove garlic
4 slices wholemeal bread
or French bread, toasted
3 oz (85g) grated Cheddar
cheese

1 Heat the oil with the fat in a pan, and fry the onions gently until they begin to colour.
2 Add the stock and seasoning, bring to the boil, then simmer for about 15 minutes.
3 Meanwhile, halve the garlic clove and rub over the toasted bread, then discard.
4 Put one piece of toast in each of 4 soup bowls, and cover with the prepared soup.
5 Divide the grated cheese between the soup bowls and place under a hot grill for a few minutes so that the cheese browns. Take to the table at once.

Serve with: A large mixed salad that includes lettuce, grated root vegetables, chopped pear and a sprinkling of nuts. Finish the meal with cashew muffins, and maybe some fresh fruit.

Tuesday
Lentil Lasagne

6 oz (170g) wholemeal
lasagne
3 tablespoons vegetable oil
1 stick celery, finely sliced
1 small onion, finely sliced
1 small red pepper, finely
sliced
1 clove garlic, crushed
2 tomatoes, coarsely
chopped
6 oz (170g) split red lentils
Approx. ½ pint (285ml)
water
½ teaspoon yeast extract,
or to taste
1-2 teaspoons oregano
Seasoning to taste
½ pint (285ml) white
sauce (see page 153)
2 eggs, beaten
2 oz (55g) grated Cheddar
cheese

1 Bring a large pan of water to the boil and add the lasagne sheets one at a time. Cook for 8 minutes, or until just tender, then drain well and rinse in cold water. Arrange the sheets on a clean tea towel, and set aside.
2 Heat the vegetable oil in a pan and gently fry the celery, onion and pepper with the garlic. After 5 minutes, add the tomatoes and cook a few minutes more.
3 Stir in the lentils with enough water to cover; add yeast extract, oregano and seasoning. Bring to the boil, then simmer the mixture for 15 minutes, or until the lentils are cooked and a thick purée has formed. Drain off any excess liquid if necessary.
4 In a greased ovenproof dish, arrange alternate layers of the lasagne and lentil mixture until all the ingredients have been used.
5 Mix together the white sauce and beaten eggs and pour evenly over the top. Sprinkle with the grated cheese. Bake at 400°F/200°C (Gas Mark 6) for 30 minutes, or until golden.

Serve with: A salad of finely grated white cabbage in a honey dressing, with chopped walnuts added.

Wednesday
Italian Rice Salad

6 oz (170g) brown rice
3 tablespoons vegetable oil
1 green pepper, sliced
1 small aubergine, peeled
  and cubed
3 tomatoes, peeled and
  chopped
3 oz (85g) cooked broad
  beans
1 oz (30g) pine nuts

For the dressing:
6 tablespoons vegetable oil
  (preferably olive)
3 tablespoons white wine
  vinegar
½-1 clove garlic, crushed
Seasoning to taste

1 Add the rice to twice the volume of water, bring to the boil, then simmer covered for 30-40 minutes, or until just cooked. Do not stir. Drain well and leave to cool.
2 Meanwhile, heat the oil in another pan and gently fry the pepper for a few minutes.
3 Add the aubergine to the pan. Continue cooking over a low heat, stirring frequently, until the vegetables are just tender. Add the tomatoes and beans and cook a minute or two more.
4 When all the ingredients are cool, use a wooden spoon to mix them together gently, including the pine nuts.
5 Combine the salad dressing ingredients in a screw-top jar and pour over the rice salad. Mix again. Chill before serving.

Serve with: Fresh wholemeal bread, and a lettuce and endive salad.

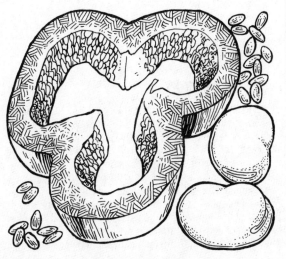

Thursday
Russian Quiche

½ lb (225g) pastry of your
  choice

For the filling:
½ oz (15g) margarine or
  butter
4 spring onions, chopped
6 oz (170g) mushrooms,
  chopped
1 teaspoon fresh dill,
  chopped
1 tablespoon fresh parsley,
  chopped
2 eggs
2 egg yolks
¼ pint (140ml) natural
  yogurt
¼ pint (140ml) milk
Seasoning to taste
4 oz (115g) grated Gruyére
  cheese
1 small cooked beetroot,
  well drained and cubed
Paprika

1 Make up the pastry mix and set aside in a cool place.
2 Melt the fat in a pan and sauté the onions and mushrooms until they begin to soften. Add the herbs.
3 Beat together the eggs, egg yolks, yogurt, milk and seasoning, making sure they are well mixed. Stir in the grated cheese and prepared vegetables. Add the beetroot.
4 Roll out the pastry and use to line a medium-sized flan dish. Bake blind at 400°F/200°C (Gas Mark 6) for 10 minutes.
5 Pour in the filling and smooth the top. Sprinkle with paprika. Bake at the same temperature for 10 minutes, then lower the heat to 350°F/180°C (Gas Mark 4) and cook for 20-30 minutes more, or until set.

Serve with: A celery and cucumber salad, plus a serving of hot buckwheat.

Friday
Ricotta Cheese Omelette

6 oz (170g) Ricotta cheese
6 large eggs
Seasoning to taste
Approx. 1 oz (30g) butter
  or margarine

1 Tip the Ricotta cheese into a bowl and use a wooden spoon to mash it until thick and creamy.
2 Whisk the eggs and stir together with the cheese, adding just a drop of cold water. Season to taste.
3 Melt a little of the fat in a heavy-based frying pan and add about a quarter of the egg and cheese mixture. Cook gently, tipping the pan frequently, until the omelette has set, but is still soft. Transfer to a plate and either serve or keep in a warm spot. Use the rest of the mixture in the same way.

Serve with: Potato croquettes, plus a salad of raw grated parsnip, carrots and watercress.

Saturday
Gado Gado

For the sauce:
2 tablespoons vegetable oil
1 large onion, finely
  chopped
2-3 cloves garlic, crushed
¼ pint (140ml) water
½ lb (225g) smooth peanut
  butter
1 tablespoon honey, or to
  taste
Squeeze of lemon juice
1 bay leaf, crushed
½ teaspoon ground ginger
½ teaspoon chilli powder
Soya sauce to taste
Seasoning to taste
Approx. ½ pint (285ml)
  milk

For the fried onion
rings:
2 large onions
A little milk
Wholemeal flour
Vegetable oil for frying

1 Heat the oil in a saucepan and sauté the onion and garlic until tender and beginning to colour.
2 Stir in the water and, when it boils, add the peanut butter,

stirring continually so that it dissolves completely.
3 Flavour with honey, lemon juice, bay leaf, spices, soya sauce and seasoning.
4 Add enough milk to make a pouring sauce and heat gently, stirring continually, before tipping into a jug or sauce boat and taking to the table.
5 Meanwhile, peel the onions and cut them across into ¼-inch (6mm) slices. Dip each ring into milk, then into flour, making sure the coating is even.
6 Deep fry the rings in hot oil until light brown and crisp. Drain on paper towels.

Serve with: Gado Gado is a Javanese dish, the sauce being served with raw or cooked vegetables. Try it with a platter of three or four different vegetables, lightly steamed and chosen for their contrasting appearance — for example, carrots, tiny new potatoes, courgettes, green beans. Serve the onion rings in a separate bowl to be sprinkled on top.

Sunday
Ratatouille Pancakes

For the batter:
4 oz (115g) wholemeal
  flour
2 oz (55g) soya flour
Pinch of salt
½ pint (285ml) water
2 teaspoons vegetable oil

For the filling:
4 tablespoons vegetable oil
1 medium aubergine, diced
2 onions, sliced
2 courgettes, sliced
2 peppers, sliced
1 lb (455g) tomatoes,
  peeled and chopped
1 clove garlic, crushed
Seasoning to taste
2 hard-boiled eggs or
  4 oz (115g) tofu, cubed
Vegetable oil for frying

1 Sift together the flours and salt, then gradually add the water, stirring continuously to remove any lumps. Whisk, then beat in the oil. Leave covered in a cool place for at least half an hour.
2 Heat the oil in a large pan and fry the diced aubergine, sliced onions and courgettes for 5 minutes.
3 Add the peppers and tomatoes to the pan with the garlic and seasoning. Mix well, cover the pan, and cook over a low heat for 15 minutes, or until all the ingredients are cooked.
4 Stir in the chopped hard-boiled eggs or tofu and leave just long enough to heat through.
5 Meanwhile, whisk the batter again and, if necessary, add a

drop more water so that it pours easily.

6 Heat a little oil in a frying pan and, when it begins to smoke, pour in a thin layer of the batter. Cook until lightly browned underneath, shaking the pan occasionally. Turn the pancake and cook the other side then keep in a warm place whilst using the rest of the batter in the same way.

7 Fill each pancake with some of the ratatouille mixture, roll up, and serve at once.

Serve with: A green salad with beansprouts and chopped stuffed olives.

Week 7:
Monday
'Beef' Curry

**1 pint (570ml) curry
    sauce (see page 154)*
*5 oz (140g) soya 'beef'
    chunks, hydrated in
    water*
2 tablespoons vegetable oil
½ onion, sliced
*4 tablespoons natural
    yogurt*

For the garnish:
2 tomatoes, sliced
*1 small green chilli,
    chopped*
*1 oz (30g) cashew nuts,
    chopped*

1 Heat the curry sauce gently.
2 Bring the soya chunks to the boil, simmer for a minute or two only, then drain.
3 Heat the oil in a clean pan and fry the onion until it begins to soften. Add the soya chunks to the pan, stir, and cook briefly.
4 Mix the contents of the two pans together, and stir in the yogurt. Heat through gently.
5 Garnish with slices of tomato, the finely chopped chilli, and a scattering of chopped nuts.

Serve with: Brown rice, a raw courgette salad, and a selection of chutneys.

**Make a day in advance and leave overnight for the flavour to develop. Reheat gently.

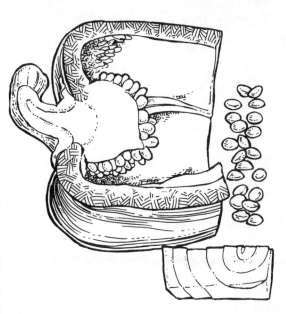

Tuesday
Spanish Lentil Patties

3 tablespoons vegetable oil
1 onion, finely chopped
*1 green pepper, finely
    chopped*
14 oz (395g) tin tomatoes
*2 tablespoons tomato
    purée*
Seasoning to taste
Pinch of garlic salt
Good pinch of oregano
½ lb (225g) split red lentils
Wholemeal flour to coat
Vegetable oil for frying
*Brown gravy to serve
    (optional)*

1 Heat the oil in a pan and add the onion and pepper. Cook gently until they begin to soften.
2 Add the contents of the tin of tomatoes, the tomato purée, seasoning, oregano and lentils. Bring to the boil and simmer, stirring frequently, until the lentils can be mashed to make a thick purée. (You may need to add a drop of water during the cooking process.)
3 Leave mixture to cool. Divide and then shape into small patties, and coat with flour.
4 Shallow fry in hot vegetable oil until golden on both sides. Drain on paper towels. Serve, if liked, with brown gravy.

Serve with: An endive and chicory salad with walnuts, plus lightly steamed new potatoes.

Wednesday
Aubergine Parmesan

2 medium aubergines
2 eggs
⅛ pint (70ml) cream or
   milk
3 tablespoons vegetable oil
2 oz (55g) wheatgerm
½ pint (285ml) tomato
   sauce (see page 153)
Chopped basil
4 oz (115g) Mozzarella
   cheese, sliced
2 oz (55g) grated
   Parmesan cheese
2 oz (55g) wholemeal
   breadcrumbs

1 Wash and trim the aubergines, then cut into ½-inch (12mm) slices.
2 Beat the eggs and cream or milk together lightly. Pour the mixture over the aubergine slices.
3 Heat the oil in a pan. Dip the aubergine slices into the wheatgerm and then fry them gently in the oil, turning once.
4 Arrange a third of the slices in a greased ovenproof dish, top with a third of the tomato sauce, a good sprinkling of basil, a third of the sliced Mozzarella cheese and a sprinkling of Parmesan cheese.
5 Repeat the layers twice more. Sprinkle the breadcrumbs over the top. Bake at 375°F/190°C (Gas Mark 5) for about 30 minutes, or until hot and bubbly. Garnish with fresh basil.

Serve with: A potato salad with cooked peas added.

Thursday
Rice with Chestnuts

6 oz (170g) dried chestnuts,
   hydrated in water
3 tablespoons vegetable oil
1 large onion, sliced
1 large pepper, sliced
1-2 cloves garlic, crushed
¾ lb (340g) brown rice
Seasoning to taste
Grated Parmesan cheese to
   serve

1 Drain the chestnuts, put into a saucepan with fresh water, and cook until soft. Carefully remove the skins. Reserve a few chestnuts, then purée the rest with the water in which they were cooked. Set aside.
2 Heat the oil in a pan and fry the onion and pepper with the garlic until soft. Stir in the rice, and cook a minute more.
3 Add water to the chestnut purée to make up to about 1½

pints (850ml) liquid, and pour into the pan. Stir well, bring to the boil. Simmer covered for 30-40 minutes, or until the rice is tender.
4 Chop the remaining nuts and stir into the mixture. Cook briefly to heat through.
5 Hand round grated Parmesan cheese for those who want it.

Serve with: A salad of raw (or very lightly steamed) young green beans, with lettuce, cucumber, fennel and tomato.

Friday
Pizza Alla Casalinga

For the dough:
½ lb (225g) wholemeal
   flour
Salt
½ oz (15g) fresh yeast
¼ pint (140ml) warm milk
1 small egg, lightly beaten
1 oz (30g) margarine

For the topping:
¾ lb (340g) tomatoes,
   sliced
1 teaspoon oregano
1 teaspoon basil
½ lb (225g) Bel Paese
   cheese, thinly sliced
1 small onion, sliced
Green olives, sliced
1 tablespoon capers
Seasoning to taste
1-2 tablespoons vegetable
   oil

1 Sift together the flour and salt. In a large bowl dissolve the yeast in the milk, add the egg, then gradually stir in the flour.
2 Soften the margarine and add to the mixture; knead until the dough is smooth and elastic, adding a little flour if it's sticky to handle. Leave in the bowl, cover with a clean cloth, and set aside in a warm, draught-free place for 45 minutes to an hour, or until the dough is well risen.
3 Knead the dough again lightly, then use your hands to shape it into two large rounds, and roll lightly so that they are an even depth. Place on a lightly greased baking sheet.
4 Arrange the tomatoes over the top of the dough. Sprinkle with half the herbs. Cover with thin slices of cheese, top with onion rings, plus scattered olives and capers. Add remaining herbs and seasoning, and trickle a little vegetable oil over all the ingredients.
5 Leave in a warm spot for 10-15 minutes. Bake at 400°F/200°C (Gas Mark 6) for 20-30 minutes, or until cheese has melted

and dough is crisp. Cut into slices to serve.

Serve with: A mixed salad. If young broad beans are available, add a few raw ones. Add walnuts or pine nuts for crunch as well as extra protein.

Saturday
Vegetable Couscous

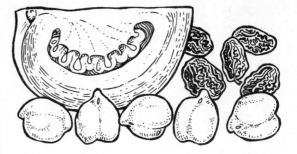

1 lb (455g) couscous
¾ pint (425ml) lukewarm
   salted water
½ lb (225g) chick-peas,
   soaked overnight
3 tablespoons vegetable oil
1 large onion, sliced
2 cloves garlic, crushed
1 green pepper, sliced
1 turnip, sliced
2 carrots, sliced
2 courgettes, sliced
2 large potatoes, cubed
1½ pints (850ml) water
3 oz (85g) raisins
½ teaspoon cayenne
2 teaspoons ground cumin
1 teaspoon ground
   coriander
1 teaspoon paprika
½ teaspoon saffron
   dissolved in 1 teaspoon
   hot water
Seasoning
2 oz (55g) almonds
½ lb (225g) tomatoes,
   quartered
2 oz (55g) butter

1 Put the couscous grains into a large bowl and pour on the lukewarm water. Set aside for an hour, then drain.
2 Drain the chick-peas, cover with fresh water, and bring to the boil. Cover the pan and simmer for 1 hour or until cooked.
3 Heat the oil in a large, heavy-based pan, and add the onion and garlic with the pepper, turnip and carrots. Fry gently for 10 minutes, stirring occasionally.
4 Add the courgettes, potatoes and water. Bring to the boil then lower heat and simmer for 15 minutes.
5 Add the drained chick-peas, the raisins, spices, saffron and seasoning. Bring mixture to the boil.
6 Put a colander over the top of the pan, line it with cheesecloth and, if necessary, seal any gap between the pan and colander with a damp rolled up cloth.*
7 Transfer the couscous grains to the top of the double pan, cover securely, cook gently for 20 minutes.

8 Stir the nuts into the vegetable mixture and add the tomatoes.
9 Transfer the couscous to a bowl and stir in the butter then return to the colander. Return the colander to the pan, cover again, and continue cooking all the ingredients for a further 10 minutes.
10 Spoon the couscous onto a large, warmed serving dish and top with the vegetable mixture, plus some of the cooking liquid.

Serve with: A simple green salad should be sufficient to complete the meal.

*Traditionally, vegetable couscous is made in a 'couscoussier'. An alternative can be put together in the way described.

Sunday
Fettucine with Pesto Sauce and Pine Nuts

10 oz (285g) wholemeal
   fettucine
1 bunch fresh basil
2-3 cloves garlic
Sea salt
3 oz (85g) grated Pecorino
   or Parmesan cheese
4 tablespoons olive oil
Cold water to mix
1-2 oz (30-55g) pine nuts

1 Cook the fettucine in a large pan of boiling water for 5-10 minutes, until just tender.
2 Meanwhile, wipe the basil to clean it, then put into a mortar and pound together with the garlic cloves and salt until you have a thick smooth pulp.
3 Add the grated cheese and mix well.
4 Add the oil drop by drop, beating continually, then stir in one or two tablespoons of cold water, so that the sauce has the consistency of thin cream.
5 Drain the hot fettucine and serve with the sauce. Top with a sprinkling of pine nuts.

Serve with: A salad of chicory, endive, raw cauliflower florets and tomatoes.

Summer

Week 8:
Monday
Curry Pie

½ lb (225g) shortcrust
  pastry (see page 151)

For the filling:
2 tablespoons vegetable oil
1 onion, chopped
1 clove garlic, crushed
1 apple, chopped
1 oz (30g) wholemeal flour
1 tablespoon curry powder,
  or to taste
⅓ pint (200ml) water
2 oz (55g) cooked beans,
  any kind
½ small cauliflower
1 large carrot, cubed
3 eggs, hard-boiled

1 Make up the pastry in the usual way. Divide into two, and use one piece to line an 8-inch (20cm) pie plate and shallow ovenproof dish.
2 Heat the oil in a large pan and fry the onion, garlic and apple for a few minutes. Add the flour and curry powder and cook briefly.
3 Pour in the water together with the beans, cauliflower florets and carrots. Cover the pan and cook gently for 30 minutes, or until the sauce is thick and the vegetables cooked.
4 Shell and quarter the eggs and stir carefully into the other ingredients. Pour onto the pastry base and spread evenly.
5 Roll out the remaining dough and use to make a topping for the pie, dampening the edges before pressing together to seal them. Prick the top.
6 Bake at 400°F/200°C (Gas Mark 6) for 25-30 minutes or until cooked.

Serve with: A crisp cucumber, lettuce and tomato salad sprinkled with chopped hazelnuts. Small potatoes, lightly steamed, could be served as well.

Tuesday
Onion and Okra Layer with Peanuts

1 lb (455g) okra
3 tablespoons vegetable oil
2 onions, sliced
½ clove garlic, crushed
1 oz (30g) margarine or
  butter
2 oz (55g) wholemeal
  breadcrumbs
2 oz (55g) peanuts,
  coarsely chopped
½-1 teaspoon oregano
Seasoning to taste
4 tomatoes, sliced
3 oz (85g) grated Cheddar
  cheese
Parsley to garnish
Natural yogurt to serve

1 Top and tail the cleaned okra and slice lengthways.
2 Heat the oil in a pan and gently sauté the onions and garlic for 5 minutes, then add the okra and cook 5 minutes more, or until the vegetables are tender.
3 In a clean pan, melt the fat and stir in the breadcrumbs, peanuts, oregano and seasoning. Fry briefly.
4 Layer the okra with the crumb mixture and sliced tomatoes. Repeat. Top with the grated cheese.
5 Bake at 375°F/190°C (Gas Mark 5) for 30 minutes. Garnish with parsley. Hand round yogurt for those who want it.

Serve with: Hot wholewheat berries and a cucumber salad.

Wednesday
Carrot Sesame Crumble

For the base:
1 lb (455g) carrots, sliced
2 oz (55g) curd or Ricotta
  cheese or 2 tablespoons
  peanut butter
Seasoning to taste
Fresh parsley

For the crumble:
4 oz (115g) wholemeal
  flour
2 oz (55g) margarine or
  butter
2 oz (55g) sesame seeds
Seasoning to taste

1 Steam or cook the carrots in the minimum amount of water for 10 minutes or until tender, then drain well.
2 Put the carrots into an ovenproof dish and stir in the cheese or peanut butter so that it melts to make a sauce. Add seasoning and chopped parsley.
3 Put the flour into a bowl and rub in the fat to make a crumb-like mixture. Stir in the seeds and season to taste.
4 Sprinkle the prepared crumble over the carrot mixture, and press down lightly and evenly.
5 Bake at 375°F/190°C (Gas Mark 5) for 20-25 minutes, or until the topping is cooked.

Serve with: Steamed spinach and jacket potatoes.

Thursday
Polenta with Vegetable Sauce

¾ pint (425ml) water
Seasoning to taste
½ lb (225g) fine polenta
*   (cornmeal)*
Approx. 2 tablespoons
*   vegetable oil*
1 onion, sliced
1 clove garlic, crushed
1 pepper, sliced
1 medium courgette, sliced
1 small aubergine, cubed
4 tomatoes, chopped
2 tablespoons tomato
*   purée*
4 oz (115g) cooked chick-
*   peas, coarsely chopped*
1-2 teaspoons marjoram
Seasoning to taste
2 oz (55g) grated Edam
*   cheese*

1 Bring the water to a boil, season, and sprinkle in the polenta. Cook gently, stirring occasionally, for 15 minutes. Spoon into a greased, ovenproof dish.
2 Heat the vegetable oil and sauté the onion, garlic, and pepper for 5 minutes. Add the courgette and aubergine, and cook 5 minutes more.
3 Stir in the tomatoes and tomato purée, and cook just long enough to thicken. Add chick-peas, marjoram and seasoning.
4 Spoon vegetable and chick-pea sauce over the polenta. Sprinkle with cheese. Bake at 350°F/180°C (Gas Mark 4) for 20 minutes.

Serve with: A salad made of two different kinds of lettuce, plus chicory, cucumber and olives. Add pumpkin seeds for protein.

Friday
Courgette and Pepper Bake

3 tablespoons vegetable oil
1 small red pepper, sliced
1 small green pepper,
*   sliced*
1 onion, sliced
1 clove garlic, crushed
1 lb (455g) courgettes,
*   sliced*
4 oz (115g) mushrooms,
*   chopped*
⅓ pint (200ml) milk
2 eggs
4 oz (115g) grated Cheddar
*   cheese*
Seasoning to taste
2 large tomatoes, sliced
Parsley sprigs to garnish

1 Heat the vegetable oil in a pan and lightly fry the peppers, onion and garlic for 7-10 minutes, or until beginning to soften.
2 Add the courgettes to the pan with the mushrooms. Stir, then cook for 10-15 minutes, or until all the vegetables are tender.
3 Transfer the prepared ingredients to a greased ovenproof dish and smooth the top.
4 Whisk together the milk, eggs, grated cheese and seasoning, and pour over the vegetables, spreading evenly. Decorate the top with tomato slices.
5 Bake at 375°F/190°C (Gas Mark 5) for 35-40 minutes, or until set. Garnish with parsley sprigs.

Serve with: A salad of raw, finely grated, root vegetables, and maybe some French bread.

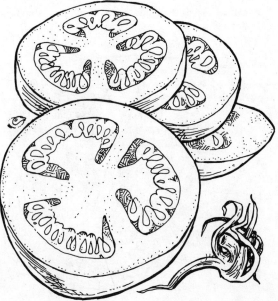

Summer

Saturday
Creamy Cucumber Flan

For the flan case:
4 oz (115g) wholemeal
   crackers or crispbread
4 oz (115g) margarine or
   butter
2 oz (55g) flaked almonds
Seasoning to taste

For the filling:
1 small cucumber
4 oz (115g) cream cheese
4 tablespoons natural
   yogurt
2 tablespoons chopped
   fresh mint
Seasoning to taste
Garlic salt
Fresh mint to garnish

1 Crush the crackers or crispbread, then use fingertips to rub in the fat as evenly as possible. Stir in the nuts and seasoning.
2 Press the mixture against the base and sides of a lightly greased, medium-sized flan dish. Bake at 400°F/200°C (Gas Mark 6) for 20 minutes. Leave to cool.
3 Finely chop all but 1-inch (25mm) of the cucumber, and press out excess moisture.
4 Mash the cream cheese with a wooden spoon to soften, then stir in the yogurt, mint and seasoning to taste. Add the prepared cucumber.
5 Spoon the cucumber mixture into the cold flan case and smooth the top. Chill well, preferably overnight. Garnish with a ring of wafer-thin cucumber slices, and a sprig of fresh mint.

Serve with: A red pepper and tomato salad, and freshly made bran muffins.

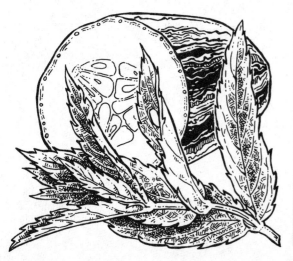

Sunday
Asparagus Almond Soufflé

½ lb (225g) fresh
   asparagus, or frozen or
   tinned equivalent
1½ oz (45g) margarine or
   butter
1 oz (30g) wholemeal flour
⅓ pint (200ml) milk
Seasoning to taste
Pinch of cayenne pepper
2 oz (55g) grated Gruyère
   cheese
1½ oz (45g) almonds,
   coarsely chopped
4 egg yolks
5 egg whites

1 Trim and cook the asparagus in the usual way (see page 38). (If using frozen, follow directions on pack.) Drain well and chop into small, even-sized pieces.
2 Melt the fat and add the flour, cooking gently. Off the heat, pour in the milk, then return to heat and continue cooking and stirring until the sauce thickens.
3 Add seasonings, grated cheese and nuts to the sauce. When well mixed, stir in the asparagus and egg yolks. Cool slightly.
4 Whisk the egg whites until stiff, and use a metal spoon to fold them carefully into the asparagus mixture.
5 Bake at once in an oven pre-heated to 375°F/190°C (Gas Mark 5) for 30-40 minutes, or until risen and golden.

Serve with: Hot herbed rice and a simple beetroot salad.

Week 9:
Monday
Tofu Fritters

1 lb (455g) tofu
1 oz (30g) walnuts, finely
   chopped
2-3 spring onions, finely
   chopped
1 tablespoon parsley,
   chopped
1 teaspoon oregano,
   chopped
Seasoning to taste
1 tablespoon soya sauce
1 large egg, beaten
Wholemeal breadcrumbs
Vegetable oil for frying
Tomato sauce to serve (see
   page 153)

1 Lay the tofu between two clean tea towels and press down with a weight. Leave for 30 minutes to drain well.
2 Crumble the tofu into a bowl and mix with the nuts and onions, the herbs and seasoning.
3 Add soya sauce, the beaten egg, and just a spoonful or two of breadcrumbs to take up any excess moisture. Knead for a minute or two.
4 Divide the mixture into small pieces and shape into fritters. Deep fry in a pan of hot oil until brown and firm. Drain on paper towels. Arrange on a warmed serving dish and pour on the sauce.

Serve with: Can be eaten with a grain dish, or maybe spaghetti as a base. A raw spinach salad sprinkled with soya 'bacon' bits would go well, too.

Tuesday
Macaroni with Pea Sauce

1 oz (30g) margarine or
 butter
1 onion, sliced
4 oz (115g) mushrooms,
 sliced
½ lb (225g) cooked peas
⅓ pint (200ml) vegetable
 stock
Seasoning to taste
Chopped parsley
10 oz (285g) wholemeal
 macaroni
2 oz (55g) walnut pieces
 for garnish

1 Melt fat and sauté the onion to soften.
2 Add the mushrooms, peas and vegetable stock. Cook covered for 10 minutes, or until vegetables are tender. Add seasoning and parsley.
3 At the same time cook the pasta in a large pan of boiling water. When tender, drain well.
4 Mix together the pasta and pea sauce. Heat for just a minute or two more.
5 Transfer to a warmed serving dish and top with a sprinkling of walnut pieces.

Serve with: A tomato, celery and basil salad.

Wednesday
Rice and Vegetable Pie

½ lb (225g) brown rice
1 pint (570ml) vegetable
 stock or water
2 tablespoons vegetable oil
1 clove garlic, crushed
1 onion, sliced
1 red pepper, sliced
2 courgettes, sliced
Seasoning to taste
4 oz (115g) cooked
 sweetcorn
4 oz (115g) grated Cheddar
 cheese
1 oz (30g) margarine or
 butter
⅛ pint (70ml) single cream
Parsley to garnish

1 Rinse the rice, then put into a saucepan with the liquid. Bring to the boil, cover, and simmer for 30-40 minutes, or until the rice is tender. (Add more liquid if necessary.)
2 Heat the oil in a large pan. Add the garlic, sliced onion, pepper and courgettes, and stir well. Cook gently for 10 minutes, or until the vegetables are beginning to soften. Season to taste. Stir in the sweetcorn.
3 Spread a third of the rice across the base of a lightly greased ovenproof dish. Top with half the vegetable mixture, then half the grated cheese. Repeat this, then finish with the remaining rice.
4 Dot with the fat and pour on the cream. Bake at 350°F/180°C (Gas Mark 4) for 30 minutes. Garnish with parsley.

Serve with: A beansprout salad sprinkled with tamari roasted soya splits.

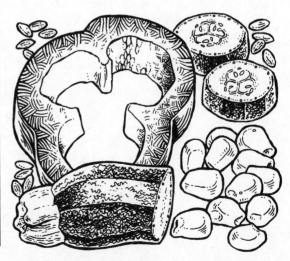

Thursday
Salad Flan

For the pastry:
6 oz (170g) wholemeal
  flour
Seasoning to taste
3 oz (85g) margarine or
  butter
1 egg, lightly beaten
Cold water to mix

For the filling:
1 chicory
½ small cauliflower
4 oz (115g) mushrooms,
  sliced
2 sticks celery, sliced
2 spring onions, sliced
4 hard-boiled eggs,
  chopped
Mayonnaise to mix
Seasoning to taste
4 cherry tomatoes
Chives to garnish

1 Sieve the flour into a bowl with the seasoning.
2 Rub in the fat to make a crumb-like mixture.
3 Use a knife to stir in the beaten egg, then add one or two tablespoons of water to make a dough.
4 Knead briefly, then roll out and use to line an 8-inch (20cm) flan ring.
5 Bake the pastry blind at 375°F/190°C (Gas Mark 5) for 20-30 minutes, or until cooked. Set aside to cool.
6 Put the pastry case onto a serving dish and remove the ring carefully. Line the flan case decoratively with the chicory leaves.
7 In a bowl mix together the cauliflower florets, mushrooms, celery and onions, and the chopped, hard-boiled eggs. Bind with mayonnaise and season to taste.
8 Spoon the mixture into the flan case. Decorate with cherry tomatoes and garnish with chopped chives.

Serve with: French bread spread with nut butter.

Friday
Potato and Pine Nut Loaf

¾ lb (340g) potatoes
Squeeze of lemon juice
Seasoning to taste
1 oz (30g) wholemeal flour
1 onion, finely chopped
2 courgettes, finely
  chopped
4 sticks celery, finely
  chopped
3 oz (85g) cooked
  sweetcorn
2 oz (55g) pine nuts
1 large egg, beaten
Tomato to garnish

1 Peel and finely grate the potatoes, then add lemon juice and seasoning, mixing well. Stir in the flour.
2 Add the onion, courgettes and celery to the potato mixture.
3 Drain and stir in the sweetcorn together with the pine nuts.
4 Stir the beaten egg into the other ingredients. The mixture should be fairly soft, so add a drop of water if necessary.
5 Turn into a greased loaf tin, smooth the top, and bake at 375°F/190°C (Gas Mark 5) for 40-50 minutes, or until cooked. Garnish with slices of tomato.

Serve with: A beansprout, carrot and apple salad, and a hot grain such as millet or kasha.

Saturday
Pepper and 'Ham' Pizza

½ lb (225g) pizza dough
  of your choice

For the topping:
¼ pint (140ml) thick
  tomato sauce (see page
  153)
2 green peppers finely
  sliced into rings
3 oz (85g) soya 'ham'
  chunks, hydrated in
  water
2 teaspoons oregano
Seasoning to taste
1 oz (30g) grated Cheddar
  cheese (optional)
1-2 tablespoons vegetable
  oil

1 Make up the pizza dough according to instructions. Divide into four and roll out to make small circles. Arrange on a baking sheet.
2 Spread the pizzas evenly with tomato sauce and top with pepper rings.
3 Drain the soya 'ham' chunks and, if tender, cut into small pieces. (You may need to boil them a few minutes first to soften.) Sprinkle over pizzas.
4 Add oregano, seasoning, cheese (optional) and a trickle of oil.
5 Bake at 400°F/200°C (Gas Mark 6) for 20 minutes or until dough is cooked.

Serve with: A green bean and cucumber salad with vinaigrette dressing.

Sunday
Turkish Vegetable Stew

2 tablespoons vegetable oil
1 onion, sliced
1 clove garlic, crushed
4 oz (115g) green beans,
    sliced
2 sticks celery, chopped
2 courgettes, chopped
2 potatoes, diced
1 teaspoon molasses
Seasoning to taste
½ pint (285ml) vegetable
    stock or water
⅓ pint (200ml) natural
    yogurt

1 Heat the oil in a pan and fry the onion and garlic gently until soft.
2 Add the remaining vegetables to the pan, and cook for a minute or two only.
3 Stir the molasses and seasoning into the stock, and pour over the vegetables. Bring to the boil.
4 Lower heat, cover pan, and simmer for 15-20 minutes, or until the vegetables are cooked but still firm. You may need to add a drop more liquid.
5 Serve with a good spoonful of yogurt on each portion.

Serve with: A dish of hot bulghur flavoured with herbs, and sprinkled with chopped roasted almonds or pistachio nuts. Add a tomato and chicory salad, if liked.

Week 10:
Monday
Macaroni Parmigiana

2 tablespoons vegetable oil
1 pepper, sliced
1 onion, sliced
1-2 cloves garlic, crushed
14 oz (395g) tin tomatoes,
    coarsely chopped
3 tablespoons tomato
    purée
Seasoning to taste
1-2 teaspoons oregano
½ lb (225g) wholemeal
    macaroni
6 oz (170g) cottage cheese
6 oz (170g) Gruyère cheese,
    sliced
3 oz (85g) grated
    Parmesan cheese

1 Heat the oil in a pan and sauté the sliced pepper and onion with the garlic.
2 Add the tomatoes, tomato purée, seasoning and oregano. Continue simmering until the sauce thickens.
3 Cook the macaroni in boiling water for 10 minutes, or until tender. Drain well.
4 Lightly grease an ovenproof dish. Put in a layer of macaroni, then half the cottage cheese, slices of Gruyère, some grated Parmesan and half the tomato sauce. Repeat to use up the rest of the ingredients, finishing with tomato sauce topped with grated Parmesan cheese.
5 Bake at 375°F/190°C (Gas Mark 5) for 20 minutes.

Serve with: A mushroom and pepper salad.

Summer

Tuesday
Green Bean and Almond Curry

1½ lb (680g) green beans

For the sauce:
2 tablespoons vegetable oil
1 teaspoon ground
*   turmeric*
1 teaspoon garam masala
Pinch of ground ginger
Pinch of chilli powder
1 small onion, chopped
1 clove garlic, crushed
3 tomatoes, chopped
Seasoning to taste
2 oz (55g) almonds
Coriander leaves to
*   garnish*

1 Top and tail the beans, and cut lengthways into thin strips. If they are very large or tough, steam them for 5-10 minutes.
2 Heat the vegetable oil and sprinkle in the spices. Cook briefly.
3 Add the chopped onion and the garlic, and cook long enough for them to begin to colour. Then stir in the tomatoes and seasoning, and simmer so that a sauce begins to form.
4 Add the prepared beans, and cook in the sauce until they are tender. Stir in the nuts and leave over the heat just long enough to warm through.
5 Garnish the curry with chopped coriander leaves.

Serve with: Hot wholewheat berries instead of rice, and cucumber with yogurt and chopped chives.

*Make the sauce a day in advance and leave overnight for the flavours to develop. Reheat gently.

Wednesday
Cheese and Spinach Dumplings

1 lb (455g) fresh spinach
*   or frozen equivalent*
2 eggs
½ lb (225g) Ricotta cheese,
*   mashed*
2 oz (55g) wholemeal
*   breadcrumbs*
2 oz (55g) grated
*   Parmesan cheese*
Seasoning to taste
Good pinch of nutmeg
2 oz (55g) wholemeal flour
2 oz (55g) grated
*   Parmesan cheese to*
*   serve*
2 oz (55g) butter

1 Cook the spinach until tender, then drain and chop.
2 Beat the eggs, and add the Ricotta cheese.
3 Stir in the breadcrumbs, Parmesan cheese, seasoning and nutmeg, mixing well. Add the spinach.
4 Divide the mixture into small balls, smooth the surface and coat with flour. Set aside for a short time, if possible.
5 Bring a pan of salted water to the boil and drop in the dumplings, a few at a time. Simmer for 5 minutes, or until they rise to the surface. Remove with a slotted spoon, and keep warm whilst cooking the rest.
6 Arrange the dumplings on a heat-proof dish, sprinkle with extra cheese and dot with butter. Grill until golden.

Serve with: Try spaghetti as a base, or serve with new potatoes. A chicory salad would also go well with these dumplings.

Thursday
Courgette and Almond Crumble

For the base:
3 tablespoons vegetable oil
1 onion, chopped
1 lb (455g) courgettes,
*   sliced*
4 oz (115g) mushrooms,
*   sliced*
4 oz (115g) cooked
*   sweetcorn*
Celery salt
Fresh ground pepper
Good pinch of basil
Soya sauce

For the crumble:
3 oz (85g) ground almonds
3 oz (85g) Weetabix or
*   equivalent wholemeal*
*   cereal*
3 oz (85g) margarine
Seasoning to taste

1 Heat the oil in a large pan, and gently fry the onion for a few minutes until soft.
2 Add the courgettes and mushrooms to the pan and cook for 5 minutes more, stirring frequently.
3 Combine the vegetables with the sweetcorn, seasoning and basil. Add soya sauce to taste. Transfer to an ovenproof dish.
4 Mix the ground almonds with the crumbled cereal, and rub in the margarine. Season generously. Sprinkle mixture over prepared vegetables.
5 Bake at 400°F/200°C (Gas Mark 6) for 15-20 minutes.

Serve with: Wholemeal bread, grilled tomatoes.

Friday
Tomato 'Sausage' Rolls

½ lb (225g) wholemeal
    flour
4 oz (115g) margarine
Tomato juice
1 medium tin soya
    'sausages'
1 oz (30g) melted
    margarine or butter

1 Put the flour into a bowl and rub in the fat to make a crumb-like mixture.
2 Use tomato juice to bind the dough. Wrap in clingfilm and chill for 30 minutes.
3 Roll out the dough thinly and cut into pieces, wrapping each one carefully around a 'sausage'. (If the 'sausages' are large, cut them in half.)
4 Arrange on a baking sheet and brush with the melted fat. Bake at 400°F/200°C (Gas Mark 6) for 15 minutes, or until cooked.

Serve with: New potatoes and a lightly steamed green vegetable such as broccoli.

Saturday
Aubergine and Tomato Stew

2 medium aubergines
Sea salt
2 tablespoons vegetable oil
1 onion, sliced
1 clove garlic, crushed
1 green pepper, chopped
4 large tomatoes, peeled
    and chopped
4 oz (115g) mushrooms,
    sliced
Seasoning to taste
Parsley, chopped
10 oz (285g) smoked tofu,
    cubed

1 Wash the aubergines, then cut into even-sized cubes. Arrange on a plate, sprinkle with salt, and set aside for 30 minutes.
2 Rinse the aubergines, drain well, then pat dry.
3 Heat the oil in a large pan and fry the onion with the garlic and pepper for 5 minutes.
4 Add the aubergine cubes and cook gently, stirring frequently, until they begin to colour.
5 Stir the tomatoes and mushrooms into the pan with the seasoning and chopped parsley, cover, and simmer for 20 minutes or until the vegetables are cooked. Add a few spoonfuls of water if necessary.

6 Mix the tofu gently into the aubergine stew and cook a few minutes longer to heat through.

Serve with: A hot grain dish — millet, for example. A raw spinach salad sprinkled with salted peanuts would also go well.

Sunday
Masala Dosai (Indian-Style Pancakes)

For the batter:
4 oz (115g) wholemeal
    flour
Pinch of salt
1 egg
¼ pint (140ml) skimmed
    milk
¼ pint (140ml) buttermilk

For the filling:
4 oz (115g) yellow split
    peas, soaked overnight
2 tablespoons vegetable oil
1 onion, finely sliced
3 oz (85g) ground sesame
    seeds
1 teaspoon curry powder
Garam masala
Vegetable oil for frying

1 Sieve together the flour and salt. Stir in the egg, then the skimmed milk, and finally the buttermilk. Whisk to lighten batter and stand it in a cool place for at least half an hour.
2 Drain the split peas and cook in water until tender. (You can use pre-cooked split peas, left over from a previous recipe, to save time.)
3 Heat the oil in a pan and sauté the onion until it begins to colour. Add the ground sesame seeds and curry powder, and cook gently for 5 minutes more. Adjust flavouring by adding garam masala to taste.
4 Stir in the drained, mashed split peas and heat through.
5 Meanwhile, whisk the batter and, if it seems too heavy, adjust its consistency by adding more liquid. Heat a drop of oil in a heavy-based pan and pour in a little of the batter. Tip the pan and cook gently until the pancake begins to colour underneath.
6 Flip the pancake, or turn with a spatula, and cook the other side. Keep cooked pancakes warm whilst using the rest of the batter in the same way.
7 Spread each pancake with some of the filling, roll up, and serve at once.

Serve with: A selection of traditional Indian sambals (side dishes), such as cucumber slices in yogurt, mango chutney, quartered tomatoes, banana chunks, salted peanuts.

Week 11:
Monday
Deep-Fried Tofu in Breadcrumbs

1¼ lb (565g) tofu
Wholemeal flour
Seasoning to taste
1 large egg, lightly beaten
Approx. 3 oz (85g)
*   wholemeal breadcrumbs*
Vegetable oil for frying
Parsley to garnish
Tartare sauce to serve

1 Wrap the tofu in a clean tea towel, put a heavy weight on top, and leave for a while so that the tofu is as dry as possible.
2 Cut into ½-inch (12mm) slices, and dip in the seasoned flour.
3 Now dip the tofu in the beaten egg and coat evenly with the fine breadcrumbs. Set aside for 10 minutes if possible.
4 Heat the oil to 350°F (180°C) in a deep pan. Deep fry some of the tofu slices until crisp and golden. Drain on paper towels, and keep warm whilst cooking the rest of the tofu in the same way. Hand round tartare sauce at the table.

Serve with: Hot rice and a salad of carrot, lettuce and spring onion with a few grapes sprinkled on top.

Tuesday
Green Bean and 'Minced Meat' Omelette

½ lb (225g) green beans
1 oz (30g) margarine or
*   butter*
1 onion, chopped
3 oz (85g) soya 'minced
*   meat', hydrated in water*
Seasoning to taste
1 teaspoon marjoram
4 eggs

1 Trim, slice and steam the beans until just tender, then drain well.
2 Melt the fat in a large clean pan and fry the onion for a few minutes until it begins to soften.
3 Bring the soya 'meat' to a boil, cook for a minute only, then drain well and stir into the onion.
4 Season and add marjoram and cook the mixture briefly. Add the beans.
5 Whisk together the eggs and pour over the other ingredients.
6 Continue cooking gently until the eggs set. Serve the omelette cut into quarters.

Serve with: New potatoes, and a tomato and raw grated courgette salad with chopped chives to garnish.

Wednesday
Spaghetti Alla Carbonara

¾ lb (340g) wholemeal
*   spaghetti*
½ oz (15g) margarine or
*   butter*
2 oz (55g) soya 'bacon' bits
2 tablespoons cream
3 eggs
4 oz (115g) grated
*   Parmesan cheese*
Seasoning to taste

1 Cook the spaghetti in a pan of boiling water for 10 minutes, or until just tender.
2 Meanwhile, melt the fat in a pan and fry the 'bacon' bits for only a minute or two. Remove from the heat, stir in the cream, and set aside.
3 Whisk the eggs and most of the grated cheese together, and season well.
4 Drain the spaghetti and return to the pan. Over a very low heat, add the 'bacon' mixture, then the egg mixture, tossing the spaghetti so that it is evenly coated with the other ingredients.
5 Cook for literally a minute, then transfer to a warmed serving dish and sprinkle with the remaining cheese.

Serve with: Fresh wholemeal rolls, and a tomato and parsley side salad.

Thursday
Stuffed Fennel Bulbs

2 large fennel bulbs
2 Weetabix or equivalent
*   wholemeal cereal*
6 oz (170g) curd cheese
2 oz (55g) hazelnuts,
*   chopped and roasted*
Seasoning to taste
Squeeze of lemon juice
Parsley to garnish

1 Trim the fennel bulbs, then cut in half lengthways and scoop out the centres to leave a fairly thick shell. Steam them briefly until just tender, then arrange close together in an ovenproof dish.
2 Crumble the Weetabix into a bowl and mix in the cheese, nuts, seasoning and lemon juice.
3 Spoon some of the filling into each of the fennel shells. Bake at 350°F/180°C (Gas Mark 4) for 15-20 minutes. Garnish with parsley.

Serve with: You could add the centres of the fennel, chopped finely, to a salad of celery, lettuce and orange segments. Steamed new potatoes would go well too.

Friday
Cabbage and Nut Meat Hash

3 medium potatoes
Medium tin nut meat
Approx. 2 oz (55g)
*   margarine or butter*
1 lb (455g) cabbage, finely
*   shredded*
Seasoning to taste

1 Boil or steam the potatoes until cooked but still firm, then drain well and cool slightly.
2 Dice the potatoes and nut meat.
3 Heat half the fat in a pan and add the potatoes and nut meat, cooking and stirring until lightly browned. Remove from the pan.
4 Melt the rest of the fat and stir in the shredded cabbage. Cook briefly, then cover and cook for 5-10 minutes, or until tender. Stir occasionally.
5 Add the potatoes and nut meat, mix well and heat through. Season to taste.

Serve with: A watercress salad, plus wholemeal toast.

Saturday
Mushroom Egg Ravioli

½ lb (225g) wholemeal
*   pasta dough (see page*
*   152)*

For the filling:
1½ oz (45g) margarine or
*   butter*
2 oz (55g) mushrooms,
*   chopped*
1 oz (30g) wholemeal flour
¼ pint (140ml) milk
Seasoning to taste
2 hard-boiled eggs, finely
*   chopped*
Chopped parsley
Parsley to garnish

1 Divide the dough into two and roll into oblongs making the dough as thin as possible. Mark one half into squares about 2 inches (5cm) across.
2 Melt the fat in a saucepan and lightly fry the mushrooms. Remove them carefully and set aside, then sprinkle in the flour and cook briefly.

3 Off the heat, stir in the milk, then continue cooking to make a thick sauce. Return the mushrooms to the pan, season, add the chopped eggs and some parsley, mixing well to make a paste.
4 Using a teaspoon, drop a little of the filling onto each of the squares. Brush the lines with water, then lay the second sheet of dough over the first and press down to remove any air pockets.
5 Press firmly along the lines, and cut into squares with a serrated-edged pastry cutter. Arrange the ravioli in a single layer on a lightly floured surface, cover with a dampened cloth, and leave for at least 30 minutes.
6 To cook, drop the ravioli a few at a time into a large pan of boiling salted water. Cook, stirring occasionally, for 5-8 minutes, or until tender. Remove with a perforated spoon and cook the rest in the same way. Garnish generously with fresh parsley.

Serve with: Cold cauliflower vinaigrette with a sprinkling of almonds.

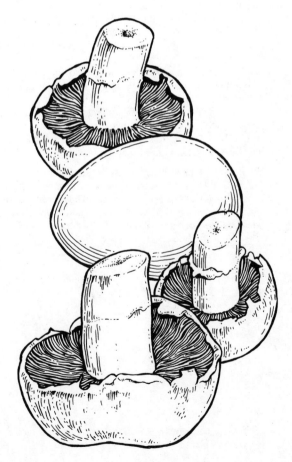

Sunday
Pissaladière

*½ lb (225g) shortcrust
pastry* (see page 151)*

For the topping:
3 tablespoons vegetable oil
1 green pepper
*¾ lb (340g) onions,
chopped*
1 clove garlic, crushed
14 oz (395g) tin tomatoes
*2 tablespoons tomato
purée*
Seasoning to taste
1 teaspoon mixed herbs
*4 oz (115g) grated Cheddar
cheese*
*12 black olives, halved and
stoned*

1 Make up the pastry, roll out in a rectangle, and arrange in
a lightly greased, Swiss-roll tin.
2 Heat most of the oil in a pan. Cut the pepper into strips and
fry until beginning to colour. Remove, drain and set aside.
3 Pour in the rest of the oil, add the onion and garlic; cook
gently until soft.
4 Add the tinned tomatoes, tomato purée, seasoning and herbs,
and continue to cook gently until a thick sauce forms. Spread
this over the pastry.
5 Top with the grated cheese. Make a lattice pattern with the
strips of green pepper and arrange the olives in between.
6 Bake at 400°F/200°C (Gas Mark 6) for 20-30 minutes or until
the cheese begins to brown. Eat hot or cold.

Serve with: A type of salad Niçoise would go well with this
French flan — just combine lettuce, cucumber, celery,
tomatoes, radishes and black olives with lightly cooked green
beans and an oil and vinegar dressing. Add chopped hard-
boiled egg for extra protein if you feel you need it.

*Self-raising flour gives a more authentic pastry base, though
you can use plain if you prefer.

Week 12:
Monday
Russian Salad

1 small cucumber, diced
*½ lb (225g) cooked
potatoes, diced*
*½ lb (225g) cooked
carrots, diced*
½ lb (225g) cooked peas
2 sticks celery, chopped
2 spring onions, chopped

For the dressing:
2 tablespoons mayonnaise
*1 tablespoon natural
yogurt*
Pinch of cayenne pepper
Pinch of dill or tarragon
Lettuce to serve
*2 hard-boiled eggs to
garnish*

1 Combine the cucumber, potatoes and carrots in a bowl. Add
the peas, celery and onions.
2 Mix together the salad dressing ingredients and stir into the
vegetables. Cover and chill well.
3 Serve the salad piled on a bed of lettuce, and garnished with
slices of hard-boiled egg.

Serve with: Fresh wholemeal bread with nut butter. If liked,
start the meal with soup.

Tuesday
Celery Provençale Crumble with Tofu

For the base:
1 large head of celery
2 tablespoons vegetable oil
1 onion, sliced
1-2 cloves garlic, crushed
14 oz (395g) tin tomatoes
*10 oz (285g) tofu, well
drained*
Parsley
Seasoning to taste

For the crumble:
*6 oz (170g) wholemeal
flour*
3 oz (85g) margarine
Parsley
Seasoning to taste

1 Clean the celery and chop coarsely.
2 Heat the vegetable oil in a pan and sauté the onion and garlic for 5 minutes, or until soft. Add the prepared celery and cook a few minutes more.
3 Stir in the contents of the tin of tomatoes, break them up, and cook gently until the sauce thickens, stirring occasionally.
4 Crumble or mash the tofu, and add to the mixture with the parsley and seasoning; mix well. Transfer to an ovenproof dish.
5 Put the flour in a bowl and rub in the margarine to make a crumb-like mixture. Add parsley and seasoning. Spread over celery and tofu.
6 Bake at 375°F/190°C (Gas Mark 5) for 20 minutes, or until crumble is cooked.

Serve with: Hot rice, and a salad of Chinese leaves, red pepper and roasted chopped hazelnuts.

Wednesday
Potato 'Sformato'

2 tablespoons vegetable oil
1 lb (455g) onions, sliced
6 tablespoons vegetable
  stock
1½ lb (680g) potatoes
1 oz (30g) margarine or
  butter
⅓ pint (200ml) milk
2 eggs, separated
2 oz (55g) grated
  Parmesan cheese
Seasoning to taste
Marjoram
Wholemeal breadcrumbs
Tomato sauce to serve (see
  page 153)

1 Heat the oil in a pan and add the onions. Sauté gently until the onions begin to soften. Pour in the stock and cover the pan; cook 10 minutes more.
2 Peel, dice, and steam the potatoes until soft. Mash well together with the margarine and milk, then cook for a short time. Combine with contents of first pan.
3 Stir in the egg yolks, cheese, seasoning and marjoram.
4 Whisk the 2 egg whites until stiff, then fold gently into the mixture. Spoon into a small, well-greased soufflé dish that has been sprinkled lightly with breadcrumbs.
5 Cover with greased foil, and then stand the soufflé dish in a pan containing 2-inches (5cm) of hot water. Bake at once at 350°F/180°C (Gas Mark 4) for about 40 minutes, or until set. Leave for a minute or two, then turn out carefully onto a warm serving plate. Pour on the sauce.

Serve with: A salad of raw cabbage, carrots and roasted sunflower seeds to contrast the rather subtle taste and smooth texture of the 'sformato'.

Thursday
Stuffed Courgettes with Yogurt

8 medium courgettes
2 tablespoons vegetable oil
1 onion, chopped
1 clove garlic, crushed
4 oz (115g) cooked brown
  rice
2 tomatoes, coarsely
  chopped
Seasoning to taste
Good pinch of sage
1 oz (30g) soya 'bacon' bits
¾ pint (425ml) vegetable
  stock

For the sauce:
1 pint (570ml) natural
  yogurt
1 teaspoon wholemeal
  flour
1 tablespoon cold water
Tomatoes to garnish

1 Trim the courgettes, and use a thin knife or apple corer to scoop a hole through the centre of each one.
2 Heat the oil in a pan and fry the chopped onion with the garlic until they begin to soften. Stir in the cooked rice, tomatoes, seasoning, sage and 'bacon' bits.
3 Carefully stuff the centres of the courgettes with the filling and arrange side by side in a large pan.
4 Pour the vegetable stock over the top, cover, and cook gently for 20 minutes.
5 Put the yogurt into a clean pan and beat well. Stir the flour into the water and add to the yogurt, mixing thoroughly. Bring to the boil, then simmer over a very low heat until the yogurt thickens.
6 Spread over the courgettes and cook, uncovered, for 10 minutes more. Garnish with quartered tomatoes.

Serve with: Lightly steamed new potatoes. A salad of broad beans, beetroot and orange on a lettuce base.

Summer

Friday
Peanut and Wheatgerm Croquettes

4 oz (115g) wholemeal
  breadcrumbs
4 oz (115g) peanuts,
  coarsely grated or
  ground
4 oz (115g) grated Cheddar
  cheese
¼ pint (140ml) milk
Parsley, chopped
Seasoning to taste
Approx. 2 oz (55g)
  wheatgerm
Extra wheatgerm for
  coating
Vegetable oil for frying

1 In a bowl mix together the fine breadcrumbs, peanuts, cheese and milk.
2 Add a generous amount of parsley, seasoning, and enough wheatgerm for the mixture to hold its shape.
3 Mould into 8 small croquettes and roll in wheatgerm.
4 Heat the vegetable oil in a frying pan and shallow fry the croquettes, turning frequently, until crisp and brown on the outside. Drain on paper towels.

Serve with: Potatoes in white parsley sauce and any colourful vegetable combination, such as a dish of broccoli, peas and carrots.

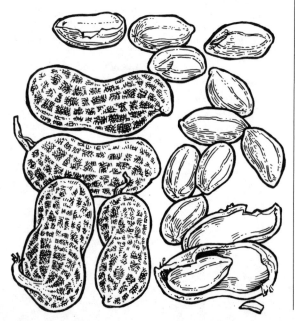

Saturday
Pastitsio

2 tablespoons vegetable oil
1 oz (30g) margarine or
  butter
2 onions, finely sliced
2 sticks celery, finely sliced
1 clove garlic, crushed
4 oz (115g) brown lentils
14 oz (395g) tin tomatoes,
  chopped
3 tablespoons tomato
  purée
1 teaspoon oregano
1 teaspoon parsley
Seasoning to taste
10 oz (285g) wholemeal
  macaroni or pasta shells
¾ pint (425ml) white
  sauce (see page 153)
2 eggs, beaten
Pinch of nutmeg
4 oz (115g) cottage cheese

1 Heat the oil and fat together in a pan and add the onions, celery and garlic, cooking gently until they begin to soften.
2 Add the lentils and cover with water. Continue to cook until lentils are soft, then stir in the tomatoes, tomato purée, herbs and seasoning, and continue simmering until the sauce thickens.
3 Meanwhile, cook the pasta in a pan of boiling water for 10 minutes, or until just tender. Drain well.
4 When the white sauce has cooled a little, add the beaten eggs, nutmeg and cottage cheese.
5 In a large, well-greased ovenproof dish, arrange the prepared ingredients in layers — start with half the pasta, then half the lentil and tomato sauce, then repeat. Top with the cheese sauce.
6 Bake at 400°F/200°C (Gas Mark 6) for 40-50 minutes, or until golden on top.

Serve with: A green salad that includes slices of avocado and some flaked almonds.

Sunday
Tofu Vegetable Flan

For the pastry:
½ lb (225g) wholemeal
  flour
1 teaspoon baking powder
Pinch of sea salt
3 tablespoons vegetable oil
3 tablespoons cold water

For the filling:
*Approx. 2 tablespoons
   vegetable oil
½-1 clove garlic, crushed
1 onion, sliced
2 oz (55g) mushrooms,
   chopped
2 sticks celery, chopped
1 large carrot, chopped
10 oz (285g) tofu, drained
   and mashed
1 tablespoon soya sauce
Seasoning to taste
1 tablespoon parsley,
   chopped
2 oz (55g) beansprouts
1 oz (30g) sunflower seeds*

1 Sift together the dry ingredients, and beat together the oil and water.
2 Combine both mixtures, stirring well. Wrap the dough in clingfilm and chill for at least 30 minutes.
3 Meanwhile, heat the vegetable oil in a pan and add the garlic and sliced onion. Cook gently for a few minutes, then add the chopped mushrooms and cook a little longer.
4 Add the celery and carrot to the pan, stirring to mix. Cook a few minutes more. Add the tofu, soya sauce, seasoning and parsley, and cook a further 5 minutes, stirring frequently. Add the beansprouts.
5 Roll out the pastry and line a medium-sized flan dish. Bake blind at 400°F/200°C (Gas Mark 6) for 15 minutes.
6 Pile the filling into the flan case and smooth the top; sprinkle with seeds. Reduce the oven temperature to 350°F/180°C (Gas Mark 4) and cook 20 minutes more, until pastry is crisp and brown.

Serve with: A raw broccoli salad, plus a side dish of hot rice or millet.

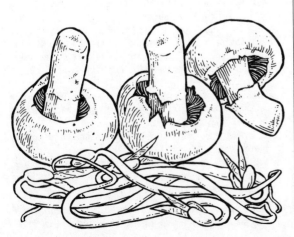

Week 13:
Monday
Gazpacho

*3 slices wholemeal bread
Approx. ¾ pint (425ml)
   tomato juice
1 lb (455g) tomatoes,
   peeled and chopped
1 cucumber, coarsely
   chopped
1 green pepper, coarsely
   chopped
1 onion, coarsely chopped
1-2 cloves garlic, crushed
⅛ pint (70ml) olive oil
3 tablespoons red wine
   vinegar
Seasoning to taste*

To serve:
*Wholemeal croûtons
4 hard-boiled eggs,
   chopped
Green stuffed olives, sliced*

1 Cube the bread and soak it in the tomato juice for 10 minutes.
2 In a blender combine the bread and juice with the tomatoes, cucumber, pepper, onion and garlic.
3 Stir the oil, vinegar and seasoning into the purée. The mixture should be the consistency of single cream, so if it seems too thick, add more tomato juice or some cold water.
4 Chill the soup for 1-2 hours, or overnight.
5 If liked, you can add a few crushed ice cubes before serving. Hand round the *croûtons*, chopped eggs and sliced olives at the table.

Serve with: French bread or wholemeal baps. A beansprout and peanut salad would also go well with gazpacho.

Tuesday
Tomato Basil Crumble

For the base:
2 oz (55g) margarine or
  butter
2 large onions, sliced
2 lb (1 kilo) tomatoes,
  sliced
Seasoning to taste
2 tablespoons fresh basil

For the crumble:
2 oz (55g) margarine or
  butter
4 oz (115g) wholemeal
  breadcrumbs
2 oz (55g) wheatgerm
2 oz (55g) sunflower seeds
Seasoning to taste

1 Melt half the fat in a pan and gently cook the onions until soft but not browned.
2 Put a layer of the onions in the bottom of a small, greased ovenproof dish. Top with a layer of sliced tomatoes, seasoning, basil, and a few knobs of fat.
3 Repeat this process until you have used up all the base ingredients.
4 In the same saucepan, melt the fat for the crumble. Stir in the crumbs, wheatgerm and sunflower seeds, and cook for just a few minutes, stirring continually. Season to taste.
5 Sprinkle the crumble evenly over the tomatoes and bake at 400°F/200°C (Gas Mark 6) for 20 minutes.

Serve with: A cold leek and pasta salad, topped with soya 'bacon' bits.

Wednesday
Mushroom Cashew Vol-au-Vents

*For the rough puff
  pastry:*
½ lb (225g) wholemeal
  flour
5 oz (140g) unsalted butter
Pinch of sea salt
1 teaspoon lemon juice
Cold water to mix

For the filling:
½ pint (285ml) white
  sauce (see page 153)
2 tablespoons vegetable oil
6 oz (170g) mushrooms,
  sliced
2 oz (55g) cashew nuts,
  chopped
1-2 tablespoons cream
Fresh chives
Seasoning to taste
1 egg, beaten
Capers to garnish
  (optional)

1 Sift the flour (the bran can be used in another recipe). Cut the butter into small pieces and stir into the flour; add salt. Mix the lemon juice with a little cold water and stir into the flour and fat, adding more water if necessary to make a fairly firm dough. (Leave the fat in lumps.)
2 Roll out into a large oblong on a floured board. Fold into three. Seal the edges, give the pastry a half-turn, and repeat the rolling process.
3 Wrap the pastry in clingfilm or a polythene bag and leave in the fridge for 30 minutes, then roll and fold twice more. Chill again.
4 Meanwhile, make up the white sauce.
5 Heat the oil in a pan and fry the mushrooms gently for just a minute or two until they are cooked, but still firm. Drain well and stir into the sauce.
6 Add the nuts, cream, plenty of chives and seasoning.
7 Roll out the pastry to a thickness of about 1-inch (2.5cm). Cut into rounds 2-inches (5cm) in diameter, then use a smaller cutter to mark a lid to a depth of about ½ an inch (12mm).
8 Brush the tops only with a mixture of beaten egg and water, and bake at 400°F/200°C (Gas Mark 6) for about 20 minutes, or until crisp and golden.
9 Remove the 'lid' and return to the oven for a minute or two more.
10 Fill at once with some of the hot mushroom and nut mixture, garnishing with the capers or, if you prefer, more chives. Balance the 'lids' on top of the filling if you like.

Serve with: A broad bean and potato salad on a lettuce base. Hot grilled tomatoes could also be served.

Thursday
Nutty Ravioli

*½ lb (225g) wholemeal
 pasta dough (see page
 152)*

For the filling:
*2 oz (55g) mixed chopped
 nuts*
*2 oz (55g) wholemeal
 breadcrumbs*
1 egg
Soya sauce to taste
1-2 teaspoons marjoram
Seasoning to taste
*½ pint (285ml) white
 sauce to serve (see page
 153)*
*3 oz (85g) grated Cheddar
 cheese*

1 Split the dough into two pieces and roll out as thinly as possible, shaping them into oblongs. Mark one half into squares about 2 inches (5cm) across.
2 In a bowl mix together the nuts, breadcrumbs, egg, soya sauce, marjoram and seasoning, mashing well to form a paste. If it is too dry, add a drop of stock. If too wet, add more nuts or bread.
3 Drop a little of the filling into the centre of each of the marked squares. Dampen the lines with water. Lay the second sheet of dough over the first, and press down to remove air pockets.
4 Press firmly along the marked lines to seal, then cut into squares, preferably using a serrated-edged cutter. Lay the ravioli on a lightly floured surface, cover with a damp cloth, and leave for at least 30 minutes.
5 Bring a large pan of salted water to the boil and drop in the ravioli, a few at a time, stirring so that they do not stick together. Continue cooking for 5-8 minutes, or until tender. Remove with a slotted spoon and keep warm whilst cooking the rest in the same way.
6 Heat the white sauce and stir in the cheese until melted. Pour over the ravioli.

Serve with: A raw spinach salad with celery, green pepper and onion, plus French bread.

Friday
Stuffed Aubergines

4 small aubergines
1 tablespoon capers
*1 oz (30g) chopped
 walnuts*
*2 oz (55g) wholemeal
 breadcrumbs, moistened
 with a drop of water*
10 black olives, chopped
3 small tomatoes, chopped
Garlic salt
*Freshly ground black
 pepper*
*1 tablespoon parsley,
 chopped*
2 tablespoons vegetable oil

1 Halve the aubergines lengthways and cut out most of the flesh, leaving a firm outer shell.
2 Chop the aubergine flesh and combine it with the capers, walnuts, breadcrumbs, olives, tomatoes, seasoning and parsley.
3 Stand the aubergine shells close together in an ovenproof dish and lightly stuff each one with some of the mixture. Trickle the tops with oil.
4 Cover the dish with a lid or silver foil, and bake at 325°F/170°C (Gas Mark 3) for about 1 hour, or until cooked through.

Serve with: A lettuce and green bean salad topped with a tahini dressing to add protein to the meal. Lightly steamed new potatoes with parsley.

Summer

Saturday
Gougère

For the filling:
2 tablespoons vegetable oil
1 onion, sliced
½ lb (225g) mushrooms,
 sliced
1 oz (30g) soya 'bacon' bits
1 oz (30g) wholemeal flour
½ pint (285ml) milk
1 tablespoon parsley,
 chopped
Seasoning to taste

For the gougère:
¼ pint (140ml) water
2 oz (55g) butter
3 oz (85g) wholemeal
 flour *
2-3 eggs
Seasoning to taste
2 oz (55g) Cheddar cheese,
 diced

1 Heat the oil in a pan and lightly fry the onion for a few minutes.
  Add the mushrooms and cook a few minutes more until just
  tender. Stir in the soya 'bacon' bits.
2 Sprinkle in the flour and cook briefly, then add the milk and
  continue cooking to thicken the sauce. Add parsley, season
  well, and set aside.
3 In a clean saucepan, bring the water to the boil, add the butter
  and, when this has melted, tip in all the flour at once. Beat
  vigorously with a wooden spoon, cooking gently at the same
  time, until the mixture forms a smooth ball.
4 Cool the mixture slightly, then whisk the eggs and add a little
  at a time, stopping when the dough is shiny and still firm
  enough to hold its shape. Season and add the diced cheese.
5 Pipe or spoon the mixture into a circle on an oiled baking
  sheet or round the edge of a shallow ovenproof dish. Pile
  the vegetables in the centre.
6 Bake at 400°F/200°C (Gas Mark 6) for 30-40 minutes, or
  until well risen and golden.

Serve with: A raw spinach salad would go especially well,
topped with wholemeal *croûtons*.

*You will get a lighter choux pastry if you use 81 per cent
wholemeal flour (or simply sift out some of the bran from
your usual flour). The heavier version is, however, just as good
to eat.

Sunday
Soya Bean Curry

*1 pint (570ml) curry
 sauce (see page 154)
½ lb (225g) cooked soya
 beans
2 medium carrots, sliced
2 medium courgettes, cut
 into chunks
2 oz (55g) peanuts
Parsley to garnish*

1 Heat the sauce gently.
2 Add the drained soya beans together with the carrots and
  the courgettes.
3 Simmer for 15 minutes, or until the vegetables are just cooked.
4 Stir in the nuts and cook for a minute or two more.
5 Garnish with parsley.

Serve with: Brown rice, and a salad of spring onions and
beetroot in yogurt.

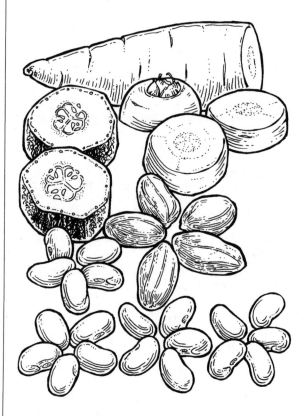

*Make a day in advance and leave overnight for the flavour
to develop. Reheat gently.

3.
AUTUMN

Week 1:
Monday
Macaroni with Eggs

10 oz (285g) wholemeal
  macaroni
4 eggs
2 tablespoons milk
Seasoning to taste
Fresh chives, chopped
2 oz (55g) margarine or
  butter
2 oz (55g) grated
  Parmesan cheese

1 Drop the pasta into a pan of fast boiling salted water and cook for 10 minutes, or until just tender. Drain and set aside.
2 Meanwhile, whisk together the eggs, milk, seasoning, and chives.
3 Melt the fat in a clean pan, and pour in the egg mixture. Cook gently, stirring continually, until the eggs begin to set.
4 Mix well with the macaroni and transfer to a serving dish. Top with grated cheese, and more chives to garnish.

Serve with: A red cabbage, pepper and onion salad with a sprinkling of sunflower seeds, plus wholemeal baps for the extra hungry.

Tuesday
Jacket Potato with Baked Beans

4 large potatoes
Small tin (7 oz/200g)
  baked beans
½-1 teaspoon molasses
2 tomatoes, coarsely
  chopped
Seasoning to taste
Soya 'bacon' bits
Parsley to garnish

1 Scrub the potatoes, pat dry, prick with a fork, and wrap each one individually in a piece of silver foil. Bake at 400°F/200°C (Gas Mark 6) for about an hour, or until soft.
2 Meanwhile, tip the beans into a saucepan and heat gently. Stir in the molasses and the tomatoes. Season to taste.
3 Cut the potatoes in half lengthways and scoop out some of the flesh. Chop it and mix with the beans.
4 Spoon the mixture back into each of the shells, piling it high. Sprinkle with soya 'bacon' bits. Return to the oven for 5 minutes to heat through, if necessary. Garnish with parsley.

Serve with: Hot peas and carrots, and a lettuce side salad.

Wednesday
Cheese and Tomato Pie

*¾ lb (340g) shortcrust
pastry (see page 151)*

For the filling:
2 tablespoons vegetable oil
*2 large onions, thickly
sliced*
4 large tomatoes, sliced
*6 oz (170g) grated Cheddar
cheese*
Seasoning to taste
1 egg

1 Make up the pastry, chill briefly, then divide into two pieces and roll out into circles. Use one to line the base of a small, shallow pie dish.
2 Heat the oil in a pan and fry the onions until they begin to soften.
3 Arrange the drained onions across the pastry, cover with the sliced tomatoes and top with the grated cheese. Season to taste.
4 Cover with the second round of pastry, pinching the edges together to seal the pie. Use any left-over pastry to decorate the top. Brush the pastry with beaten egg and then prick lightly with a fork.
5 Bake at 375°F/190°C (Gas Mark 5) for 30-40 minutes, or until cooked.

Serve with: Braised celery, plus jacket potatoes.

Thursday
Khichiri

3 tablespoons vegetable oil
1 onion, sliced
1-2 cloves garlic, crushed
*1 teaspoon ground
turmeric*
1 teaspoon ground ginger
1 teaspoon ground cumin
½ teaspoon garam masala
*½ lb (225g) mung beans,
soaked overnight*
1 potato, cubed,
*3 tomatoes, coarsely
chopped*
½ lb (225g) brown rice
1½ pints (850ml) water
1 tablespoon lemon juice
Parsley to garnish
Natural yogurt to serve

1 Heat the oil in a saucepan, and fry the onion with the garlic for 5 minutes. Add the spices, stir, and cook a few minutes more.
2 Drain the beans well and add to the pan with the potato, tomatoes, rice and the water. Bring to the boil, then lower the heat, cover, and simmer for 40-50 minutes, or until everything is cooked. (Although Khichiri should be dry, check that it isn't too dry when cooking.) Add the lemon juice.
3 Garnish with parsley, and hand round yogurt at the table for those who want it.

Serve with: Wholemeal popadums. A broccoli and mushroom salad with garlic and lemon dressing would complete the meal.

Friday
Quick Pan-Fried Pizzas

For the dough:
*½ lb (225g) plain
wholemeal flour*
*2 teaspoons baking
powder*
Salt and pepper
2 tablespoons vegetable oil
¼ pint (140ml) cold water
Vegetable oil for frying

For the topping:
2 tomatoes, sliced
4 large mushrooms, sliced
½ small onion, sliced
*4 oz (115g) grated Cheddar
cheese*
Seasoning to taste
Sprinkling of oregano

1 Sieve together the flour, baking powder and seasoning. Mix the oil into the water and add to the dry ingredients, mixing well. Knead. (If necessary add a drop more water.)
2 Divide the dough into two and roll out.
3 Pour a little oil into a heavy-based pan and heat until hot but not smoking. Turn down the heat and lift the dough into the pan. Cook until lightly browned underneath, then turn and cook the other side in the same way. Repeat this process with the second pizza.
4 On one side of the pizzas arrange the sliced tomatoes, mushrooms and onion rings, top with grated cheese and season well. Add the oregano.
5 Put the pizzas under a moderate grill for a few minutes to cook the topping and melt the cheese.

Serve with: Wholemeal baps, and a coleslaw and walnut salad.

Saturday
Cauliflower and Chick-Pea Flan

For the flan case:
6 oz (170g) rolled oats
3 oz (85g) margarine
1 oz (30g) sesame seeds
Pinch of sea salt

For the filling:
1 small cauliflower
3 tablespoons vegetable oil
1 small onion, sliced
1½ oz (45g) wholemeal
*   flour*
2 tablespoons tahini
6 oz (170g) cooked
*   chick-peas*
Seasoning to taste
2 tomatoes, sliced

1 Put the oats in a bowl, and use fingertips to rub in the fat. Add seeds and salt, stirring well.
2 Lightly grease a medium-sized flan dish and press the oat mixture evenly against the sides and base. Bake at 400°F/200°C (Gas Mark 6) for 15 minutes.
3 Break the cauliflower into florets and cook in boiling water until just tender. Drain, but reserve the water.
4 Heat the oil in a clean pan and sauté the onion until it begins to colour. Sprinkle in the flour, cook briefly, then pour in about ½ pint (285ml) of the reserved water and simmer until the sauce thickens. (Use more water if necessary.)
5 Add the tahini to the sauce and mix well, then stir in the cauliflower florets, chick-peas and seasoning. Spoon into the flan case and smooth the top. Decorate with a ring of tomato slices.
6 Bake at the same temperature for 10-15 minutes more, or until the case is cooked.

Serve with: A red cabbage and apple salad. Rye bread could be served too.

Sunday
Onion Soufflé

2 tablespoons vegetable oil
1 lb (455g) onions,
*   chopped*
1 oz (30g) margarine or
*   butter*
1 oz (30g) wholemeal flour
⅓ pint (200ml) vegetable
*   stock*
3 tablespoons creamy milk
4 eggs, separated
Seasoning to taste
Good pinch of tarragon or
*   basil*
1 tablespoon sesame seeds

1 Heat the oil in a saucepan and gently sauté the onion until it begins to soften. Drain well and mash, sieve or liquidize the onions.
2 Melt the fat, add the flour, and cook gently, stirring. Then, off the heat, add the stock. Return to heat and cook until the sauce thickens.
3 Remove from heat again, cool slightly, then stir in the milk, egg yolks, seasoning and herbs.
4 Whisk the egg whites until stiff. Use a metal spoon to fold them into the onion mixture. Spoon into a 2-pint soufflé dish and sprinkle with seeds.
5 Bake at once in an oven pre-heated to 375°F/190°C (Gas Mark 5) for 30 minutes, or until well risen.

Serve with: Raw grated beetroot mixed with orange segments and served on a bed of endive, plus potato salad.

Autumn

Week 2:
Monday
Cheese and Sweetcorn Chowder

2 oz (55g) margarine or
butter
2 sticks celery, finely
chopped
1 onion, finely chopped
2 oz (55g) wholemeal flour
1¾ pints (1 litre) milk and
water mixed
½ lb (225g) fresh, tinned
or frozen sweetcorn
kernels
4 oz (115g) grated Cheddar
cheese
Seasoning to taste
Chopped chives to garnish

1 Melt the fat and cook the celery and onion for 5 minutes to soften.
2 Sprinkle in the flour and cook a minute more, then remove from heat, and stir in the milk and water. Return the pan to the heat and bring to the boil. Simmer until the soup thickens.
3 Add the corn and cook until tender.
4 Stir in the grated cheese and seasoning. Cook gently for a minute longer until cheese melts. Garnish generously with chopped chives.

Serve with: A tomato and onion salad, plus toast spread with low-fat cheese.

Tuesday
Wholewheat Bake

½ lb (225g) wholewheat
berries
3 tablespoons vegetable oil
1 small onion, sliced
1 lb (455g) spinach
4 oz (115g) peanuts
Seasoning to taste
2 oz (55g) grated Cheddar
cheese

1 Rinse the wholewheat berries and drain well.
2 Heat half the oil in a saucepan and add the berries, stirring so that they are well coated. Cook briefly, then cover with water, bring to the boil, and simmer for about an hour, or until tender. (Add more water if necessary.)
3 Meanwhile, fry the onion in the remainder of the oil.
4 Wash, shred and steam the spinach for just a few minutes until it begins to wilt. Drain.
5 Add the peanuts to the onion and cook until they begin to

colour. Stir in the spinach and cook a few minutes more. Season to taste.
6 Put half the wholewheat berries into an ovenproof dish, top with half of the spinach mixture. Repeat this to use up the rest of the ingredients.
7 Top with the grated cheese. Bake at 350°F/180°C (Gas Mark 4) for 20-30 minutes.

Serve with: A mushroom, celery and red pepper salad.

Wednesday
Lasagne with Ricotta

½ lb (225g) wholemeal
lasagne
1 oz (30g) margarine or
butter
1 onion, sliced
½-1 clove garlic, crushed
½ lb (225g) mushrooms,
sliced
Seasoning to taste
¾ lb (340g) spinach
6 oz (170g) Ricotta cheese
2 tablespoons milk
2 oz (55g) grated
Parmesan cheese
1 oz (30g) sunflower seeds
1 oz (30g) wholemeal
breadcrumbs
1 oz (30g) grated Cheddar
cheese

1 Cook the lasagne in a large pan of boiling water, dropping them in one sheet at a time, and simmering for 8 minutes, or as long as directed on the packet. Drain, rinse in cold water, and set aside on a clean tea towel.
2 Melt the fat in a pan, and fry the onion and garlic until they begin to soften. Add the mushrooms and cook a few minutes more, stirring occasionally. Season to taste.
3 Wash and shred the spinach, and steam until soft. Drain well, and chop finely.
4 Beat together the Ricotta cheese, milk and Parmesan cheese.
5 In a greased ovenproof dish, arrange a layer of lasagne, top with some of the mushrooms, then some of the spinach. Repeat to use up all the ingredients, finishing with a layer of lasagne.
6 Pour on the prepared cheese sauce, spreading it evenly. Sprinkle with the seeds, breadcrumbs and grated Cheddar cheese. Bake at 375°F/190°C (Gas Mark 5) for 30-40 minutes, or until crisp on top.

Serve with: A chicory, tomato and pepper salad.

Thursday
Autumn 'Beef' Bake

*3 oz (85g) soya 'minced
 beef', hydrated in water*
*1 small onion, finely
 chopped*
*Small tin (½ lb/225g)
 tomatoes, mashed*
½ teaspoon curry powder
Sea salt
*6 oz (170g) cooked
 sweetcorn*
*6 oz (170g) cooked broad
 beans*
1 green pepper, chopped
*1 medium potato, thinly
 sliced*
*1 oz (30g) margarine or
 butter*
*2 oz (55g) wholemeal
 breadcrumbs*

1 Simmer the 'minced beef' for 5 minutes, then drain well.
2 Mix the 'beef' with the onion, tomatoes, curry powder and salt.
3 In an ovenproof dish, arrange layers of the 'beef' mixture,
  sweetcorn, broad beans, pepper and potato. Continue until
  all ingredients have been used. You may need to add a drop
  of liquid (water, stock or tomato juice) if mixture seems dry.
4 Melt the fat in a small pan, mix with the breadcrumbs, and
  sprinkle over the top.
5 Bake at 350°F/180°C (Gas Mark 4) for 30 minutes or until
  vegetables are cooked and top is crisp.

Serve with: Brussels sprouts, and French-fried potatoes.

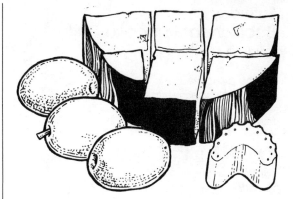

Friday
Caponata (Sweet and Sour Vegetables)

4 sticks celery
*Approx. 4 tablespoons
 vegetable oil*
*2 medium aubergines,
 cubed*
1 large onion, sliced
*⅛ pint (70ml) wine
 vinegar*
1 teaspoon raw cane sugar
*2 large tomatoes, peeled
 and chopped*
⅓ pint (200ml) water
1 tablespoon capers
10 green olives
*1 tablespoon parsley,
 chopped*
Seasoning to taste
2 oz (55g) pine nuts

1 Clean, chop and steam or boil the celery until just tender.
  Set aside.
2 Heat the oil in a large, clean pan and add the aubergine with
  the onion. Cook gently until just tender, then remove the
  vegetables from the pan with a slotted spoon.
3 Add a drop more oil if the pan seems very dry, and then pour
  in the vinegar with the sugar, tomatoes and the water.
4 Cook gently, stirring occasionally, for 5 minutes.
5 Stir in the cooked vegetables, the capers, olives and parsley.
  Season to taste. Simmer the mixture for about 10 minutes,
  or until all the vegetables are tender and the sauce has
  thickened.
6 Serve at once, sprinkled with the pine nuts, or chill overnight
  and serve as a cold dish.

Serve with: Warm wholemeal baps maybe spread with nut
butter and a green salad.

Autumn

Saturday
Buckwheat Pancakes with Marrow Filling

For the pancakes:
3 oz (85g) buckwheat flour
2 oz (55g) wholemeal flour
Pinch of salt
1 egg
½ pint (285ml) cold water

For the filling:
½ oz (15g) butter
1 tablespoon vegetable oil
1 onion, sliced
½ small marrow, peeled
* and cubed*
4 tomatoes, coarsely
* chopped*
1 teaspoon mixed herbs
Seasoning to taste
Vegetable oil for frying

For the sauce:
½ pint (285ml) white
* sauce (see page 153)*
Milk to thin
2 oz (55g) grated Cheddar
* cheese*

1 Sift together the two flours and salt, add the egg, then gradually add the water, stirring continually to keep the batter smooth. Whisk to lighten, then leave in a cool place for at least half an hour.
2 Heat the butter and oil together and add the onion. Cook until soft.
3 Add the marrow and tomatoes. Stir well. Flavour with herbs and seasoning. Cover and cook gently until the marrow is just tender.
4 Meanwhile, check the consistency of the pancake batter, adding a drop more water if necessary to make it easy to pour.
5 Heat a drop of oil in a heavy-based frying pan; pour in a little of the batter and spread evenly. Cook until it begins to colour underneath, then turn and cook the other side.
6 Keep cooked pancakes warm whilst using the rest of the batter in the same way.
7 Fill each of the pancakes with some of the marrow mixture; roll up, and place side by side in an ovenproof dish.
8 Thin the white sauce to a pouring consistency. Add the grated cheese and spread over the pancakes. Bake at 350°F/180°C (Gas Mark 4) for 15-20 minutes to heat through.

Serve with: French bread, and a carrot and raisin salad sprinkled with sesame seeds.

Sunday
Soya Bean Casserole

6 oz (170g) soya beans,
* soaked for 24 hours*
3 tablespoons vegetable oil
1 onion, finely sliced
1 clove garlic, crushed
2 sticks celery, chopped
14 oz (395g) tin tomatoes,
* mashed*
1 crushed bay leaf
1 teaspoon thyme
3 tablespoons red wine
1 tablespoon soya sauce
Seasoning to taste
4 oz (115g) grated Cheddar
* cheese*
2 oz (55g) wheatgerm

1 Drain the beans, put into a pan with fresh water, and fast boil for 10 minutes. Lower the heat, cover, and simmer the beans for 2-3 hours, or until tender.
2 Meanwhile, heat the oil in another pan and fry the onion, garlic and celery for 5 minutes. Add the tomatoes and their juice, and stir in the herbs, wine, soya sauce and seasoning. Cook gently until the sauce thickens.
3 Drain the beans and put half of them into a lightly greased ovenproof dish. Top with half the sauce, and half the cheese mixed with half the wheatgerm.
4 Repeat this. Cover the dish and bake at 350°F/180°C (Gas Mark 4) for 20-30 minutes.

Serve with: Jacket potatoes, and cabbage and onion sautéed in butter.

Note: As soya beans take so long to cook it is well worth doing double the quantity, and keeping the unused portion in the fridge or freezer.

Week 3:
Monday
Spanish Bulgur

*1 oz (30g) margarine or
  butter
1 onion, finely chopped
1 large stick celery, finely
  chopped
1 small green pepper,
  finely chopped
½ lb (225g) bulgur
¾ pint (425ml) vegetable
  stock
Seasoning to taste
Garlic salt
2 oz (55g) cooked peas
3 tomatoes, quartered
3 hard-boiled eggs, sliced
Stuffed olives to garnish*

1 Melt the fat in a pan and fry the onion, celery and pepper
  for 5 minutes, stirring occasionally.
2 Add the bulgur and cook briefly to colour. Stir in the stock,
  bring to a boil, and simmer covered for about 20 minutes, or
  until vegetables are cooked.
3 Add seasoning, garlic salt, the cooked peas and quartered
  tomatoes. Stir and cook a minute more to heat through.
4 Drain if necessary and turn onto a heated serving dish. Top
  with egg slices and sprinkle with the olives.

Serve with: A beansprout salad, and French bread.

Tuesday
Avocado Salad

*1 medium crisp lettuce
1 large grapefruit
2 avocados
Squeeze of lemon juice
2 sticks celery, finely
  chopped
2 oz (55g) roasted flaked
  almonds
4 oz (115g) low-fat cream
  cheese
1-2 tablespoons fruit juice
Watercress to garnish*

1 Shred the lettuce and spread over a shallow serving dish.
2 Peel and segment the grapefruit; peel and slice the avocados,
  tossing the slices gently in lemon juice. Arrange the grapefruit
  and avocado slices in an overlapping pattern on top of the
  lettuce.

3 Pile up the celery in the centre of the dish. Sprinkle with
  almonds.
4 Mash the cheese together with the fruit juice and spoon onto
  the salad. Garnish with watercress.

Serve with: Freshly made corn muffins, spread with nut butter.

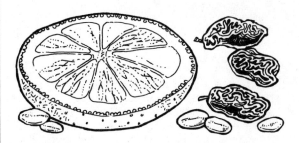

Wednesday
Imam Bayeldi

*2 large aubergines
3 tablespoons olive oil
1 onion, finely chopped
1 clove garlic, crushed
½ teaspoon ground cumin
½ teaspoon ground
  coriander
2 tomatoes, skinned and
  chopped
1 oz (30g) oats
1 oz (30g) sultanas
Squeeze of lemon juice
Seasoning to taste
Approx. 4 tablespoons
  tahini
1 oz (30g) wholemeal
  breadcrumbs*

1 Trim the aubergines, then cut in half lengthways. Scoop out
  the flesh with a teaspoon, leaving a shell about ¼-inch (6mm)
  thick. Sprinkle the flesh and shells with salt, and leave to
  drain for 30 minutes. Rinse well and pat dry.
2 Heat the oil in a pan and fry the onion and garlic for a few
  minutes. Add the spices and cook a few minutes more.
3 Stir in the tomatoes with the cubed aubergine flesh and the
  oats, and cook until the aubergine is soft and the tomatoes
  have broken down.
4 Add the sultanas, a squeeze of lemon juice, and seasoning
  to taste, mixing well.
5 Stand the aubergine shells close together in an ovenproof
  dish and fill them with the prepared mixture. Top each one
  with a trickle of tahini and breadcrumbs.
6 Bake at 400°F/200°C (Gas Mark 6) for 35-40 minutes.

Serve with: Hot brown rice and a cucumber salad with mint
dressing.

Thursday
Swiss Cheese Omelette

6 large eggs
2 tablespoons single cream
Seasoning to taste
1 oz (30g) margarine or
  butter
6 oz (170g) Gruyère cheese,
  grated
Chives to garnish

1 Lightly whisk together the eggs, cream and seasoning.
2 Heat a little of the fat in a small pan. Pour in a quarter of the egg mixture and lower the heat. Cook until the omelette begins to set underneath, then lift up the sides and tilt the pan so that any liquid runs underneath. Continue cooking until the top begins to set.
3 Top with 1½ oz (45g) of the grated cheese, fold and serve.
4 Use the remaining ingredients to make three more omelettes in the same way. Garnish each one with fresh chives.

Serve with: A crisp salad of briefly steamed marrow cubes with tomatoes, onions, parsley and chives, plus fresh wholemeal baps.

Friday
Peanut Curry (Thai-Style)

3 tablespoons vegetable oil
1 large onion, thickly
  sliced
½ pint (285ml) coconut
  milk
1-2 tablespoons curry
  paste*
4 oz (115g) peanuts
½ lb (225g) green beans,
  fresh or frozen
1 teaspoon lemon juice
2 teaspoons raw cane sugar
2 teaspoons soya sauce
Seasoning to taste

1 Heat the oil in a large pan. Fry the onion gently until beginning to soften.
2 Add the coconut milk, bring it to a boil, then lower the heat and stir in the curry paste. Simmer for a few minutes.
3 Add the peanuts and the trimmed, sliced green beans (if using frozen, cook them first, then drain off any excess liquid). Stir in the remaining ingredients.
4 Simmer the mixture gently for 15 minutes, or until the vegetables are cooked and the sauce begins to thicken. Adjust flavouring if necessary. Stir occasionally and add a drop more coconut milk if the mixture is too dry.

Serve with: Brown rice and a tomato, cucumber and watercress salad.

*You can use any curry paste for this recipe — adjust the amount according to the strength. Matsaman curry paste is traditionally used in Thai cooking, and should be available from any shop or supermarket stocking oriental foods.

Saturday
Tortellini

¾ lb (340g) basic pasta
  dough (see page 152)
10 oz (285g) Ricotta cheese
3 oz (85g) grated
  Parmesan cheese
1 egg, lightly beaten
Seasoning to taste
1 tablespoon fresh parsley
Pinch of nutmeg
Tomato sauce to serve (see
  page 153)
Parsley to garnish

1 Roll out the prepared dough and cut into circles approximately 2-inches (5cm) across.
2 Mash together the two cheeses, beaten egg, seasoning, parsley and nutmeg.
3 Drop a small amount of the mixture onto each of the pasta circles, and fold to make a semi-circle, pressing the edges together firmly, then bring the points together to make a ring. Arrange on a tea towel and leave for at least an hour.
4 Bring a large pan of water to the boil and drop in the tortellini. Cook for about 5 minutes, or until they rise to the top. Remove with a perforated spoon, drain well, tip into a serving dish and top with the tomato sauce. Garnish with parsley.

Serve with: A raw fennel and apple salad with maybe a few coarsely chopped, cooked chick-peas sprinkled over the top.

Sunday
Harvest Pie

¾ lb (340g) shortcrust
  pastry (see page 151)

For the filling:
2 potatoes
¾ lb (340g) spinach
3 tomatoes, sliced
1 tablespoon vegetable oil
1 large onion, sliced
3 hard-boiled eggs, sliced
Seasoning to taste

1 Make up the pastry in the usual way. Divide into two pieces and use one of them to line a small, greased flan dish.
2 Steam the potatoes until just cooked (or use left-overs). Cut into slices.
3 Steam the washed spinach, drain well and chop coarsely.
4 Arrange the potato in the flan case, cover with the spinach and then the sliced tomatoes.
5 Heat the oil in a pan and fry the onion until soft. Spread over the tomatoes and top with the sliced eggs. Add seasoning. (If liked, you can season between the layers.)
6 Roll out the remaining pastry and spread over the flan dish. Seal the dampened edges, and decorate with any left-over dough. Prick lightly with a fork.
7 Bake at 400°F/200°C (Gas Mark 6) for about 30 minutes, or until the pastry is cooked.

Serve with: A large green salad, adding some cooked beans or nuts for protein.

Week 4:
Monday
French-Style Vegetable Soup

2 tablespoons olive oil
1-2 cloves garlic, crushed
1 large onion, sliced
1½ pints (850ml) water
1 potato, diced
1 stick celery, sliced
1 carrot, sliced
1 leek, sliced
1 courgette, sliced
½ lb (225g) cooked haricot
  beans
½ tablespoon basil
Seasoning to taste
2 tomatoes, skinned and
  chopped
½ lb (225g) green beans
2 oz (55g) small
  wholemeal pasta shapes
2 oz (55g) grated Cheddar
  cheese

1 Heat the oil in a heavy-based saucepan, then add the garlic and onion. Cook briefly.
2 Pour in the water and bring to a boil. Add the potatoes, celery, carrots, leeks and courgettes, followed by the haricot beans, basil and seasoning, and cook covered for about 20 minutes, or until the vegetables begin to soften.
3 Add the tomatoes and prepared green beans with the pasta. Cook 10 minutes more or until all the ingredients are tender.
4 Divide between 4 bowls and top each one with a spoonful of cheese.

Serve with: This filling soup is virtually a meal in itself, although some fresh bran muffins would make a good accompaniment.

Tuesday
Acapulco Pizza

½ lb (225g) pizza dough
  of your choice

For the topping:
¼ pint (140ml) thick
  tomato sauce (see page
  153)
6 oz (170g) refried beans
  (see page 148)
1 onion, sliced into rings
1 teaspoon chilli pepper
  (or to taste), finely
  chopped
2 tablespoons cooked
  sweetcorn
4 oz (115g) grated Cheddar
  cheese

1 Make up the dough according to instructions. Divide into four portions and roll out to make four small circles.
2 Top each one with some of the tomato sauce, then the bean mixture.
3 Arrange onion rings on top of the beans with the chilli pepper and sweetcorn. Finish with grated cheese.
4 Bake at 400°F/200°C (Gas Mark 6) for 20-30 minutes or until cooked.

Serve with: A green salad of crisp lettuce, cucumber, radishes and slices of avocado. Nuts could be sprinkled on top.

Note: Fresh chilli peppers vary considerably in strength, though most of them are fiery, so go carefully until you are used to them. If unavailable, use chilli powder instead.

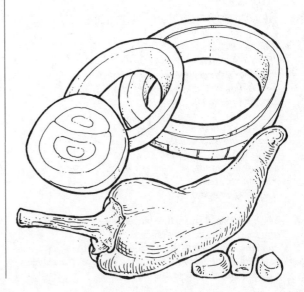

Wednesday
West Indian Beans

*½ lb (225g) kidney beans,
  soaked overnight
1 onion, sliced
1-2 cloves garlic, crushed
1 large green pepper,
  chopped
1 large carrot, chopped
4 tomatoes, chopped
1 teaspoon marjoram
4 oz (115g) creamed
  coconut
2 oz (55g) peanuts
Seasoning to taste
Parsley to garnish*

1 Put the beans into a saucepan, cover with fresh water, and fast boil for 10 minutes.
2 Add the onion, garlic, pepper, carrot and tomatoes, and the marjoram.
3 Cover and cook until the beans are just tender, which can take anything from 45 minutes to 1½ hours. Keep checking, as the beans will break up if overcooked. You may also need to add a drop more water.
4 Grate the coconut and stir into the other ingredients. Add the nuts. Season to taste. Heat through, transfer to a serving dish, and garnish generously with fresh parsley.

Serve with: Hot brown rice and a mixed green salad.

Thursday
Soya Spinach Crumble

For the base:
*1½ lb (680g) spinach
1 tablespoon vegetable oil
6 oz (170g) tofu
1 oz (30g) sesame seeds*

For the crumble:
*2 oz (55g) wholemeal flour
1-2 oz (30-55g) soya grits
1 teaspoon marjoram
Seasoning to taste
2 oz (55g) margarine*

1 Wash, shred and steam the spinach until tender, then drain and chop it as fine as possible.
2 Heat the oil and stir in the mashed tofu with the seeds. Cook briefly. Add the spinach. Spoon the mixture into a shallow casserole dish.

3 Combine the flour, soya grits, marjoram and seasoning in a bowl, and use fingertips to rub the margarine in to make a crumble. Spread this over the spinach mixture.
4 Bake at 400°F/200°C (Gas Mark 6) for 20 minutes, or until crumble is cooked.

Serve with: A dish of sliced potatoes and onions, plus a red cabbage and sultana salad.

Friday
Risotto Filled Ravioli

*½ lb (225g) wholemeal
  pasta dough (see page
  152)*

For the filling:
*2 tablespoons vegetable oil
½ small onion, finely
  chopped
¼-½ teaspoon curry
  powder
3 oz (85g) brown rice
Approx. ½ pint (285ml)
  vegetable stock
1 oz (30g) pine nuts
Seasoning to taste
Tomato sauce to serve (see
  page 153)
2 oz (55g) grated
  Parmesan cheese to
  serve*

1 Divide the dough into two and roll into oblongs, making the dough as thin as possible. Mark one half into squares about 2-inches (5cm) across.
2 Heat half the oil in a pan and fry the onion to soften. Add the curry powder and cook a minute more, then stir in the rice. Pour in the stock, bring to the boil and simmer until rice is tender. Drain off any excess liquid.
3 Heat the remaining oil in a clean pan and cook the pine nuts briefly until golden. Drain them and add to the rice with seasoning.
4 Drop a small amount of the rice mixture into the centre of each of the marked squares. Brush the lines lightly with water. Lay the second sheet of dough on top and press down to remove air pockets.
5 Cut along the lines with a serrated-edged pastry cutter and press to seal. Leave on a floured surface, covered with a damp cloth, for 30 minutes.
6 Drop the ravioli, a few at a time, into a large pan of boiling salted water. Cook, stirring occasionally, for 5-8 minutes, or until tender. Remove with a perforated spoon and keep warm whilst cooking the rest. Top with tomato sauce, and serve with Parmesan cheese.

Serve with: Brussels sprouts, steamed then fried together with peanuts, and served hot.

Note: Left-over risotto can be used instead of rice, in which case no cooking will be required.

Saturday
Egg Curry

6 eggs

*For the sauce:
2 tablespoons vegetable oil
1 small onion, finely
*   chopped*
½ clove garlic, crushed
1 small apple, chopped
1-2 tablespoons curry
*   powder*
½ oz (15g) wholemeal
*   flour*
½ pint (285ml) vegetable
*   stock*
Squeeze of lemon juice
1 oz (30g) desiccated
*   coconut*
1-2 tablespoons mango
*   chutney, chopped*
Cucumber slices to garnish

1 Hard-boil the eggs and set aside.
2 Heat the oil in a pan and fry the onion with the garlic for a few minutes. Add the apple and cook a minute more, then sprinkle in the curry powder and flour. Cook briefly.
3 Pour in the vegetable stock, stir well, and simmer to make a thick sauce.
4 Add the lemon juice, coconut and chopped mango chutney. Carefully stir in the halved eggs and cook over a low heat just long enough to heat through.
5 Garnish with thinly sliced cucumber.

Serve with: Tomato, onion and parsley salad. Serve on a base of hot millet.

Sunday
Cheese and Pumpkin Turnovers

½ lb (225g) shortcrust
*   pastry (see page 151)*

For the filling:
¾ lb (340g) pumpkin
6 oz (170g) grated
*   Lancashire cheese*
2 small eggs
Seasoning to taste
1 teaspoon mixed spice, or
*   to taste*
Milk to glaze
Parsley to garnish

1 Make up the pastry and roll out. Cut into 4 squares about 4-inches (10cm) in diameter.
2 Peel, cube and steam the pumpkin until tender. Drain very well, then tip into a bowl and mash. Mix with the cheese, eggs, seasoning and spice.
3 When the filling has cooled slightly, spoon a little onto each of the pastry squares. Fold over to form a triangle, dampen the edges, and press down firmly. Brush lightly with milk.
4 Transfer carefully to a baking sheet and cook in the oven at 400°F/200°C (Gas Mark 6) for 20-30 minutes, or until pastry is cooked. Garnish with parsley.

Serve with: Creamy mashed potatoes and a salad of lettuce, carrots, raw parsnip and a handful of raisins.

*Make a day in advance and leave overnight for the flavour to develop. Reheat gently.

Week 5:
Monday
Aduki Cabbage Casserole

1 medium white cabbage
1 tablespoon vegetable oil
1 onion, sliced
1 oz (30g) wholemeal flour
¼ pint (140ml) vegetable
   stock
½ pint (285ml) cider
1 large cooking apple,
   peeled and chopped
Seasoning to taste
6 oz (170g) cooked aduki
   beans

1 Trim and coarsely slice the cabbage, removing the hard stalk. Blanch in boiling water for 5 minutes, then drain well and arrange in an ovenproof dish.
2 Heat the oil in a clean pan and fry the onion until it begins to soften. Sprinkle in the flour and cook a minute more, then remove from the heat and pour in the stock and cider. Stir well.
3 Continue simmering until the sauce thickens. Add the apple, and seasoning to taste.
4 Drain the aduki beans and spoon them over the cabbage, then top with the sauce. Cover the casserole and bake at 350°F/180°C (Gas Mark 4) for about an hour, or until cooked.

Serve with: Brown rice, plus a green pepper and watercress salad with a few chopped apricots and almonds.

Tuesday
Pasta Shells with Beetroot

6 oz (170g) wholemeal
   pasta shells
1 oz (30g) margarine or
   butter
1 lb (455g) cooked
   beetroot, diced
½ pint (285ml) white
   sauce (see page 00)
3 tablespoons soured
   cream
Seasoning to taste
2 oz (55g) grated Cheddar
   cheese
1 oz (30g) wholemeal
   breadcrumbs

1 Cook the pasta shells in boiling water for 10 minutes, or till just tender.
2 Melt the fat in a clean pan and gently fry the beetroot for just a few minutes. Drain well.
3 Heat the sauce; remove from heat and stir in the soured cream

and then the beetroot. Season to taste.
4 Add the drained pasta and turn the mixture into a lightly greased ovenproof dish.
5 Top with the grated cheese and breadcrumbs, and bake at 400°F/200°C (Gas Mark 6) for 15 minutes, or until crisp and brown.

Serve with: A crisp green salad sprinkled with chopped walnuts.

Wednesday
Sweetcorn and 'Bacon' Risotto

¾ lb (340g) brown rice
2 tablespoons vegetable oil
1 large onion, sliced
1½ pints (850ml) vegetable
   stock or water
6 oz (170g) cooked
   sweetcorn kernels
4 oz (115g) grated Cheddar
   cheese
1 oz (30g) soya 'bacon' bits
Seasoning to taste
Watercress to garnish

1 Rinse the rice through with water, then drain well.
2 Heat the oil in a pan, and lightly fry the onion until it begins to soften. Stir in the rice with the liquid. Bring to the boil, then simmer covered for 30-40 minutes, or until the rice is cooked. (Add more liquid if necessary.)
3 Stir in the sweetcorn, grated cheese, soya 'bacon' bits and seasoning. Heat a minute more only.
4 Garnish generously with watercress.

Serve with: A raw spinach and tomato salad.

Thursday
Herb Pancakes

½ pint (285ml) pancake
   batter (see page 152)
1-2 tablespoons mixed
   fresh herbs
Seasoning to taste
Vegetable oil for frying
6-8 oz (170-225g) low-fat
   cream, curd or Ricotta
   cheese

1 Make up the batter, add the finely chopped herbs and seasoning. Cover and set aside in a cool place for a minimum of half an hour.
2 Heat a little of the oil in a heavy-based frying pan. Whisk

the batter, and pour in just enough to cover. Cook gently until lightly browned underneath, tipping the pan occasionally to make sure the pancake doesn't stick.

3 Flip or use a spatula to turn the pancake. Cook briefly, then keep warm while using the rest of the batter in the same way.

4 Roll up the pancakes and top each one with a spoonful or two of the cheese, spreading it gently so that the heat of the pancake causes the cheese to become creamy.

Serve with: A salad of lettuce, celery and beetroot generously sprinkled with chopped roasted hazelnuts. Add wholemeal baps if liked.

Friday
Quick Beany Vegetable Bake

*1 lb (455g) mixed frozen
  vegetables
6 oz (170g) cooked beans
  (haricot are ideal)
2 oz (55g) peanuts
¼ pint (140ml) vegetable
  stock
2 tablespoons peanut
  butter
Seasoning to taste
½ oz (15g) margarine or
  butter
2 oz (55g) wheatgerm*

1 Cook the vegetables according to instructions. Drain well. Combine with the cooked beans and peanuts.

2 Put the vegetable mixture into an ovenproof dish. Mix the vegetable stock with the peanut butter and seasoning, and pour over the vegetables.

3 Melt the fat and mix it with the wheatgerm. Sprinkle over the vegetables.

4 Bake at 350°F/180°C (Gas Mark 4) for 20 minutes, or until heated through.

Serve with: A hot grain such as kasha, and a tomato and watercress salad.

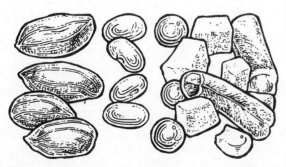

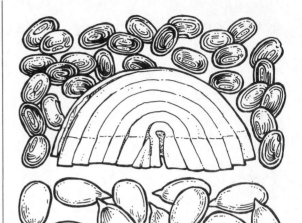

Saturday
Pumpkin Flan

*8 oz (225g) pastry of your
  choice*

*For the filling:
1 lb (455g) pumpkin
1 tablespoon vegetable oil
1 onion, sliced
8 oz (225g) spinach
3 oz (85g) cooked aduki
  beans
Seasoning to taste
Good pinch of nutmeg
1 large egg, beaten
  (optional)
1 oz (30g) pumpkin seeds*

1 Make up pastry mix and set aside in a cool place.

2 Peel and cube the pumpkin; steam until soft.

3 Heat the oil in a pan and sauté the sliced onion so that it begins to colour. Mash the pumpkin and add to the onion, mixing well.

4 Steam the spinach, drain well, and chop coarsely. Stir into the pumpkin mixture. Add the beans, seasoning, nutmeg and beaten egg, if using. (The filling won't set as firm without egg, but will taste just as good.)

5 Roll out the pastry and line a medium-sized flan dish. Bake blind at 400°F/200°C (Gas Mark 6) for 10 minutes.

6 Spoon the pumpkin mixture into the flan case and smooth the top before sprinkling with pumpkin seeds. Lower the oven temperature to 375°F/190°C (Gas Mark 5) and cook for 30 minutes more, or until set.

Serve with: A salad of beansprouts, pepper, onion, cucumber, plus wholemeal baps.

Sunday
Blue Cheese and Celery Soufflé

4 large sticks celery
1 oz (30g) margarine or
*   butter*
1 oz (30g) wholemeal flour
⅓ pint (200ml) milk
3 oz (85g) Gorgonzola or
*   other blue cheese,*
*   crumbled*
4 eggs, separated
Seasoning to taste
1 oz (30g) walnuts,
*   chopped*

1 Chop the celery as thin as possible and cook in boiling salted water until soft, then drain and press through a sieve or liquidize to make a purée.
2 Melt the fat in a pan and add the flour; cook briefly. Remove from the heat and stir in the milk, then return to heat and cook, stirring, to thicken.
3 Add the crumbled cheese and the celery purée, the egg yolks and seasoning.
4 Whisk the egg whites until stiff, and use a metal spoon to fold them carefully into the other ingredients.
5 Pour the mixture into a greased, 2-pint soufflé dish. Top with the coarsely chopped nuts. Bake at once in an oven pre-heated to 375°F/190°C (Gas Mark 5) for 30 minutes, or until risen.

Serve with: A potato salad with Chinese leaves, celery and watercress.

Week 6:
Monday
Oriental Rice

½ lb (225g) brown rice
1 pint (570ml) water
2-3 tablespoons vegetable
*   oil*
1 onion, sliced
½ small cauliflower
1 stick celery, sliced
1 carrot, sliced
2 oz (55g) beansprouts
½ bunch watercress
Soya sauce
Seasoning to taste
2 oz (55g) sesame seeds,
*   roasted*
2 hard-boiled eggs,
*   chopped*

1 Rinse the rice, then cook in the water for 30-40 minutes or until just tender, adding more water during cooking if necessary. Drain well.
2 Meanwhile, heat the oil in a pan and sauté the onion for 5 minutes.
3 Stir in the cauliflower florets, sliced celery and carrot. Cook gently for 5-10 minutes more.
4 Add the beansprouts and watercress and continue cooking for literally a minute.
5 Combine the hot rice and vegetables. Flavour to taste with soya sauce and seasoning. Stir in the seeds.
6 Transfer to a serving dish and top with the chopped eggs.

Serve with: A salad of lightly cooked marrow cubes in a creamy dressing, garnished with mint, served on a lettuce base.

Tuesday
Miso Soup with Tofu

2 tablespoons vegetable oil
1 large onion, sliced
2 carrots, sliced
½ small cauliflower
2 strips dried wakame*,
*   soaked briefly*
2 pints (1 litre) vegetable
*   stock*
1-2 tablespoons miso
½ lb (225g) tofu, well
*   drained*
2 oz (55g) beansprouts

1 Heat the oil in a saucepan and fry the onion for 5 minutes. Add the carrot and cauliflower florets, and stir well. Cook for 5 minutes more.
2 Drain and slice the wakame and add to the pan with the vegetable stock. Bring to the boil, then simmer for 10 minutes, or until the vegetables are tender.
3 Cream the miso with a little of the broth and add to the other ingredients. Stir in the diced tofu and the beansprouts.
4 Heat for literally a few minutes more.

Serve with: A cucumber and raw mushroom salad, and maybe a cold rice bowl sprinkled with sunflower seeds.

*This is a variety of seaweed which can be bought in health-food, wholefood and speciality shops. If unavailable, try any other variety, or just omit it.

Wednesday
Butter Bean Casserole

½ lb (225g) butter beans,
  soaked overnight
4 medium leeks, sliced
4 tomatoes, quartered
⅓ pint (200ml) vegetable
  stock
1 teaspoon thyme
Seasoning to taste
4 oz (115g) Cheddar
  cheese, grated
2 oz (55g) wholemeal
  breadcrumbs

1 Drain the butter beans, put in a pan and cover with fresh water. Boil for 30 minutes, then lower the heat and simmer for 30-40 minutes, or until just tender. Be careful not to overcook them.
2 Steam the leeks until just tender.
3 Mix the tomatoes with the drained beans and leeks. Transfer to an ovenproof dish. Add the stock, thyme and seasoning.
4 Bake uncovered at 350°F/180°C (Gas Mark 4) for 10 minutes.
5 Mix the cheese and breadcrumbs and sprinkle over the top. Bake 10 minutes more, or until all the ingredients are heated through and the top is golden.

Serve with: A beetroot and apple salad on a lettuce base — add a handful of chopped brazil nuts, if liked. Fresh wholemeal bread could also be served.

Thursday
'Chicken' Chow Mein

3 tablespoons vegetable oil
1 clove garlic, crushed
4 oz (115g) green beans,
  sliced
2 sticks celery, chopped
2 oz (55g) mushrooms,
  chopped
1 red pepper, chopped
¼ small white cabbage,
  chopped
Small tin bamboo shoots,
  drained and diced
½ pint (285ml) vegetable
  stock
3 oz (85g) soya 'chicken'
  pieces, hydrated in water
⅛ pint (70ml) water
1 oz (30g) wholemeal flour
2 tablespoons soya sauce
1 oz (30g) almonds,
  coarsely chopped

1 Heat the oil in a pan and add the garlic. Cook for 5 minutes.
2 Add the prepared vegetables to the pan with the bamboo shoots.
3 Stir in the stock, cover the pan, and simmer for 5 minutes. Add the shredded 'chicken' pieces and continue cooking for 5-10 minutes, or until all the ingredients are tender.
4 Mix the water with the flour and soya sauce, add to the pan, and cook to thicken.
5 Sprinkle the nuts over the mixture.

Serve with: Wholemeal noodles and a tomato, onion, and parsley salad.

Friday
Potato Gnocchi with Gorgonzola Sauce

1 lb (455g) potatoes
6 oz (170g) wholemeal
  flour
1 large egg
½ oz (15g) margarine or
  butter
Seasoning to taste
Pinch of nutmeg

For the sauce:
3 oz (85g) Gorgonzola
  cheese
⅓-½ pint (200-285ml) milk
1 oz (30g) walnuts,
  chopped

1 Peel and cube the potatoes, them steam until tender. Drain well and mash to make a thick purée.
2 Add all the other ingredients and mix thoroughly to make a fairly firm dough. Knead until smooth. With floured hands divide the dough into rolls the shape of a finger, cut into 1-inch (2.5cm) pieces, and twist to make a crescent. If time allows, set aside in the cool for 15 minutes,
3 Bring a pan of salted water to a gentle boil and add the gnocchi, a few at a time. Cook for 5-10 minutes, or until they rise to the surface. Remove with a perforated spoon, drain, and keep warm whilst cooking the rest.
4 To make the sauce, mash the Gorgonzola together with the milk (warming it if necessary). Adjust the consistency to make it easy to pour. Serve over gnocchi, sprinkled with chopped walnuts.

Serve with: Something light and crisp to contrast the richness of this dish. A salad of raw mushrooms, celery and watercress would go well.

Saturday
Hazelnut Tomato Loaf

½ lb (225g) roasted
  hazelnuts
1 tablespoon vegetable oil
1 onion, finely chopped
½ lb (225g) tomatoes,
  peeled and chopped
2 eggs, separated
Seasoning to taste
1 tablespoon chopped
  parsley
Parsley sprigs to garnish

1 Coarsely grind most of the nuts, reserving just a few.
2 Heat the vegetable oil and fry the onion until it begins to colour.
3 Mix together the nuts, tomatoes and fried onion. Add the egg yolks, seasoning and parsley.
4 Beat the egg whites until stiff but not too dry. Fold carefully into the other ingredients. Spoon into a small, greased loaf tin. Sprinkle with reserved nuts.
5 Bake at 400°F/200°C (Gas Mark 6) for 30 minutes, or until golden and risen. Garnish each serving with parsley sprigs.

Serve with: Spinach salad sprinkled with chopped spring onions. You could also serve steamed potatoes.

Sunday
Leek Quiche in Brown Rice Case

6 oz (170g) cooked brown
  rice

For the filling:
8 oz (225g) leeks
2 large eggs
¼ pint (140ml) milk
¼ pint (140ml) natural
  yogurt
Seasoning to taste
Pinch of nutmeg
Soya 'bacon' bits

1 Grease a medium-sized flan dish. Drain the rice well, then spoon into the flan dish, using the back of a spoon to press the rice firmly and evenly against the base and sides.
2 Bake at 350°F/180°C (Gas Mark 4) for 5-10 minutes or until crisp. Set aside.
3 Trim, chop and steam the leeks until just tender. Drain well and spread across base of the flan.
4 Beat together the eggs, milk, yogurt, seasoning and nutmeg.
5 Sprinkle the soya 'bacon' bits over the leeks, then carefully pour in the mixture. Bake at 375°F/190°C (Gas Mark 5) for 30-40 minutes, or until set.

Serve with: A cucumber and yogurt salad.

Week 7:
Monday
Salsify Cheese Crumble

For the base:
1 lb (455g) salsify
½ pint (285ml) vegetable
  stock
1 oz (30g) margarine
1 oz (30g) wholemeal flour
4 oz (115g) Lancashire
  cheese, grated
Pinch dry mustard
Seasoning to taste

For the crumble:
3 oz (85g) wholemeal flour
1 oz (30g) bran
2 oz (55g) margarine
Pinch thyme

1 Scrub the salsify and cut into small, even-sized pieces.
2 Pour on the stock, bring to boil, then simmer covered for about 20 minutes or until tender. Drain, but reserve the liquid.
3 In a clean saucepan melt the margarine, then stir in the flour and cook for a few minutes. Add the reserved stock, stir well, and continue cooking until the sauce thickens.
4 Add the grated cheese, mustard and seasoning. Mix the salsify into the sauce. If it seems too thick, add a drop of water. Spoon the mixture into an ovenproof dish.
5 Sift together the flour and bran, rub in the margarine, and flavour with thyme. Sprinkle the crumb-like mixture over the salsify.
6 Bake at 375°F/190°C (Gas Mark 5) for about 20 minutes, or until top is cooked.

Serve with: Jacket potatoes, with a raw spinach, celery, pepper and peanut salad.

Tuesday
Creamy Cabbage Turnovers

*½ lb (225g) shortcrust
pastry (see page 151)
2 oz (55g) sesame seeds*

For the filling:
*½ medium-sized white
cabbage, finely shredded
2 tablespoons vegetable oil
1 onion, chopped
½-1 clove garlic, crushed
Seasoning to taste
Approx. 3 tablespoons
tahini
2 oz (55g) sunflower seeds*

1 Make up the pastry in the usual way, adding the seeds and making sure they are evenly distributed. Chill briefly.
2 Roll out and cut into 4 squares about 4-inches (10cm) in diameter.
3 Steam the cabbage for 5 minutes, then drain well.
4 Heat the oil in a pan and fry the onion and garlic until they begin to soften. Stir in the cabbage and cook a few minutes more, or until all the vegetables are tender.
5 Remove pan from the heat and add seasoning plus enough tahini to coat the vegetables. Sprinkle in the seeds.
6 Put a spoonful or two onto each of the pastry squares. Fold across to make a triangle. Dampen the edges and press firmly to seal.
7 Transfer the turnovers to a baking sheet and cook at 400°F/200°C (Gas Mark 6) for 20-30 minutes, or until pastry is cooked.

Serve with: Hot Kasha, plus a red cabbage, beetroot and apple salad on a lettuce base.

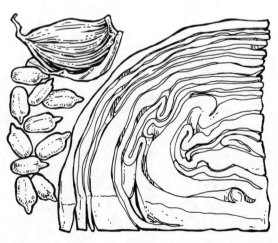

Wednesday
Hawaiian Rice with Pineapple

*6 oz (170g) brown rice
1 pint (570ml) water
3 tablespoons vegetable oil
1 small onion, finely
chopped
1 clove garlic, crushed
Small piece fresh ginger,
finely chopped
¼ small white cabbage,
finely shredded
½ green pepper, chopped
Seasoning to taste
1 tablespoon soya sauce
Small tin pineapple chunks
in natural juice
2 teaspoons arrowroot
2 oz (55g) flaked almonds,
lightly roasted*

1 Cook the rinsed rice in the water until just tender. This will take approximately 30-40 minutes, and you may need to add a drop more water during the cooking process. Drain well.
2 Meanwhile, heat half the oil in another pan and fry the onion and garlic for a few minutes.
3 Add the ginger and cook a minute more, then add the cabbage and pepper. Cook over a medium heat for 3-5 minutes, stirring continually, and adding seasoning and soya sauce half-way through. Turn out onto a dish and keep warm.
4 Pour the remaining oil into the pan and add the rice and drained pineapple chunks (reserving the juice). Season and mix well. Cook for a few minutes to heat through, then add the vegetables and stir.
5 Mix together the pineapple juice and the arrowroot. Add to the pan, and mix thoroughly. Lower the heat and cook until a sauce forms.
6 Turn the rice mixture out onto a serving dish and sprinkle with the nuts.

Serve with: A tomato, endive and chicory salad.

Thursday
Mixed Bean and Leek Stew

3 oz (85g) borlotti beans,
  soaked overnight
3 oz (85g) chick-peas,
  soaked overnight
3 oz (85g) haricot beans,
  soaked overnight
4 tablespoons vegetable oil
1 clove garlic, crushed
1 onion, sliced
1 leek, chopped
1½ pints (850ml) vegetable
  stock
½ small cabbage,
  shredded
Small tin (½ lb/225g)
  tomatoes
Seasoning to taste
1 teaspoon basil, or to
  taste
½ oz (15g) wholemeal
  flour
Natural yogurt to serve
Parsley to garnish

1 Drain the beans, put in a pan and cover with fresh water. Cook for an hour, or until tender.
2 Heat the oil in a large saucepan and fry the garlic and onion for 5 minutes, stirring frequently.
3 Add the leek and cook a minute more, then pour in the stock and bring to the boil. Add the cabbage and simmer for 5 minutes.
4 Add the drained beans, tomatoes, seasoning and basil. Continue simmering until all the ingredients are cooked.
5 Mix a little of the cooking liquid with the flour, then stir it into the pan. Cook for a few minutes more to thicken the sauce. Adjust the seasoning.
6 Stir in yogurt, or hand round at the table for those who want to help themselves. Garnish with parsley.

Serve with: Jacket potatoes, plus a watercress salad.

Friday
Buckwheat Noodles with Cauliflower

9 oz (255g) buckwheat
  flour
3 oz (85g) wholemeal flour
Pinch of salt
2 small eggs, beaten
⅛ pint (70ml) milk
Warm water to mix

For the topping:
½ small cauliflower
2 tablespoons vegetable oil
1 oz (30g) wholemeal flour
½ pint (285ml) vegetable
  stock or water
Seasoning to taste
2-3 tablespoons tahini
Chopped red pepper to
  garnish

1 Combine the two flours and the salt. Mix in the beaten eggs and milk, then add enough water to make a firm but pliable dough. Knead until smooth.
2 Divide into two pieces, and roll them out as thinly as possible. Set aside for an hour.
3 Roll up each piece to make a sausage shape and use a sharp knife to cut carefully into thin strips. Unroll noodles and set aside until needed.
4 Trim the cauliflower and break into florets. Steam briefly
5 Heat the oil in a clean pan and sprinkle in the flour. Cook until it begins to colour, then add the stock. Continue simmering, stirring frequently, to make a thick sauce.
6 Add seasoning and tahini to sauce, then mix in the cauliflower florets. Heat gently.
7 Drop the noodles into a pan of boiling water and cook for 5 minutes, then drain well. Serve topped with the cauliflower sauce and sprinkled with finely chopped red pepper.

Serve with: A salad of Chinese leaves, mushrooms, and dried apricot pieces.

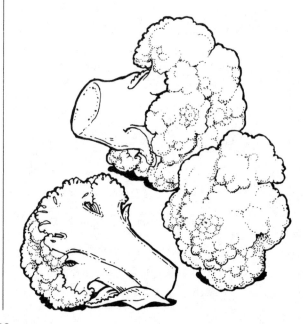

Saturday
Stuffed Cucumber with Soured Cream Sauce

2 large cucumbers
2 tablespoons vegetable oil
½ small onion, sliced
½ clove garlic, crushed
2 oz (55g) wholemeal breadcrumbs
Good squeeze lemon juice
1 tablespoon parsley
Seasoning to taste
2 oz (55g) pine nuts or walnuts
1 oz (30g) margarine or butter

For the sauce:

2 oz (55g) margarine or butter
6 oz (170g) mushrooms, chopped
1 oz (30g) wholemeal flour
½ pint (285ml) vegetable stock
¼ pint (140ml) soured cream
Seasoning to taste
Parsley sprigs to garnish

1 Trim the cleaned cucumbers, cut into halves or thirds, then cut lengthways and scoop out the seeds. Arrange close together in a greased ovenproof dish.
2 Heat the vegetable oil in a pan and lightly fry the onion with the garlic, until they begin to soften.
3 Stir in the crumbs, lemon juice, parsley, seasoning and nuts. Spoon some of the mixture into each of the cucumber shells, piling it up if necessary.
4 Dot the stuffing with fat and bake at 350°F/180°C (Gas Mark 4) for 20 minutes.
5 Meanwhile, heat the fat for the sauce in a clean pan and lightly fry the mushrooms.
6 Sprinkle in the flour and cook a minute or two more before pouring in the stock.
7 Stir well, then cook the mixture gently until a thick sauce forms.
8 Off the heat, stir in the soured cream and seasoning, then return to cooker and simmer gently just long enough to heat through.
9 Pour the sauce over the stuffed cucumber and garnish with parsley.

Serve with: Steamed potatoes and a raw spinach, carrot and peanut salad.

Note: This could also be made with courgettes — trim, cut lengthways and proceed as above.

Sunday
Omelette Pie

6 eggs
2 tablespoons vegetable oil
1 small onion, sliced
6 stuffed olives, sliced
2 oz (55g) grated Cheddar cheese
1 small courgette, sliced
Seasoning to taste
1-2 oz (30-55g) butter or margarine
½ pint (285ml) tomato sauce (see page 153)
Parsley to garnish

1 Beat together two eggs at a time, using three bowls.
2 Heat half the oil in a pan and sauté the onion until it begins to colour. Drain well and add to the eggs in one of the bowls with the sliced olives.
3 Add the cheese to the eggs in the second bowl.
4 Heat the remaining oil and fry the courgette. Drain well and stir into the egg mixture in the third bowl. Season all the ingredients.
5 Melt a little of the fat in a frying pan and, when hot, pour in the first mixture. Cook until set. (If liked you can finish it off under the grill.)
6 Set the omelette aside in the warm, add more fat to the pan if necessary, and cook the contents of the second bowl in the same way.
7 Do the same with the third egg mixture.
8 Pile the omelettes up to make a stack and pour tomato sauce over the top. Garnish with parsley. Serve cut in wedges.

Serve with: Herbed rice and a fresh tomato salad.

Week 8:
Monday
Polenta with Mushrooms

1½ pints (850ml) water
Seasoning to taste
½ lb (225g) fine polenta
 (cornmeal)
1 tablespoon vegetable oil
1 onion, sliced
½ lb (225g) mushrooms,
 sliced
½ pint (285ml) white
 sauce (see page 153)
Pinch of nutmeg
2 oz (55g) grated
 Parmesan cheese
Cress to garnish

1 Bring the water to a boil, add seasoning, and sprinkle in the polenta. Stir, then cook gently for about 20 minutes, stirring occasionally. When the mixture is thick, turn it out on a wetted plate or tin and smooth the top. Set aside to cool.
2 Heat the vegetable oil and lightly sauté the onion until it begins to soften, then add the mushrooms and cook a few minutes more.
3 Stir the vegetables into the white sauce, and add the nutmeg.
4 Cut the polenta into small circles and arrange half of it in a shallow, greased ovenproof dish. Top with half the sauce, and a little of the cheese. Repeat to use up the rest of the ingredients, finishing with cheese.
5 Bake at 375°F/190°C (Gas Mark 5) for 15 minutes, or until heated through and golden on top. Garnish with cress.

Serve with: A salad of fennel, lettuce, apple, radishes and chopped, roasted hazelnuts.

Tuesday
Baked Bean and 'Bacon' Loaf

1 lb (455g) tin baked beans
3 oz (85g) wholemeal
 breadcrumbs
½ onion, finely chopped
½ green pepper, finely
 chopped
1 oz (30g) soya 'bacon' bits
1 large egg, lightly beaten
1 oz (30g) margarine or
 butter
Seasoning to taste

1 Mash the beans and mix with the breadcrumbs.
2 Stir in the onion and pepper.

3 Add the 'bacon' bits, beaten egg and the fat. Season well.
4 Turn into a small, greased loaf tin, and smooth the top. Bake at 350°F/180°C (Gas Mark 4) for 40-50 minutes, or until set.

Serve with: French-fried potatoes, plus grilled tomatoes and mushrooms.

Wednesday
Quiche Paysanne

6 oz (170g) pastry of your
 choice

For the filling:
1 oz (30g) margarine or
 butter
1 onion, sliced
½ clove garlic, crushed
4 oz (115g) mushrooms,
 sliced
1 large cooked potato,
 diced
2 tomatoes, chopped
3 tablespoons cooked peas
2 large eggs
¼ pint (140ml) creamy
 milk
Chopped parsley
Seasoning to taste
2 oz (55g) grated Cheddar
 cheese

1 Make up the pastry mix and set aside in a cool place.
2 Melt most of the margarine and fry the onion and garlic until soft.
3 Add the mushrooms and cook a few minutes more, stirring occasionally.
4 Add the rest of the fat and, when melted, mix in the potato. Cook for 5 minutes. Stir in the tomatoes and peas.
5 Roll out the pastry and use to line a medium-sized flan dish. Bake blind at 400°F/200°C (Gas Mark 6) for 10 minutes.
6 Spoon the vegetable mixture into the flan case. Beat together the eggs, milk, parsley and seasoning. Pour into flan case, and top with the grated cheese.
7 Bake at 375°F/190°C (Gas Mark 5) for 30 minutes, or until set.

Serve with: French bread and a tomato salad with a garlic dressing.

Thursday
Jambalaya

2 tablespoons vegetable oil
½ oz (15g) wholemeal
  flour
3 oz (85g) soya 'ham'
  chunks, hydrated in
  water
½ lb (225g) tomatoes,
  chopped
1 onion, chopped
1 green pepper, chopped
½ clove garlic, crushed
Seasoning to taste
Pinch of paprika
1 pint (570ml) water
½ lb (225g) brown rice
Holbrook's Worcestershire
  sauce
Parsley to garnish

1 Heat the oil in a large saucepan and stir in the flour, cooking
  briefly.
2 Drain and coarsely chop the 'ham', and add to the pan with
  the tomatoes, onion, pepper, garlic, seasoning, paprika and
  water. Stir well.
3 Bring to the boil, then simmer for 10 minutes.
4 Stir in the rice, cover the pan, and cook for 30-40 minutes,
  or until all the ingredients are tender. If necessary, add a drop
  more water.
5 Flavour with Worcestershire sauce and garnish generously
  with chopped parsley.

Serve with: A celery, cabbage and apple salad.

Friday
Tagliatelle with Vegetables and Cashew Nuts

¾ lb (340g) wholemeal
  tagliatelle
4 tablespoons vegetable oil
½-1 clove garlic, crushed
2 courgettes, finely
  chopped
4 oz (115g) mushrooms,
  finely chopped
2 oz (55g) cashew nuts
Seasoning to taste
Oregano
Grated Parmesan cheese to
  serve (optional)

1 Cook the tagliatelle in a large pan of boiling water for 10
  minutes, or until just tender.
2 Meanwhile, heat the oil and fry the garlic, courgettes and
  mushrooms over a gentle heat, stirring continually, for 3
  minutes.
3 Add the nuts, seasoning and oregano, stir, and cook a few
  minutes longer.
4 Toss the drained tagliatelle with the sauce, and serve at once.
  Hand the cheese around at table for those who want it.

Serve with: A grated carrot and chopped date salad on a crisp
lettuce base.

Saturday
Peanut and Parsnip Curry

*1 pint (570ml) curry
  sauce (see page 154)
2 parsnips, peeled and
  cubed
4 oz (115g) peanuts
4 tomatoes, skinned and
  chopped
2 oz (55g) freshly grated
  coconut
Onion rings
Parsley to garnish

1 Heat the curry sauce gently in a pan.
2 Add the parsnips, stir well, and cook gently for 10 minutes.
3 Add the nuts, the tomatoes, and the coconut. Continue
  cooking gently until the parsnip is tender.
4 Top with thinly sliced onion rings, and garnish with parsley.

Serve with: Brown rice. Add a lettuce, tomato and cucumber
salad sprinkled with radishes.

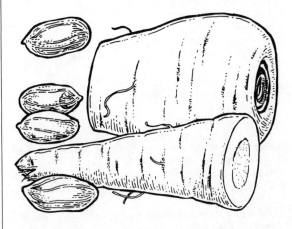

*Make a day in advance and leave overnight for the flavour
to develop. Reheat gently.

Sunday
Moussaka

3 tablespoons vegetable oil
2 aubergines, sliced
2 onions, sliced
5 oz (140g) soya 'minced
*   meat', hydrated in water*
2 tablespoons tomato
*   purée*
3 large tomatoes, sliced
2 eggs
6 tablespoons creamy milk
Seasoning to taste

1 Heat half of the oil in a large pan. Fry the aubergine slices, turning once, until they begin to soften. Drain and set aside.
2 Add the rest of the oil to the pan and fry the onion for 5 minutes.
3 Stir in the soya 'meat' with a little of its liquid, add the tomato purée, and cook for 10 minutes, or until tender.
4 Layer the aubergine and 'meat' mixture in a greased ovenproof dish. Slice the tomatoes and arrange over the top.
5 Whisk together the eggs, milk and seasoning, and pour over the other ingredients. Bake at 350°F/180°C (Gas Mark 4) for 20 minutes, or until set.

Serve with: New potatoes cooked with mint, and a chicory and pepper salad.

Week 9:
Monday
Green Bean and Egg Salad

1 lb (455g) green beans
3 tablespoons vegetable oil
2 oz (55g) margarine or
*   butter*
Seasoning to taste
Good pinch raw cane
*   sugar*
Good pinch of nutmeg
2 tablespoons vegetable oil
2 large eggs
Lemon slices to serve

1 Pick young, tender beans only. Trim the ends and, if at all stringy, the sides. Wipe to clean.
2 Heat the oil together with the fat in a pan, and add the beans. Cook covered for a few minutes only, until beans are cooked but still firm.
3 Tip into a serving dish and stir in seasoning, sugar and nutmeg. Chill well.
4 Meanwhile, heat the oil in a frying pan. Beat the eggs with a drop of water, season well, and add to pan. Cook until lightly

set, then transfer to a plate. Roll up and leave to cool.
5 Serve the bean salad topped with the omelette cut into thin slices, and garnished with lemon twists.

Serve with: A bowl of hot rice, or cold rice salad sprinkled with peanuts.

Tuesday
Macaroni Burgers

4 oz (115g) wholemeal
*   macaroni*
1 oz (30g) margarine or
*   butter*
1 onion, finely chopped
Good pinch of thyme
Seasoning to taste
1 oz (30g) wholemeal flour
2 eggs, beaten
Wholemeal breadcrumbs
*   to coat*
Vegetable oil for frying

1 Cook the macaroni in a pan of boiling water until just tender. Drain well.
2 Melt the fat and sauté the finely chopped onion until soft, then add the thyme and seasoning. Off the heat, stir in the flour, then the macaroni and half the beaten eggs. If the mixture seems too wet, add a little more flour. Set aside to cool slightly.
3 Divide the mixture into small portions and shape into burgers. Dip each one in the remaining beaten egg and then coat well with breadcrumbs.
4 Deep fry the burgers a few at a time in the vegetable oil. When crisp and brown, drain well on paper towels.
Serve with: A root vegetable salad with finely grated, raw Brussels sprouts and a few beansprouts added, maybe with a blue cheese or tofu garlic dressing.

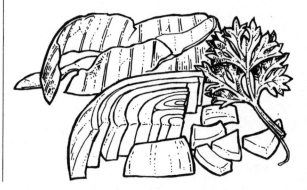

Wednesday
Tomato Sweetcorn Flan

*8 oz (225g) pastry of your
   choice*

For the filling:
*½ oz (15g) margarine or
   butter*
1 small onion, sliced
½-1 clove garlic, crushed
*6 oz (170g) cooked
   sweetcorn*
4 tomatoes, quartered
3 eggs, separated
*1 tablespoon fresh
   chopped parsley*
Seasoning to taste
*1 oz (30g) wholemeal
   breadcrumbs*
Parsley to garnish

1 Make up the pastry mix, cool briefly. Roll out and use to line a medium-sized flan dish. Bake blind at 400°F/200°C (Gas Mark 6) for 10 minutes.
2 Melt the fat and lightly fry the onion and garlic until the onion begins to soften. Drain.
3 Mix together with the sweetcorn, tomatoes, egg yolks, parsley and seasoning.
4 Whisk the egg whites until stiff and fold carefully into the other ingredients. Spoon into the flan case, and top with breadcrumbs. Bake at 375°F/190°C (Gas Mark 5) for 30-40 minutes, or until set. Garnish with fresh parsley.

Serve with: Wholemeal scones and a green salad.

Thursday
Leek and Pasta Omelette

*½ oz (15g) butter or
   margarine*
1 tablespoon vegetable oil
2 small leeks, sliced
*2 oz (55g) wholemeal
   noodles, cooked*
4 eggs, lightly beaten
*2 oz (55g) grated Edam
   cheese*
Seasoning to taste
*3 tablespoons soured
   cream*
*1 oz (30g) roasted
   hazelnuts, chopped*

1 Melt most of the fat together with most of the oil. Add the leeks to the pan and sauté gently, stirring frequently, until the leeks soften. Remove pan from the heat.

2 Combine the drained, coarsely chopped noodles with the beaten eggs, grated cheese and seasoning.
3 Add remaining fat and oil to the pan containing the leeks, and heat until the fat melts. Pour in the egg mixture.
4 Cover the pan and cook gently for 15 minutes, or until the omelette sets.
5 Serve cut into wedges, each one topped with some soured cream and a sprinkling of chopped nuts.

Serve with: A salad of lettuce, cucumber, celery and tomatoes. Granary bread could also be served.

Friday
Pumpkin Pizza

*½ lb (225g) pizza dough
   of your choice*

For the topping:
½ small pumpkin
2 tablespoons vegetable oil
1 onion, sliced
1 green pepper, sliced
2-3 tablespoons tahini
Seasoning to taste
*3 oz (85g) walnuts,
   coarsely chopped*

1 Make up the pizza dough according to instructions.
2 Peel and cube the pumpkin; steam gently until tender, then drain well.
3 Heat the oil in a pan and sauté the onion and pepper until soft. Add the pumpkin and lightly mash the ingredients together so that they are thoroughly blended.
4 Stir in enough tahini to give the vegetables a creamy texture; season to taste.
5 Divide the dough into two circles and bake at 400°F/200°C (Gas Mark 6) for 10 minutes.
6 Remove from the heat and spread with the pumpkin mixture. Sprinkle with the nuts. Return to the oven and continue cooking for 15 minutes, or until the dough is crisp. Cut in half to serve.

Serve with: A raw cauliflower and tomato salad.

Saturday
Cheese Charlotte

8 thin slices wholemeal
  bread
⅓ pint (200ml) milk
1½ oz (45g) butter
3 eggs, separated
½ oz (15g) wholemeal
  flour
Seasoning to taste
Pinch of ground nutmeg
½ lb (225g) Cheddar
  cheese
6 tablespoons single cream
1 oz (30g) roasted flaked
  almonds
Watercress to garnish

1 Trim crusts from the bread. Chop one slice into cubes and put them into a small dish. Cover with half of the milk. Spread out the remaining slices in a shallow dish. Sprinkle with the remaining milk and leave to soak.
2 In a bowl cream together the butter, egg yolks, flour, seasoning, nutmeg, grated cheese and soaked bread cubes.
3 Add the cream. Mix all the ingredients together thoroughly.
4 Whisk the egg whites until stiff, and use a metal spoon to fold this into the first mixture.
5 Line a greased, straight-sided heatproof dish or small cake tin with the soaked bread slices. Spoon the cheese mixture into the centre.
6 Bake at 350°F/180°C (Gas Mark 4) for 30-40 minutes, or until set. Sprinkle with the nuts and garnish with watercress.

Serve with: French-fried potatoes and a tomato and onion salad.

Sunday
Autumn Vegetable Curry

*1 pint (570ml) curry
  sauce (see page 154)
2 large potatoes, peeled
  and cubed
½ medium-sized marrow,
  peeled and cubed
4 oz (115g) cooked
  sweetcorn
4 oz (115g) almonds
Tomatoes and parsley to
  garnish

1 Heat the curry sauce gently in a pan.
2 Add the potatoes and marrow to the curry sauce, stir well, and simmer for 10-15 minutes, or until just cooked.
3 Stir in the sweetcorn and the nuts, and cook a few minutes more to heat through.
4 Decorate the curry with quartered tomatoes and fresh parsley sprigs.

Serve with: Hot buckwheat as a base, with a simple green salad. Add cubed cheese for more protein if you feel you need it.

*Make a day in advance and leave overnight for the flavour to develop. Reheat gently.

Week 10:
Monday
Peanut Butter Croquettes

1 onion, finely grated
1 carrot, finely grated
4 oz (115g) peanut butter
Seasoning to taste
Good pinch of marjoram
1 egg, beaten
5 oz (140g) dry wholemeal
  breadcrumbs
Vegetable oil for frying

1 Mix the onion and carrot with the peanut butter, seasoning, marjoram and beaten egg. Add most of the breadcrumbs to make a mixture that holds its shape, but is not too dry.
2 Divide into smaller pieces and shape into croquettes. Roll in the remainder of the crumbs.
3 Shallow or deep fry the croquettes in vegetable oil until golden and crisp. Drain on paper towels.

Serve with: Steamed potatoes with parsley, plus a crisp green salad.

Tuesday
Egg and Celery Flan

For the flan case:
4 oz (115g) rolled oats
2 oz (55g) wholemeal flour
2 tablespoons vegetable oil
Pinch of sea salt
Water to mix

For the filling:
½ small head of celery
1 onion, sliced
2 oz (55g) margarine or
* butter*
3 hard-boiled eggs,
* coarsely chopped*
½ pint (285ml) white
* sauce (see page 153)*
½ teaspoon dry mustard
Seasoning to taste
Good pinch of tarragon
1 oz (30g) wholemeal
* breadcrumbs*
Parsley to garnish

1 Stir together the oats and flour, then add the oil and seasoning with just enough cold water to make a dough. Press this evenly against the base and sides of a medium-sized flan dish.
2 Trim the celery and chop into even-sized pieces. Melt the margarine and fry the celery and onion, stirring frequently, until beginning to soften.
3 Stir the eggs gently into the celery mixture. Flavour the white sauce with the mustard and then add to the other ingredients with the seasoning and tarragon.
4 Spoon into the flan case, smooth the top, sprinkle with breadcrumbs. Bake at 375°F/190°C (Gas Mark 5) for 30 minutes. Garnish with parsley.

Serve with: A coleslaw of cabbage, carrots, green pepper, chopped dried apricots and cashew pieces.

Wednesday
Oriental 'Pork'

5 oz (140g) soya 'pork'
* chunks, hydrated in*
* water*
Approx. 1 oz (30g)
* margarine or butter*
2 sticks celery, chopped
6 oz (170g) tin pineapple in
* natural juice*
1 small onion, finely
* chopped*
1 oz (30g) wholemeal flour
1 teaspoon raw cane sugar
2 teaspoons soya sauce
2 teaspoons tomato purée
2 tablespoons white wine
* vinegar*
½ pint (285ml) vegetable
* stock*
Seasoning to taste

1 Drain the 'pork' chunks well. Melt the fat and fry the chunks gently, turning frequently so that all sides are cooked. Transfer to an ovenproof dish.
2 Add the celery and drained pineapple (reserving the juice) to the 'pork'.
3 In the remaining fat fry the onion until it begins to brown (adding more fat if necessary).
4 In a bowl mix together the flour, sugar, soya sauce, tomato purée, vinegar and stock. Add the juice from the pineapple.
5 Stir the onion into the 'pork', then pour on the prepared liquid. Season to taste.
6 Cover the dish and bake at 375°F/190°C (Gas Mark 5) for about 45 minutes, or until well cooked.

Serve with: Any grain dish goes well. Try millet for a change from the more usual rice.

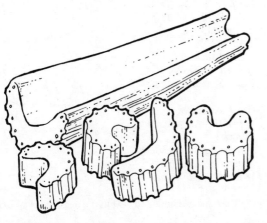

Thursday
Ravioli with Cheese Filling

½ lb (225g) wholemeal
   pasta dough (see page
   152)

For the filling:
1 tablespoon vegetable oil
½ small onion, chopped
½ lb (225g) Ricotta cheese
4 oz (115g) grated
   Parmesan cheese
Squeeze of lemon juice
Seasoning to taste
2 egg yolks
Tomato sauce to serve (see
   page 153)

1 Divide the dough into two and roll each piece into an oblong, making the dough as thin as possible. Mark one half into squares about 2-inches (5cm) across.
2 To make the filling, heat the oil in a pan and fry the onion until it begins to colour. Drain well, and then mix with the two cheeses, lemon juice, seasoning and egg yolks. The mixture should have a paste-like consistency.
3 Using a teaspoon, place a little of the filling in the centre of each of the marked squares. Brush the lines lightly with water.
4 Place the rest of the dough carefully on top of the first piece, and press lightly to remove any air that may be trapped. Then press more firmly along the lines before cutting into squares, preferably with a serrated-edged pastry cutter.
5 Separate the ravioli and place in a single layer on a lightly floured surface, cover with a dampened cloth, and leave for at least 30 minutes.
6 Drop the ravioli a few at a time into a large pan of boiling salted water, stirring occasionally so they do not stick together. Cook for approximately 5-8 minutes, or until tender, then remove with a perforated spoon and drain well. Cook the rest in the same way. Top with tomato sauce.

Serve with: Hot broccoli with butter, lemon juice and a sprinkling of Brazil nuts.

Friday
Spaghetti with Chilli Beans

10 oz (285g) wholemeal
   spaghetti
3 tablespoons vegetable oil
2-3 cloves garlic, crushed
1 small chilli pepper,
   seeded and finely
   chopped
Seasoning to taste
2 large tomatoes, peeled
   and chopped
4 oz (115g) cooked kidney
   beans
Parsley to garnish

1 Cook the spaghetti in a pan of boiling water for 10 minutes or until just tender. Drain well.
2 Meanwhile heat the vegetable oil and sauté the garlic and chilli pepper. After a few minutes add the seasoning, tomatoes and beans. Cook for 5-10 minutes more.
3 Serve the spaghetti with the sauce poured over the top. Garnish generously with fresh parsley.

Serve with: Mixed root vegetable salad on a lettuce base with cheese or yogurt dressing.

Saturday
Tempura Vegetables

For the batter:
4 oz (115g) wholemeal
   flour
3 large eggs, whisked
⅛ pint (70ml) water
Garlic salt

For the filling (about
1 lb (455g) in total):
2 courgettes
2 carrots
2 celery sticks
½ small cauliflower
2 oz (55g) mushrooms

For the sauce:
¼ pint (140ml) vegetable
   stock
2 tablespoons soya sauce
2 tablespoons sherry
Vegetable oil for frying

1 Put the flour in a bowl and beat in the eggs, water and salt

to make a batter. Adjust the liquid if necessary. Set aside in a cool place until needed.
2 Cut the courgettes, carrots and celery into chunks; break the cauliflower into fair-sized florets. Cook them in boiling water for 5 minutes, then drain well and pat dry.
3 Wash and dry the mushrooms.
4 Make the sauce by combining all the ingredients in a saucepan, bring to the boil, then simmer for a few minutes. Cool before using.
5 Dip the vegetable pieces into the batter and deep fry until crisp and brown. Drain well, and keep warm whilst cooking the rest of the ingredients in the same way.
6 Hand round the sauce at the table.

Serve with: Brown rice.

Sunday
Parsnip and Carrot Soufflettes

6 oz (170g) parsnips,
  peeled and diced
6 oz (170g) carrots, peeled
  and diced
Seasoning to taste
3 egg yolks
5 egg whites
1 oz (30g) margarine or
  butter
1½ oz (45g) wholemeal
  breadcrumbs
Parsley to garnish

1 Steam the vegetables gently until soft. Push through a sieve, mash, or liquidize them to make a purée. Cool slightly.
2 Season to taste, then stir in the egg yolks.
3 Whisk the egg whites to stiffen, and use a metal spoon to fold them into the vegetables.
4 Lightly grease four ramekins and divide the mixture between them.
5 Melt the fat and stir in the breadcrumbs. Sprinkle this over the soufflettes.
6 Bake at once in an oven preheated to 375°F/190°C (Gas Mark 5) for 20 minutes, or until the soufflettes are puffed up, and the crumbs browned. Garnish with parsley.

Serve with: French-fried potatoes and a salad of grated cabbage, onion, lettuce and salted peanuts.

Week 11:
Monday
Curried Rice Salad

6 oz (170g) brown rice
3 tablespoons vegetable oil
1 onion, sliced
1 teaspoon curry powder,
  or to taste
3 sticks celery
1 small red pepper
3 oz (85g) cashew nuts

For the yogurt
  dressing:
¼ pint (140ml) natural
  yogurt
1 tablespoon vegetable oil
1 tablespoon white wine
  vinegar·
Seasoning to taste

1 Cook the rice in twice the volume of water for 30-40 minutes, or until just tender. Drain well and set aside.
2 Heat the oil in a clean pan and fry the onion until it begins to soften; add the curry powder and cook a few minutes more. Stir in the rice, mixing well, and remove from the heat.
3 Chop the celery and pepper as fine as possible and add to the rice with the nuts. Set aside to get completely cold.
4 Stir together the ingredients for the dressing. Hand this round at the table for those who want it.

Serve with: Popadums, mango chutney, and a fresh tomato salad.

Tuesday
Black Bean Soup

6 oz (170g) black beans,
  soaked overnight
2 tablespoons vegetable oil
1 large onion, chopped
1 large green pepper,
  chopped
1-2 cloves garlic, crushed
1 pint (570ml) vegetable
  stock
2 tomatoes, chopped
2 tablespoons tomato
  purée
Seasoning to taste
Parsley to garnish

1 Drain the beans and put into a pan. Cover with fresh water, bring to the boil, then cover and simmer for an hour or until tender. Drain well.
2 Heat the oil in a clean pan and fry the onion, pepper and garlic.
3 When soft, add the stock, tomatoes, tomato purée, seasoning, and the beans. Continue cooking for 20-30 minutes. Add more stock or water if the soup is too thick, and adjust seasoning as necessary.
4 Serve the soup as it is, or purée to make a smoother soup. Garnish with plenty of fresh parsley.

Serve with: Wholemeal baps, peanut butter, and a chicory salad.

Wednesday
Quick Vegetable Lasagne

1 lb (455g) frozen mixed
  vegetables
6 oz (170g) wholemeal
  lasagne
6 oz (170g) grated Cheshire
  cheese
½ pint (285ml) white
  sauce (see page 153)
A few potato crisps

1 Cook the frozen vegetables as specified on the pack.
2 Meanwhile, bring a large pan of water to the boil and add the lasagne, one sheet at a time. Cook for 8 minutes, or until just tender. Drain well and rinse with cold water.
3 Arrange a third of the lasagne in the base of a lightly greased, ovenproof dish, top with half the well-drained vegetables and

2 oz (55g) of the grated cheese. Repeat this once more, and then finish with the remaining lasagne.
4 Pour the white sauce over the top, sprinkle with the final 2 oz (55g) of grated cheese and some crumbled crisps.
5 Bake at 375°F/190°C (Gas Mark 5) for 30 minutes.

Serve with: A simple watercress and mushroom salad sprinkled with a few nuts or deep-fried soya beans to add crunch.

Thursday
Marrow with Beans

3 oz (85g) flageolet beans,
  soaked overnight
1 oz (30g) margarine or
  butter
1 tablespoon vegetable oil
1 large onion, sliced
4 tomatoes, peeled and
  chopped
⅛ pint (70ml) tomato juice
1 teaspoon marjoram
Seasoning to taste
1½ lb (680g) marrow,
  peeled and cubed
2 oz (55g) grated Cheddar
  cheese
2 oz (55g) wholemeal
  breadcrumbs

1 Drain the beans and put in a pan. Cover with fresh water, bring to the boil, and continue boiling for 10 minutes. Lower the heat and simmer the beans for about an hour, or until just cooked.
2 In a saucepan melt the fat together with the oil, and fry the onion for a few minutes. Stir in the tomatoes with the juice, marjoram and seasoning, and cook for 5 minutes.
3 Add the marrow to the tomato mixture, and stir well. Cover the pan and simmer for 15-20 minutes, or until the marrow is just tender.
4 Drain the beans and stir into the vegetables. Cook for a few minutes more to heat through.
5 Tip the mixture into a shallow heatproof dish and sprinkle with the mixed cheese and breadcrumbs. Put under the grill briefly until crisp and golden.

Serve with: Potato slices in a cream sauce garnished with watercress.

Friday
Venetian Pizza

½ lb (225g) pizza dough
of your choice
Approx. 2 tablespoons
bran

For the topping:
3 tablespoons tomato
purée
4 oz (115g) Mozzarella
cheese, thinly sliced
1 onion, thinly sliced into
rings
1 oz (30g) pine nuts
1 oz (30g) raisins
Seasoning to taste
1-2 tablespoons vegetable
oil

1 Make up the pizza dough according to instructions. Divide into two and roll out on the bran to make medium-sized circles. Arrange on a baking sheet.
2 Spread the tomato purée over the tops of the pizza circles, taking it right to the edges. Arrange the Mozzarella cheese slices on top.
3 Spread the onion rings over the cheese. Sprinkle with pine nuts and raisins, seasoning to taste and a little oil.
4 Bake at 400°F/200°C (Gas Mark 6) for 20 minutes, or until the dough is cooked.

Serve with: A raw mushroom and red pepper salad generously garnished with fresh basil or parsley. Add chopped, hard-boiled egg or tofu dressing for protein, if liked.

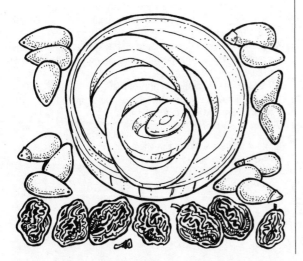

Saturday
Onion Dumplings

For the pastry:
¾ lb (340g) shortcrust
pastry (see page 151)
4 oz (115g) grated Cheddar
cheese
Pinch of dry mustard

For the filling:
4 large onions
2 tablespoons vegetable oil
1 red pepper, chopped
½ oz (15g) wholemeal
flour
¼ pint (140ml) vegetable
stock
½-1 teaspoon tarragon
Seasoning to taste
4 oz (115g) cooked
sweetcorn kernels
1 oz (30g) cashew nuts
Milk to glaze

1 Make up the pastry in the usual way, adding the finely grated cheese and the mustard. Adjust the liquid to make a fairly firm dough, then set aside in a cool place.
2 Peel the onions and remove a slice from the top of each one. Use a sharp knife to scoop out the flesh, leaving a shell 3 layers thick. Cook the shells in boiling water for 5 minutes, then remove them and drain well.
3 Heat the oil in a pan and add the chopped onion flesh with the pepper, cooking gently until they begin to soften.
4 Stir in the flour and cook briefly, then add the vegetable stock. Continue cooking until a sauce forms.
5 Add the tarragon, seasoning, sweetcorn and cashew nuts.
6 Roll out the pastry and cut into 4 squares about 6-inches (15cm) in diameter. Stand a shell in the centre of each one.
7 Fill the shells with the prepared mixture.
8 Fold the pastry around the onions, moulding it with your hands, and dampening the edges as you push them together so that they seal well. Brush lightly with milk.
9 Transfer the dumplings to a baking sheet and bake at 375°F/190°C (Gas Mark 5) for 30 minutes, or until the pastry is crisp and golden.

Serve with: Jacket potatoes and a hot vegetable such as Brussels sprouts or green beans.

Sunday
Crispy Cauliflower Cheese

1 medium cauliflower
¾ pint (425ml) white
  sauce (see page 153)
2 tablespoons vegetable oil
1 small onion, sliced
1 small pepper, sliced
½ clove garlic, crushed
6 oz (170g) cottage cheese
2 oz (55g) grated
  Parmesan cheese
½ small packet corn chips
  or potato crisps

1 Wash and trim the cauliflower, then break into florets. Steam these gently until just tender.
2 Meanwhile, make the white sauce.
3 Heat the oil in another pan and fry the onion, pepper and garlic until they begin to soften.
4 Stir the onion mixture and the cottage cheese into the sauce, mixing well.
5 Arrange the drained cauliflower in a shallow ovenproof dish. Pour on the sauce, making sure the cauliflower is well covered. Sprinkle with grated Parmesan cheese and the coarsely crushed chips or crisps.
6 Bake at 375°F/190°C (Gas Mark 5) for 10-15 minutes.

Serve with: French-fried potatoes and grilled tomatoes with chives.

Week 12:
Monday
Potato Cakes

1 lb (455g) potatoes
1 large egg, beaten
4 oz (115g) grated
  Lancashire cheese
2-3 spring onions, finely
  chopped
4 oz (115g) mushrooms,
  finely chopped
1 tablespoon fresh parsley
Seasoning to taste
Wholemeal flour to mix
Sesame seeds to coat
Vegetable oil for frying
Parsley to garnish

1 Peel, cube and steam the potatoes. Drain, then mash well.
2 Mix the beaten egg with the potatoes, together with the grated cheese, onions and mushrooms, parsley and seasoning.

3 Add enough flour to make a firm mixture, though be careful not to make it too dry.
4 Divide and shape into small cakes. Dip in sesame seeds. Shallow fry on both sides until evenly brown. Drain on paper towels. Garnish with parsley.

Serve with: Hot spinach with peanuts added, and a pepper, beetroot and onion side salad.

Tuesday
Buckwheat Bake

6 oz (170g) buckwheat
2 bay leaves
1 pint (570ml) water
1 oz (30g) margarine or
  butter
1 clove garlic, crushed
1 onion, chopped
1 red pepper, chopped
4 oz (115g) cooked green
  beans
4 oz (115g) cooked
  sweetcorn
1 tablespoon parsley
1 oz (30g) peanuts
Seasoning to taste
Soya sauce
¾ pint (425ml) thin white
  sauce (see page 153)
4 oz (115g) grated Cheddar
  cheese

1 Dry roast the buckwheat in a heavy-based pan for a few minutes, shaking frequently until it is lightly browned.
2 Add the bay leaves and water, and bring to the boil. Then cover the pan and cook gently for about 20 minutes, adding more liquid if necessary. Remove bay leaves.
3 Meanwhile, melt the fat in another pan and fry the garlic with the onion and pepper.
4 When soft, stir in the well-drained buckwheat, green beans, sweetcorn, parsley and peanuts. Add seasoning and soya sauce to taste.
5 Transfer to a shallow ovenproof dish.
6 Heat the sauce, add the cheese, and spread over the buckwheat and vegetable mixture.
7 Bake at 350°F/180°C (Gas Mark 4) for 20-30 minutes.

Serve with: A salad of radishes, onion and watercress on a Chinese cabbage base.

Wednesday
Creamy Cauliflower Curry

1 large cauliflower
4 oz (115g) cooked peas
Roasted or deep-fried
  chick-peas

For the sauce:
1 oz (30g) margarine
1 oz (30g) wholemeal flour
2 tablespoons curry
  powder, or to taste
¼ pint (140ml) single
  cream
¼ pint (140ml) milk
Tomatoes for garnish

1 Trim the cauliflower into florets, and steam until just tender. Drain and add to the well-drained peas.
2 Melt the fat in a saucepan and sprinkle in the flour and curry powder. Cook for a minute or two, stirring occasionally.
3 Pour in the cream and milk and bring gently to the boil, then simmer until the sauce thickens. If it seems too thick, add a drop of the water in which the cauliflower was cooked.
4 Stir in the vegetables and continue cooking gently for 5 minutes. Serve topped with roasted or deep-fried chick-peas for crunch, and slices of tomato to add colour.

Serve with: Brown rice, and a cucumber, pepper, tomato and spring onion salad. Add nuts if liked.

*Make a day in advance and leave overnight for the flavour to develop. Reheat gently.

Thursday
Beany Lasagne

6 oz (170g) wholemeal
  lasagne
2 × 14 oz (395g) tins
  baked beans
4 tomatoes, coarsely
  chopped
1 tablespoon molasses
Good pinch of ground
  ginger
½ pint (285ml) white
  sauce (see page 153)
4 oz (115g) grated Cheddar
  cheese
Parsley to garnish

1 Drop the lasagne in a large pan of boiling water, one sheet at a time, and cook for 8 minutes, or until just tender. Drain

well, rinse in cold water, and lay out on a clean tea towel.
2 Turn the contents of the tins of beans into a saucepan and add the tomatoes, molasses and ginger. Simmer gently for 10 minutes.
3 Arrange some of the lasagne in the base of a greased ovenproof dish and top with some of the bean mixture. Repeat until all the ingredients have been used up.
4 Heat the white sauce and stir in most of the cheese. Pour over the lasagne, and top with the remaining cheese. Bake at 350°F/180°C (Gas Mark 4) for 30 minutes to heat through. Garnish generously with parsley.

Serve with: A raw cauliflower salad.

Friday
Almond and Beansprout Pancakes

½ pint (285ml) pancake
  batter (see page 152)
Vegetable oil for frying

For the filling:
4 tablespoons vegetable oil
4 spring onions, sliced
3 oz (85g) almonds,
  coarsely chopped
2 teaspoons cornflour
Pinch of salt
2 tablespoons soya sauce
2 tablespoons sherry
6 oz (170g) beansprouts

1 Whisk the batter. Heat a little oil in a heavy-based pan and pour in a few spoonfuls of batter, cooking gently and tipping the pan frequently. When set, remove the pancake from the pan and keep it warm whilst using the rest of the batter in the same way.
2 In another pan, heat the oil and add the onions, cooking until they become transparent. Stir in the almonds.
3 Mix together the cornflour, salt, soya sauce and sherry. Add to the pan, stir, and continue cooking gently until the sauce thickens. Add the beansprouts. Adjust seasoning.
4 Use the filling mixture to stuff each of the pancakes, fold and serve at once.

Serve with: A millet and watercress salad.

Saturday
'Sausage' Meat Balls with Spaghetti

*6 oz (170g) soya 'sausage'
  mix*
*1 teaspoon oregano, or to
  taste*
Vegetable oil for frying
*10 oz (285g) wholemeal
  spaghetti*
*Tomato sauce to serve (see
  page 153)*
*Grated Parmesan cheese to
  serve (optional)*

1 Hydrate the soya 'sausage' mix according to instructions on packet. Add the oregano.
2 Shape the mixture into balls about 1-inch (2.5cm) across.
3 Heat the vegetable oil in a frying pan and fry the balls gently, turning them frequently, until browned all over.
4 Meanwhile, cook the spaghetti in boiling water for 12 minutes, or until just tender.
5 Drain the spaghetti and turn into a warmed serving dish. Top with the meat balls and tomato sauce. Hand round Parmesan cheese at the table for those who want it.

Serve with: A crisp green salad — try fresh young dandelion leaves with Italian dressing for a change.

Sunday
Parsnip Soufflé Crumble

For the base:
1 lb (455g) parsnips
*2 oz (55g) margarine or
  butter*
3 eggs, separated
A good pinch of nutmeg
Seasoning to taste

For the crumble:
*2 oz (55g) sunflower seeds,
  roasted*
2 oz (55g) wholemeal flour
*2 oz (55g) margarine or
  butter*

1 Peel, cube and steam the parsnips until soft enough to mash. Add the fat and stir well.
2 Add the egg yolks to the parsnip with the nutmeg and seasoning.
3 Make the crumble by grinding the sunflower seeds to make

a coarse meal, and stirring into the flour. Rub in the fat to make a crumb-like mixture.
4 Whisk the egg whites until stiff and fold into the parsnip purée with a metal spoon. Turn into a lightly greased soufflé dish.
5 Sprinkle lightly and evenly with the crumble. (The topping must not be heavy or the soufflé will not rise. If there is too much of the crumble mixture, reserve the surplus for use another time.)
6 Bake at 375°F/190°C (Gas Mark 5) for 30-40 minutes, or until cooked.

Serve with: Jacket potatoes and a green vegetable such as spinach.

Week 13:
Monday
Quick Beany Macaroni Bake

*½ lb (225g) wholemeal
  macaroni*
1 lb (455g) tin baked beans
4 tomatoes, sliced
Seasoning to taste
*4 oz (115g) grated Cheddar
  cheese*
*½ oz (15g) margarine or
  butter*
*1 oz (30g) wholemeal
  breadcrumbs*

1 Cook the macaroni in boiling water for 10 minutes, or until just tender. Drain well.
2 Lightly grease an ovenproof dish. Arrange alternate layers of cooked macaroni, beans, tomatoes, seasoning and grated cheese, until all the ingredients have been used.
3 Melt the fat in a small pan and stir in the crumbs. Sprinkle them over the top of the other ingredients.
4 Bake at 375°F/190°C (Gas Mark 5) for 20 minutes, or until crumbs are crisp and brown.

Serve with: A celery, apple and walnut salad.

Tuesday
Sweetcorn Fritters

¾ lb (340g) sweetcorn
1 green pepper, chopped
*4 oz (115g) wholemeal
  flour*
1 egg, lightly beaten
Seasoning to taste
*¼ pint (140ml) creamy
  milk*
*2 oz (55g) grated Cheddar
  cheese*
Vegetable oil for frying

1 Cook the sweetcorn in boiling water until just tender.
2 In a bowl, mix the pepper with the flour and beaten egg, seasoning, milk, grated cheese and drained sweetcorn.
3 Heat a little oil in a pan and drop in spoonsful of the mixture, cooking until lightly browned all over. Drain on paper towels.

Serve with: Broccoli in a tomato sauce, sprinkled with chopped, roasted hazelnuts, plus French-fried potatoes.

Wednesday
Marrow Rings with Bulgur and Lentils

1 large marrow
2 tablespoons vegetable oil
1 onion, sliced
3 oz (85g) split red lentils
½ pint (285ml) vegetable
* stock*
3 oz (85g) bulgur
2 tomatoes, chopped
1 tablespoon tomato purée
Seasoning to taste
1 oz (30g) walnuts,
* chopped*
Tomato sauce to serve (see
* page 153)*

1 Cut the marrow into a 2-inch (5cm) rings and scoop out the seeds. Arrange the rings in a greased ovenproof dish.
2 Heat the oil in a saucepan and fry the onion until it begins to colour. Add the lentils, stir, then pour in the vegetable stock.
3 Bring to the boil, then simmer until the lentils are soft.
4 Add more water and the bulgur, bring to the boil again, and simmer for a few minutes only. Cover and leave the saucepan to stand for 10 minutes, or until the bulgur is tender.
5 Stir in the tomatoes, tomato purée and seasoning. Spoon the filling into the marrow rings, piling it on top if necessary. Sprinkle with chopped nuts.
6 Bake covered at 350°F/180°C (Gas Mark 4) for 30-40 minutes, or until the marrow rings are cooked. Hand round tomato sauce at the table.

Serve with: Roast potatoes, and a lettuce and red pepper salad with cubes of cheese sprinkled on top.

Thursday
Butter Bean and Cauliflower Salad

1 small cauliflower
1 red pepper, sliced
2 oz (55g) mushrooms,
* sliced*
6 oz (170g) cooked butter
* beans*

For the cream
dressing:
2 tablespoons lemon juice
4 tablespoons single cream
Pinch of raw cane sugar
Seasoning to taste

1 Trim the base and leaves from the cauliflower and break into small florets. These can be left raw, or lightly steamed then plunged into cold water if you prefer a softer texture.
2 In a bowl mix together the cauliflower florets, pepper, mushrooms and the beans.
3 Mix together the dressing ingredients and pour over the prepared salad. Leave to stand briefly.

Serve with: Hot fried rice or — for a quicker meal — wholemeal toast. Add nuts or nut butter for extra protein.

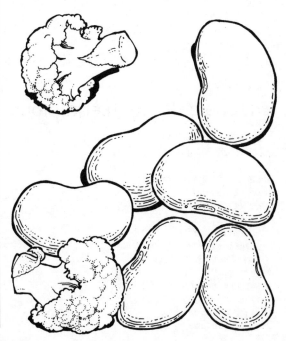

Friday
Millet Soufflé

2 oz (55g) millet
1 oz (30g) margarine or
butter
1 oz (30g) wholemeal flour
⅓ pint (200ml) milk
Seasoning to taste
Pinch of dry mustard
2 oz (55g) grated Cheddar
cheese
4 egg yolks
5 egg whites
Fresh chopped chives to
garnish

1 Cover the millet with twice its volume of water (or vegetable stock if you have some handy), and cook for 25 minutes, or until tender. Drain very well.
2 Melt the fat in a pan and sprinkle in the flour, cooking for a few minutes only. Off the heat, pour in the milk, then return to the cooker and simmer, stirring, until the sauce thickens.
3 Add seasoning, mustard, cheese, egg yolks and the millet. Mix very well.
4 Whisk the egg whites until stiff. Use a metal spoon to fold into the other ingredients.
5 Grease a 2-pint soufflé dish and spoon in the mixture. Bake at once in a preheated oven, temperature 375°F/190°C (Gas Mark 5) for 30-40 minutes, or until risen and golden.

Serve with: A light salad to contrast a rather heavy soufflé. Beansprouts, mushrooms, celery and a garnish of tamari roasted pumpkin seeds would be ideal.

Saturday
Shepherd's Pie with Beansprouts

1 lb (455g) potatoes
½ oz (15g) margarine or
butter
2 tablespoons vegetable oil
1 onion, chopped
5 oz (140g) soya 'minced
meat', hydrated in water
2 tablespoons tomato
purée
1 teaspoon yeast extract,
or to taste
1 teaspoon mixed herbs, or
to taste
3 oz (85g) beansprouts
Seasoning to taste

1 Peel, slice and steam the potatoes until soft enough to mash to a stiff paste; add half the fat, and set aside.
2 Heat the oil in a saucepan and lightly fry the onion for a few minutes. Spoon in the well-drained soya 'minced meat', mix well with the onion, then add the tomato purée, yeast extract and herbs.
3 Pour in just enough water to cover and simmer for 10 minutes.
4 Add the beansprouts, mix well and spoon into an ovenproof dish. If you like a moist-textured mixture, add a little of the liquid in which it was cooked; if not, drain well.
5 Top with the mashed potatoes spread as evenly as possible. Dot with a little extra fat. Bake at 375°F/190°C (Gas Mark 5) for about 20 minutes.

Serve with: A ratatouille of courgettes, aubergine, onions and tomatoes. Could be served hot or cold.

Sunday
Swiss Chard Quiche

½ lb (225g) pastry of your
choice

For the filling:
1½ lb (680g) Swiss chard
½ oz (15g) margarine or
butter
1 medium onion, chopped
3 large eggs
6 oz (170g) grated Cheddar
cheese
Seasoning to taste
½ teaspoon dry mustard
Soya 'bacon' bits

1 Make up the pastry mix and put aside in a cool place.
2 Trim the leaves and tops of the Swiss chard stalks (use the lower stalks in a separate recipe). Wash well and chop coarsely.
3 Melt the fat in a pan and sauté the chard together with the onion for 5-10 minutes, or until the onion begins to soften.
4 Beat the eggs lightly. Stir in the grated cheese, seasoning, mustard, and the cooled vegetables.
5 Roll out the pastry and line a medium-sized flan dish. Pour in the prepared mixture, and sprinkle with soya 'bacon' bits.
6 Bake at 400°F/200°C (Gas Mark 6) for 30 minutes, or until pastry is cooked and filling set.

Serve with: Potato salad and a sweetcorn, celery and apple salad.

4.
WINTER

Week 1:
Monday
Baked Bean and 'Ham' Crumble

For the base:
1 lb (455g) tin baked beans
5 oz (140g) soya 'ham'
chunks, hydrated in
water
2 tablespoons vegetable oil
1 large green pepper,
sliced
Seasoning to taste

For the crumble:
4 oz (115g) wholemeal
flour
2 oz (55g) margarine or
butter
Seasoning to taste

1 Tip the beans into an ovenproof dish. Drain the soya 'ham' chunks.
2 Heat the oil in a pan and lightly fry the pepper. When it begins to soften, add the soya chunks and cook a few minutes more, stirring occasionally.
3 Mix the soya chunks and pepper in with the beans, seasoning well.
4 Put the flour in a bowl and rub in the fat. Add seasoning. Sprinkle the crumble over the bean mixture.
5 Bake at 375°F/190°C (Gas Mark 5) for 20 minutes, or until crumble is cooked.

Serve with: A beansprout, watercress and mushroom salad, plus potato croquettes.

Tuesday
Winter Vegetable Flan

½ lb (225g) shortcrust
pastry (see page 151)
1 oz (30g) sesame seeds

For the filling:
1 medium onion
1 medium swede
1 medium potato
2 medium carrots
2 sticks celery
½ lb (225g) tofu
Water
Seasoning to taste
1 teaspoon marjoram
Parsley to garnish

1 Make up the pastry mix, distributing the sesame seeds evenly. Set aside in a cool place.
2 Peel and cube or slice the onion, swede, potato and carrots; chop the celery. Steam the vegetables until just tender, then drain well.
3 Beat the tofu with enough cold water to make a thick sauce, then season well and add the marjoram. Stir the vegetables into the sauce.
4 Roll out the pastry and line a medium-sized flan dish. Bake blind at 400°F/200°C (Gas Mark 6) for 10 minutes.
5 Arrange the vegetable mixture in the flan case. Bake at 375°F/190°C (Gas Mark 5) for 20 minutes, or until pastry is cooked. Garnish generously with parsley.

Serve with: Salad of finely grated Brussels sprouts, chopped tomatoes and apple, with walnuts. Also, creamed potatoes.

Wednesday
Yogurt Herb Omelette

8 eggs
¼ pint (140ml) natural
* yogurt*
2 tablespoons chopped
* parsley*
1 tablespoon chopped
* chives*
½ tablespoon chopped
* basil*
½ tablespoon chopped
* chervil*
Seasoning to taste
1½ oz (45g) margarine or
* butter*
Tomato slices to garnish

1 Beat together the eggs; add the yogurt, fresh herbs and seasoning, making sure they are thoroughly mixed.
2 Melt a quarter of the fat in a small frying pan. Pour in a quarter of the egg mixture and cook over a moderate heat until it begins to set underneath. Lift the sides to allow any liquid to run underneath.
3 When the omelette sets, fold it in half, and serve, or put aside in a warm spot. Use up the remaining ingredients in the same way to make three more omelettes.
4 Garnish each omelette with thin slices of tomato.

Serve with: A hot grain dish such as bulgur. Add a red cabbage salad sprinkled with caraway seeds.

Thursday
Three-Cheese Lasagne

½ lb (225g) wholemeal
* lasagne*
¾ lb (340g) Ricotta cheese
6 oz (170g) Mozzarella
* cheese*
¾ pint (425ml) tomato
* sauce (see page 153)*
1-2 teaspoons oregano
2 oz (55g) grated
* Parmesan cheese*
Soya 'bacon' bits

1 Bring a large pan of water to the boil and add the lasagne, one sheet at a time. Cook for 8 minutes or as long as directed on the packet. Drain, rinse in cold water, and lay out on a clean tea towel.
2 Crumble the Ricotta cheese and slice the Mozzarella.
3 Mix together the tomato sauce and oregano.
4 Spoon a little of the sauce into a lightly greased casserole, then arrange alternate layers of lasagne, Ricotta, Mozzarella

and Parmesan cheese and sauce. When all the ingredients have been used up (finishing with tomato sauce) sprinkle with soya 'bacon' bits.
5 Bake at 375°F/190°C (Gas Mark 5) for 30 minutes.

Serve with: A beansprout, carrot and celery salad, with a vinaigrette dressing and a sprinkling of roasted sunflower seeds.

Friday
Vegetable Curry-in-a-Hurry

1 lb (455g) mixed frozen
* vegetables*
3 tablespoons vegetable oil
1 onion, chopped
1 clove garlic, crushed
2 teaspoons curry powder,
* or to taste*
Sea salt
1 oz (30g) creamed
* coconut*
2 oz (55g) cashew nuts

1 Cook the frozen vegetables in boiling water until tender.
2 Meanwhile, heat the oil in a pan and fry the onion and garlic over a medium heat for 5 minutes, or until lightly browned.
3 Stir in the curry powder and salt, and cook for 5 minutes.
4 Cream the coconut in a little of the water from the vegetables, and add to the pan. Mix well.
5 Add the vegetables and cashew nuts. Cook gently for 10 minutes to heat through.

Serve with: Hot brown rice or millet, plus chutney, yogurt and a cucumber salad.

Saturday
Chinese Cabbage Bake

1 medium head of Chinese
* cabbage*
⅓ pint (200ml) white
* sauce (see page 153)*
3 tablespoons single cream
Seasoning to taste
1 tablespoon vegetable oil
½ small onion, sliced
4 oz (115g) mushrooms,
* sliced*
2 oz (55g) cashew nuts
2 oz (55g) wholemeal
* breadcrumbs*
2 oz (55g) grated Cheddar
* cheese*
Tomato slices to garnish

1 Trim and slice the cabbage and drop into a pan of boiling water. Cook for 5 minutes, then drain well.
2 Heat the white sauce and stir in the cabbage with the cream and seasoning.
3 In a clean pan, heat the oil and fry the onion until it begins to soften; add the mushrooms and fry a few minutes more.
4 Mix into the sauce with the cashew nuts. Transfer to an ovenproof dish.
5 Top with the breadcrumbs and grated cheese and bake at 350°F/180°C (Gas Mark 4) for 30 minutes. Garnish with tomato slices round the edge of the dish.

Serve with: Jacket potatoes and a crisp green salad, maybe with a tofu dressing for added protein.

Sunday
Carrot and Cottage Cheese Tarts

For the pastry:
½ lb (225g) wholemeal flour
2 teaspoons baking powder
4 oz (115g) margarine or butter
2 oz (55g) cottage cheese
1 teaspoon lemon juice
Cold water to mix

For the filling:
1½ lb (680g) carrots, sliced
½ pint (285ml) vegetable stock
4 oz (115g) cottage cheese
Seasoning to taste
2 oz (55g) beansprouts
Chives, chopped
1 large egg, lightly beaten
1 oz (30g) wholemeal breadcrumbs (optional)
Chives to garnish

1 Sift together the flour and baking powder, then use your fingertips to rub in the fat to make a crumb-like mixture.
2 Stir in the cottage cheese. Add the lemon juice to a few tablespoons of cold water and mix in to make a smooth dough, using more water as necessary. Wrap in clingfilm or a polythene bag and chill for at least 30 minutes.
3 Cook the carrots in the stock until soft. Drain well and purée, or rub them through a sieve.
4 Mix the carrot purée with the cottage cheese, plenty of seasoning, the beansprouts and chopped chives, plus the beaten egg. If the mixture is very moist, add the crumbs.
5 Roll out the pastry and use to line 8 small tartlet tins.

6 Spoon some of the carrot mixture into each of the pastry cases. Bake at 375°F/190°C (Gas Mark 5) for 20-30 minutes, or until the pastry is cooked and the filling set. Garnish with chopped chives.

Serve with: Fresh wholemeal baps, plus a salad of cucumber, lettuce, raw courgettes, mushrooms and sunflower seeds.

Week 2:
Monday
Toad-in-the-Hole

4 oz (115g) wholemeal flour
Pinch of sea salt
1 large egg
½ pint (285ml) milk
½ oz (15g) margarine or butter
Medium tin soya 'sausages'

1 Sift together the flour and salt. Use a wooden spoon to beat in the egg, then gradually add the milk, making sure the batter is smooth and free of lumps.
2 Whisk lightly, then cover and set aside in a cool place.
3 Melt the fat in a medium-sized ovenproof dish. Place the 'sausages' in the dish, turn them so that they are coated with fat.
4 Bake at 400°F/200°C (Gas Mark 6) for 10 minutes, turning occasionally, until the sausages are browned.
5 Pour the batter into the dish, tipping to spread it evenly. Lower oven temperature to 350°F/180°C (Gas Mark 4).
6 Bake for 30 minutes or until the batter is cooked.

Serve with: Roast potatoes, and cabbage cooked with onion and sprinkled with chopped peanuts.

Tuesday
Vegetable Soup with Pine Nut Dumplings

For the dumplings:
3 oz (85g) wholemeal flour
2 oz (55g) margarine or
   butter
2 oz (55g) wholemeal
   breadcrumbs
1 large egg
1½ oz (45g) pine nuts
Seasoning to taste

For the soup:
1 oz (30g) margarine or
   butter
1 onion, sliced
1 oz (30g) wholemeal flour
1¾ pints (1 litre) vegetable
   stock
2 tomatoes, coarsely
   chopped
2 courgettes, coarsely
   chopped
2 leeks, coarsely chopped
½-1 teaspoon oregano
Seasoning to taste

1 Put the flour into a bowl, rub in the fat to make a crumb-like mixture, then stir in the breadcrumbs, egg, pine nuts and seasoning. The mixture should be firm but not too dry — add a drop of cold water if necessary. Roll into small balls and set aside.
2 Melt the fat in a saucepan and fry the sliced onion until it becomes translucent.
3 Sprinkle in the flour, cook for a minute or two. Off the heat, stir in the vegetable stock, then return pan to the cooker and bring gently to the boil.
4 Add the tomatoes, courgettes, leeks, oregano and seasoning. Stir well, then drop in the dumplings.
5 Lower the heat, cover, and simmer for 15 minutes or until all the vegetables are tender and the dumplings are cooked.

Serve with: Freshly made scones, and a celery and orange salad.

Wednesday
Winter Kasha with Cashews

1 egg
½ lb (225g) kasha*
2 tablespoons vegetable oil
1 large leek, chopped
1 large parsnip, cut into
   cubes
¾ pint (425ml) vegetable
   stock
½ bunch watercress,
   chopped
2 oz (55g) cashew nuts
Seasoning to taste
6 oz (170g) grated Cheddar
   cheese

1 Beat the egg lightly and stir in the kasha so that each grain is coated.
2 Heat the vegetable oil in a pan and cook the kasha gently for a few minutes, stirring frequently.
3 Add the leek and parsnip, stir, and cook a few minutes more.
4 Pour in the vegetable stock, bring to the boil, then lower the heat and cover the pan. Cook gently for 10 minutes.
5 Add the watercress, cashew nuts and seasoning. Cover and continue cooking for 10 minutes more, or until the kasha is light and fluffy. (Add a drop more liquid if necessary.)
6 Hand round grated cheese at the table for those who want it.

Serve with: Braised celery and hot wholemeal baps.

*Kasha is another name for roasted buckwheat. If you cannot buy it ready roasted, follow instructions as for *Buckwheat Bake* (page 110).

Thursday
Polenta and Pepper Croquettes

½ pint (285ml) milk
2 oz (55g) fine polenta
   (cornmeal)
Seasoning to taste
4 oz (115g) grated Cheddar
   cheese
1 tablespoon vegetable oil
1 medium pepper, finely
   chopped
1 oz (30g) wholemeal flour
1 egg, beaten
Wholemeal breadcrumbs
Vegetable oil for frying

1 Bring the milk to a gentle boil and sprinkle in the polenta, stirring continually. Lower the heat and cook for 20-30

minutes, stirring now and again, until thick and smooth.
2 Add the seasoning and grated cheese.
3 Heat the oil and fry the pepper for a few minutes to soften, then stir into the polenta mixture. Turn out onto a wet surface, smooth the top, and leave to get cold.
4 Cut into even-sized pieces and shape into croquettes. Dip them into the flour, the beaten egg and then the breadcrumbs, coating them evenly.
5 Heat the oil in a frying pan and fry the croquettes until golden and crisp. Drain on paper towels.

Serve with: Brussels sprouts cooked with tomatoes, and jacket potatoes.

Friday
Watercress Quiche

½ lb (225g) pastry of your choice

For the filling:
1 bunch watercress
1 oz (30g) margarine or butter
1 small onion, finely sliced
⅓ pint (200ml) milk
2 large eggs
Seasoning to taste
Good pinch of nutmeg

1 Make up the pastry mix, and leave in a cool place.
2 Wash and trim the watercress; chop the leaves coarsely. Heat the fat in a pan. Add the watercress and onion, and cook together until the onion softens.
3 In a bowl, beat together the milk, eggs, seasoning and nutmeg. Add the prepared vegetables.
4 Roll out the pastry, and line a medium-sized flan dish. Bake blind at 400°F/200°C (Gas Mark 6) for 10 minutes.
5 Pour the mixture into the pastry case, lower the oven heat to 350°F/180°C (Gas Mark 4), and continue cooking the quiche for 30 minutes, or until lightly set.

Serve with: A kidney-bean salad with cucumber, tomatoes, and lettuce, plus fresh French bread.

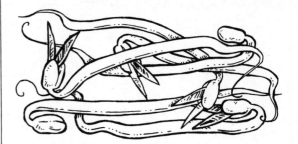

Saturday
Chinese Spring Rolls

For the rolls:
¾ lb (340g) wholemeal flour
⅓ pint (200ml) water
1 egg, lightly beaten

For the filling:
2 tablespoons vegetable oil
6 oz (170g) mushrooms, sliced
6 oz (170g) beansprouts
2 sticks celery, chopped
2 tablespoons soya sauce
Seasoning to taste
2 oz (55g) cashew nut pieces
2 tablespoons chopped watercress
Small piece fresh ginger (optional)
Vegetable oil for frying

1 Sift the flour into a bowl, add the water and a good half of the beaten egg. Mix to a dough, and knead briefly.
2 On a floured board, roll out the pastry as thinly as possible, and cut into 12 squares of equal size.
3 Heat the oil in a pan and fry the mushrooms, beansprouts and celery for a few minutes only, stirring. They should be cooked but still crisp.
4 Mix in the soya sauce, seasoning, nuts and watercress. Cool slightly. Add the sliced ginger, if using.
5 Divide the vegetables between the squares. Fold in the sides then roll up to make a small packet. Brush the edges with the remaining egg, and seal by pressing firmly.
6 Deep fry the spring rolls, a few at a time, in hot oil. When crisp, drain well and keep warm whilst cooking the rest.

Serve with: A dish of hot rice or millet with peas and a shredded omelette stirred into the grain. A Chinese cabbage salad would go well, too.

Winter

Sunday
Brussels Sprouts Soufflé

1 lb (455g) Brussels
  sprouts
½ lb (225g) potatoes
1 oz (30g) margarine or
  butter
4 tablespoons single cream
Seasoning to taste
Pinch of nutmeg
3 egg whites
1½ oz (45g) grated
  Gruyère cheese

1 Trim the Brussels sprouts, peel and dice the potatoes, and steam both vegetables until just cooked. Drain well, then put into a liquidizer, mash, or press through a sieve to make a thick purée.
2 Add butter, cream, seasoning and nutmeg, mixing well.
3 Beat the egg whites until stiff, and use a metal spoon to fold them into the puréed vegetables.
4 Turn the mixture into a greased, 2-pint soufflé dish, and sprinkle with the grated cheese. Bake at once in an oven pre-heated to 375°F/190°C (Gas Mark 5) for 25-30 minutes, or until risen and golden.

Serve with: Potatoes cooked with garlic and parsley, plus a pepper and tomato salad.

Week 3:
Monday
Chilli Bean Loaf

½ lb (225g) cooked kidney
  beans
14 oz (395g) tin tomatoes,
  chopped
1 onion, chopped
1-2 teaspoons mixed herbs
¼-½ teaspoon chilli
  powder, or to taste
4 oz (115g) wholemeal
  breadcrumbs
2 eggs, lightly beaten
Seasoning to taste
Natural yogurt to serve

1 Drain the kidney beans and then put them into a saucepan with the tomatoes and onion, the herbs and chilli powder.
2 Cook gently for 20-30 minutes, or until the sauce thickens and the beans are soft. Cool slightly.
3 Mash to a fairly coarse consistency and stir in the crumbs. Add the beaten eggs and seasoning to taste. Mix well.

4 Turn the mixture into a greased loaf tin and smooth the top. Bake at 400°F/200°C (Gas Mark 6) for 30-40 minutes, or until set.
5 Natural yogurt can be handed round at the table for those who want it.

Serve with: Brown rice and a salad of raw cauliflower, cucumber and tomatoes, sprinkled with walnuts.

Tuesday
Spaghetti Sicilienne

10 oz (285g) wholemeal
  spaghetti
2 tablespoons vegetable oil
1 large onion, sliced
1-2 cloves garlic, chopped
4 oz (115g) button
  mushrooms, sliced
10 black olives, stoned and
  chopped
Parsley
Seasoning to taste
Soya 'bacon' bits to
  garnish
Grated Parmesan cheese to
  serve (optional)

1 Cook the spaghetti in a pan of boiling water for about 10 minutes, or until just tender.
2 Meanwhile, heat the oil in a pan and fry the onion and garlic until soft.
3 Add the mushrooms and stoned chopped olives, and cook 5-10 minutes more, stirring frequently. Add a generous amount of parsley, and seasoning to taste. Stir in soya 'bacon' bits.
4 Drain the spaghetti and mix with the vegetables. Serve topped with cheese, if liked.

Serve with: A green salad of endive, lettuce and chicory with an Italian dressing.

Wednesday
Cheese Croquettes

1 tablespoon vegetable oil
1½ oz (45g) wholemeal
  flour
¼ pint (140ml) milk
5 oz (140g) grated Cheddar
  cheese
1 egg, beaten
Seasoning to taste
2 oz (55g) dried
  wholemeal breadcrumbs
1 oz (30g) bran
Vegetable oil for frying

1 Heat the oil in a saucepan and sprinkle in the flour. Cook briefly, stirring continually, then pour in the milk and bring the mixture gently to the boil.
2 Stir the finely grated cheese into the sauce. Cool slightly before adding the beaten egg and seasoning, then leave to cool completely.
3 When firm, divide the mixture into four portions and shape them into croquettes. Combine the breadcrumbs and bran. Roll the croquettes in the mixture to coat completely, and set aside for a short time.
4 Heat the oil in a pan, and when ready, drop the croquettes into it, and deep or shallow fry until golden crisp on the outside, creamy smooth inside.
5 Drain well, and serve hot.

Serve with: A pasta salad on a lettuce base, with plenty of tomato, sweetcorn and green pepper for colour, plus chopped almonds for texture.

Thursday
Fennel Flan

*8 oz (225g) pastry of your
   choice*

For the filling:
*1½ lb (680g) fennel bulbs
2 oz (55g) margarine or
   butter
6 oz (170g) Mozzarella
   cheese, thinly sliced
Seasoning to taste
2 oz (55g) grated
   Parmesan cheese
Capers*

1 Make up the pastry mix and set aside in a cool place.
2 Trim the fennel bulbs and cut lengthways into ½-inch (12mm) slices. Melt the fat in a pan and gently fry the slices, turning once, until both sides are lightly browned and the fennel begins to soften.
3 Roll out the pastry and use to line a medium-sized flan dish. Bake blind at 400°F/200°C (Gas Mark 6) for 10 minutes.
4 Lay a third of the fennel slices across the base of the flan dish, cover with half the sliced Mozzarella cheese, and season well. Repeat this, then finish with a final layer of fennel. Sprinkle with the Parmesan cheese and capers.

5 Bake at 375°F/190°C (Gas Mark 5) for 15 minutes more, or until pastry is cooked. Garnish with a few of the feathery fennel leaves.

Serve with: A rice bowl, hot or cold, with peas and sliced radishes added, plus a garnish of cress.

Friday
Millet with Brussels

*½ lb (225g) millet
1½ pints (850ml) vegetable
   stock
1 lb (455g) Brussels
   sprouts
½ pint (285ml) white
   sauce (see page 153)
4 oz (115g) grated
   Lancashire cheese
Seasoning to taste
1 oz (30g) wholemeal
   breadcrumbs*

1 Put the washed millet in a saucepan with the vegetable stock, bring to the boil, then simmer, covered, for 10 minutes.
2 Clean and trim the Brussels sprouts, halve them if large, and add to the pan. Continue cooking for 15-20 minutes more, adding water if necessary, until both the millet and sprouts are cooked.
3 Meanwhile, make the white sauce, then stir in most of the grated cheese. Season to taste.
4 Combine the sauce and millet mixture. Turn into a heatproof serving dish and sprinkle with the breadcrumbs and remaining cheese.
5 Put under a hot grill for a few minutes to brown the topping.

Serve with: A watercress and orange salad sprinkled with chopped nuts.

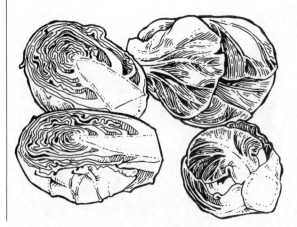

Winter

Saturday
Vegetable Peanut Crumble

For the base:
1 oz (30g) margarine or
   butter
2 tablespoons vegetable oil
1 onion, sliced
2 sticks celery, sliced
2 carrots, sliced
¼ small white cabbage,
   finely shredded
5 tablespoons cooked peas
Approx. 3 tablespoons
   peanut butter
Seasoning to taste

For the crumble:
4 oz (115g) wholemeal
   flour
2 oz (55g) margarine
2 oz (55g) salted peanuts,
   chopped

1 Heat the fat and oil together in a pan, and gently fry the onion, celery and carrots for 5 minutes, stirring frequently.
2 Add the shredded cabbage and cook until all the vegetables are just tender.
3 Add the peas, enough peanut butter to coat, and seasoning. Transfer to an ovenproof dish.
4 Put the flour in a bowl and rub in the margarine. When well mixed, stir in the coarsely chopped nuts.
5 Sprinkle the crumble over the vegetables. Bake at 375°F/190°C (Gas Mark 5) for 20 minutes, or until the topping is cooked.

Serve with: Steamed potatoes and a salad of lettuce, mushrooms and avocado slices.

Sunday
Corn and Leek Lasagne

6 oz (170g) wholemeal
   lasagne
2 oz (55g) margarine or
   butter
1 small onion, sliced
1 small pepper, sliced
2 leeks, sliced
6 oz (170g) sweetcorn
   kernels
1 tablespoon parsley
Seasoning to taste
½ pint (285ml) white
   sauce (see page 153)
2 eggs
1 oz (30g) wholemeal
   breadcrumbs
1 oz (30g) sunflower seeds

1 Drop the lasagne, one sheet at a time, into a pan of boiling water and cook for 8 minutes, or for the time indicated on the packet. Drain, rinse through with cold water, and lay on a clean tea towel.
2 Melt the fat in a pan and fry the onion, pepper and leeks for 5-10 minutes, stirring frequently. Add the sweetcorn, parsley and seasoning, cover the pan and cook 5-10 minutes more.
3 In a greased ovenproof dish arrange alternate layers of lasagne and the leek and corn mixture, continuing until all the ingredients have been used.
4 Whisk together the sauce and eggs.
5 Pour the sauce over the lasagne. Mix the breadcrumbs and seeds and sprinkle them over the top. Bake at 400°F/200°C (Gas Mark 6) for 20-30 minutes, or until set.

Serve with: A root vegetable salad on a crisp lettuce base.

Week 4:
Monday
'Beef' Cobbler

For the scone dough:
6 oz (170g) self-raising
   wholemeal flour
1 teaspoon baking powder
Pinch of sea salt
1 oz (30g) margarine or
   butter
Milk to bind

For the 'beef':
*5 oz (140g) soya 'beef'
  chunks, hydrated in
  water*
2 tablespoons vegetable oil
1 large onion, sliced
2 carrots, sliced
*4 oz (115g) split green
  peas, soaked overnight*
*½ pint (285ml) vegetable
  stock*
4 tomatoes, chopped
Seasoning to taste
Parsley to garnish

1 Sieve together the flour, baking powder and salt, then use fingertips to rub in the fat to make a crumb-like mixture.
2 Bind the dough with a drop of milk, knead briefly, then roll out to ½ an inch (12mm) thick. Cut in rounds and set aside.
3 Drain the 'beef' chunks.
4 Heat the oil in a large pan and fry the onion for a minute or two, then stir in the 'beef' chunks, carrots, and peas.
5 Add the vegetable stock, bring to the boil, then simmer for 30 minutes or until the peas have formed a thick sauce.
6 Stir the tomatoes into the mixture, and add seasoning. Transfer to an ovenproof dish and top with the cobbler rounds.
7 Bake at 400°F/200°C (Gas Mark 6) for 20 minutes, or until the dough is cooked. Garnish with parsley.

Serve with: Brussels sprouts, plus creamy mashed potatoes.

Tuesday
Mushroom and Artichoke Pizza

For the dough:
*8 oz (225g) wholemeal
  self-raising flour*
¼ pint (140ml) milk
1 tablespoon vegetable oil

For the topping:
2 tablespoons vegetable oil
1 onion, sliced
*4 oz (115g) mushrooms,
  sliced*
*14 oz (395g) tin tomatoes,
  drained*
*Small tin artichoke hearts,
  drained*
*4 oz (115g) Bel Paese
  cheese, thinly sliced*
12 black olives, sliced
1 teaspoon oregano
Seasoning to taste
*1 oz (30g) grated
  Parmesan cheese*

1 Put the flour in a bowl and add the milk, mixing well to form a dough. Roll out quickly into an oblong and put onto a baking sheet, or an oblong-shaped tin.
2 Heat the vegetable oil in a pan and fry the onion to soften. Add the mushrooms and cook a few minutes more, stirring frequently. Remove from the heat.
3 Chop the well-drained tomatoes and spread over the prepared dough. Top with the onion and mushroom mixture.
4 Slice the drained artichokes and arrange on top of the pizza. Cover everything with thin slices of the cheese, then sprinkle with sliced olives, oregano, seasoning and Parmesan cheese.
5 Bake at 425°F/220°C (Gas Mark 7) for about 20 minutes, or until dough is cooked. Cut into slices to serve.

Serve with: A chicory and endive salad sprinkled with roasted cashew nuts.

Wednesday
Chick-Pea Salad

*½ lb (225g) chick-peas,
  soaked overnight*
3 sticks celery, chopped
2 carrots, chopped
1 green pepper, chopped
*1 oz (30g) walnuts,
  chopped*
French dressing
Lettuce
Watercress to garnish

1 Drain the chick-peas, put in a pan and cover with fresh water. Bring to the boil, lower heat and simmer for an hour, or until cooked. Cool slightly.
2 Mix the celery, carrots, pepper and walnuts with the drained chick-peas. Add dressing.
3 Chill the mixed ingredients.
4 Pile into the centre of a bed of lettuce and garnish with fresh watercress sprigs.

Serve with: A grain dish, hot or cold, maybe with a yogurt dressing.

Thursday
Pasta with Peppers

2 tablespoons vegetable oil
½ oz (15g) margarine or
  butter
1 onion, sliced
1 red pepper, sliced
1 yellow pepper, sliced
Seasoning to taste
1 teaspoon mixed herbs, or
  to taste
10 oz (285g) wholemeal
  pasta shapes
3 oz (85g) cooked
  sweetcorn kernels
Grated Parmesan cheese
  or 2 oz (55g) peanuts to
  serve

1 Heat the vegetable oil together with the fat, and fry the onion and peppers until beginning to soften. Add seasoning and herbs.
2 Cook the pasta shapes in boiling water for 10 minutes or until just tender. Drain and add to the peppers and oil, mixing well. Add the sweetcorn. Cook for a few minutes more only.
3 Turn onto a warmed serving dish and top with cheese or nuts.

Serve with: An endive and cucumber salad, plus warm wholemeal baps.

Friday
Kedgeree Flan

For the base:
6 oz (170g) shortcrust
  pastry (see page 151)

For the filling:
1 tablespoon vegetable oil
Pinch ground cumin seeds
Pinch turmeric
Pinch garam masala
1 small onion, chopped
3 oz (85g) brown rice
3 oz (85g) cooked lentils
1 oz (30g) margarine or
  butter
1 large egg, beaten
Parsley and tomato slices
  to garnish

1 Make up the pastry and set aside in a cool place.
2 Heat the vegetable oil in a pan and gently fry the spices for a few minutes, then add the onion and cook until it softens.

3 Add the rice, stirring to coat the grains. Pour in just enough water to cover and cook for 15 minutes. Stir in the lentils and continue cooking until the rice is soft. Drain if necessary.
4 Add the fat and beaten egg.
5 Roll out the pastry and use to line a medium-sized flan dish. Bake blind at 400°F/200°C (Gas Mark 6) for 15 minutes.
6 Tip the rice and lentil mixture into the flan case, smooth the top, and cook for 15-20 minutes more at 300°F/150°C (Gas Mark 2), or until heated through. The parsley and tomato slices can be added with the filling, and served hot; or add them just before putting the flan on the table.

Serve with: A light, crisp green salad, maybe with a few slices of hard-boiled egg included.

Saturday
Avocado Soufflé

1½ oz (45g) margarine or
  butter
3 oz (85g) wholemeal flour
1 pint (570ml) milk
4 eggs, separated
Seasoning to taste
1 small red pepper
1 large ripe avocado
Chopped pistachios to
  garnish (optional)

1 Melt the fat in a saucepan and gently fry the flour for a minute or two. Remove from the heat and stir in the milk, then return pan to the heat and continue simmering and stirring until sauce thickens.
2 Cool slightly, then add the egg yolks and seasoning.
3 Finely chop or mash the pepper together with the avocado. Stir into the first mixture.
4 Whisk the egg whites until stiff and use a metal spoon to fold them into the other ingredients.
5 Pour into a greased, 2-pint soufflé dish, and bake at once in an oven pre-heated to 375°F/190°C (Gas Mark 5) for 30-40 minutes, or until puffed up and golden. Garnish with chopped pistachio nuts.

Serve with: Jacket potatoes, and a beetroot and Chinese leaves salad with a sprinkling of finely chopped spring onions.

Sunday
Tofu Casserole

2 tablespoons vegetable oil
2 onions, sliced
1 large red pepper, sliced
1 clove garlic, crushed
½ lb (225g) cooked
*   sweetcorn kernels*
1 lb (455g) tofu, sliced
⅓ pint (200ml) vegetable
*   stock*
Soya sauce to taste
Seasoning to taste
2 oz (55g) pumpkin seeds

1 Heat the oil in a pan and fry the onions and pepper with the garlic. When soft, put half of the mixture in a small ovenproof dish.
2 Arrange half the sweetcorn over the vegetables. Top with half of the sliced tofu.
3 Repeat this to use up the rest of these ingredients.
4 Heat the vegetable stock, add soya sauce and seasoning, and pour over the mixture.
5 Sprinkle the seeds over the top. Bake at 350°F/180°C (Gas Mark 4) for 30 minutes.

Serve with: A rice salad with fresh herbs and cress added.

Week 5:
Monday
Semolina Cheese Bake

2 oz (55g) margarine or
*   butter*
1 small onion, sliced
1 pint (570ml) water
4 oz (115g) wholemeal
*   semolina*
Seasoning to taste
1 tablespoon chopped
*   parsley*
½ teaspoon dry mustard
10 oz (285g) grated
*   Cheddar cheese,*
*   preferably matured*
2 egg whites
Watercress to garnish

1 Melt half the fat in a saucepan and cook the onion for 5 minutes to soften.
2 In a separate pan, bring the water to the boil, then sprinkle in the semolina, stirring continually. Simmer for a few minutes until thick.

3 Add the onion to the semolina with the seasoning, parsley and mustard, mixing well.
4 Stir in most of the grated cheese and the rest of the fat.
5 Whisk the egg whites until stiff, and use a metal spoon to fold carefully into the semolina mixture.
6 Turn into a lightly greased, ovenproof dish and sprinkle with the remaining cheese. Bake at 400°F/200°C (Gas Mark 6) for 20-30 minutes, or until puffed up and golden. Garnish with sprigs of watercress.

Serve with: Shredded red and white cabbage sprinkled with chopped dates and sunflower seeds.

Tuesday
'Ham' Croquettes

1 oz (30g) margarine or
*   butter*
½ onion, finely chopped
½ pepper, finely chopped
1 oz (30g) wholemeal flour
¼ pint (140ml) milk
5 oz (140g) soya 'ham'
*   chunks, hydrated in*
*   water*
4 oz (115g) cooked peas
Seasoning to taste
Good pinch of mint
Wholemeal breadcrumbs
*   to coat*
Vegetable oil for frying

1 Melt the fat and fry the onion and pepper. Stir in the flour and cook for a few minutes, then stir in the milk and continue cooking until the sauce thickens.
2 Bring a pan of water to the boil, and cook the soya 'ham' for 5 minutes, to soften. Drain well and chop coarsely.
3 Mix the coarsely chopped 'ham' into the sauce together with the peas, seasoning and mint. If the mixture is too moist, add some breadcrumbs. Leave to cool.
4 Divide the mixture and shape into croquettes. Roll in more breadcrumbs. Deep fry in the hot vegetable oil until crisp, then drain well on paper towels.

Serve with: Jacket potatoes, plus Swiss chard salad with parsley, and a French dressing.

Wednesday
Rye with Lentils

½ lb (225g) cracked rye*
½ lb (225g) lentils, soaked
  overnight
3 tablespoons vegetable oil
1 large onion, coarsely
  chopped
1 large swede. coarsely
  chopped
1 large carrot, coarsely
  chopped
2 sticks celery, coarsely
  chopped
¼ pint (140ml) vegetable
  stock
Soya sauce to taste
Seasoning to taste
4 oz (115g) smoked tofu

1 Dry roast the rye for a minute or two, then cover well with water and cook for about 40 minutes or until tender. Add more water as necessary.
2 Drain the lentils and cook in a separate pan of water. When just cooked, drain them well.
3 Meanwhile, heat the oil in another pan and fry the onion, swede, carrot and celery, stirring frequently.
4 As they begin to colour, add the vegetable stock and cook briefly until tender but not soggy.
5 Gently mix together the drained rye, lentils and vegetables, adding soya sauce and seasoning to taste. Pile onto a warmed serving dish.
6 Lightly grill the sliced tofu, arrange over the top. Serve at once.

Serve with: A cucumber, tomato and parsley salad.

*If you can only buy whole rye grains, crack them with a rolling pin. This speeds up what can be a very slow cooking process.

Thursday
Mushroom Walnut Omelette

2 oz (55g) margarine or
  butter
4 oz (115g) mushrooms,
  thinly sliced
2 oz (55g) walnuts
8 eggs
Seasoning to taste
3 tablespoons cold water
Parsley to garnish

1 Melt half the fat in a pan and add the mushrooms with the walnuts. Cook gently, stirring occasionally, for 5 minutes, or until the mushrooms begin to colour.
2 Meanwhile, whisk the eggs together with seasoning and water.
3 Heat half the remaining fat in an omelette or frying pan, and pour in half the egg mixture. Reduce the heat and cook until the omelette begins to set underneath. Lift the edges and tilt the pan so that any liquid runs underneath.
4 Continue cooking until the omelette is almost set. Top with half the mushroom and walnut mixture, fold over to make a semi-circle, and divide in half.
5 Use up the rest of the ingredients in the same way to make two more servings. Garnish with plenty of parsley.

Serve with: A raw cauliflower, watercress and carrot salad. Hot wholemeal muffins could be served instead of potatoes for a change.

Friday
Parsnip Pancakes

½ pint (285ml) pancake
  batter (see page 152)
Vegetable oil for frying

For the filling:
1 lb (455g) parsnips,
  peeled and cubed
4 oz (115g) fresh or frozen
  peas
1 oz (30g) margarine
½ small onion, finely
  chopped
1 oz (30g) wholemeal flour
⅓ pint (200ml) milk
1 tablespoon chopped
  parsley
1 tablespoon cream
Seasoning to taste
1 oz (30g) almonds,
  coarsely chopped
Watercress to garnish

1 Make up the batter according to instructions and set aside in a cool place for at least half an hour.
2 Meanwhile, cook the parsnips in boiling water with the peas (if fresh) for 10-15 minutes, or until just tender. (If using frozen peas, add them a few minutes before the parsnip is ready.)
3 In a separate pan, melt the margarine and sauté the onion for a few minutes, until soft.
4 Remove the pan from the heat and pour in the milk, then return to the heat and bring to the boil, stirring continually to make a thick, smooth sauce. Add the parsley and cook another minute only.
5 Off the heat, stir in the cream and seasoning, and the well-drained vegetables. Add the nuts. Keep the mixture warm.

6 Whisk the batter and, if too thick, adjust consistency by adding a drop of water.

7 Heat a little oil in a frying pan and pour in enough batter to cover the base. Cook gently, tipping frequently, until lightly browned underneath, then flip or turn the pancake with a spatula. Cook the other side. Keep warm while using the rest of the batter in the same way.

8 Fill the pancakes with the parsnip mixture, roll up, and serve at once, garnished with watercress. (If necessary they can be put in an ovenproof dish and heated through briefly in a hot oven or under the grill.)

Serve with: Crisps or potato croquettes, and grilled tomatoes topped with grated cheese.

Saturday
Leek and Banana Curry

*For the sauce:
3 tablespoons vegetable oil
1 onion, chopped
¼ teaspoon ground
    coriander
¼ teaspoon ground mace
¼ teaspoon ground ginger
¼ teaspoon ground
    cinnamon
¼ teaspoon ground chilli
Seasoning to taste
1 oz (30g) wholemeal flour
1 pint (570ml) vegetable
    stock
Squeeze of lemon juice

1 lb (455g) leeks
2 large bananas (or
    equivalent in dried
    bananas)
1 oz (30g) raisins
1 oz (30g) pine nuts

1 Heat 2 tablespoons of the vegetable oil in a pan and fry the chopped onion to soften.

2 Sprinkle in the spices, seasoning and flour, stir briefly, and cook for a few minutes. Stir in the stock and bring to the boil, then simmer for 20-30 minutes to make a thick sauce. Add the lemon juice.

3 Meanwhile, clean, trim and chop the leeks into even-sized pieces. Steam until tender. Drain well and add to the sauce.

4 Peel and chop the bananas. Stir into the other ingredients and heat gently for just a minute or two more.

5 Heat the remaining oil and fry the raisins and pine nuts, stirring frequently, until plump and golden. Sprinkle over the curry.

*Make a day in advance and leave overnight for the flavour to develop. Reheat gently.

Serve with: Brown rice and a raw cauliflower salad, maybe with deep-fried soya beans to add crunch.

Sunday
Chestnut Loaf

½ lb (225g) cooked
    chestnuts, mashed, or
    tinned equivalent.
4 oz (115g) wholemeal
    breadcrumbs
4 oz (115g) peanuts,
    ground
1 onion
2 sticks celery
3 eggs, lightly beaten
Seasoning to taste
Good pinch of marjoram

1 Mash the cooked chestnuts to a smooth purée.

2 Mix the purée with the breadcrumbs and peanuts.

3 Chop the onion and celery as finely as possible, and add to the first mixture with the beaten eggs, seasoning and marjoram.

4 Spoon into a greased loaf tin and smooth the top.

5 Bake at 350°F/180°C (Gas Mark 4) for 45 minutes, or until firm to the touch.

Serve with: Jacket potatoes and a green vegetable such as steamed Brussels sprouts.

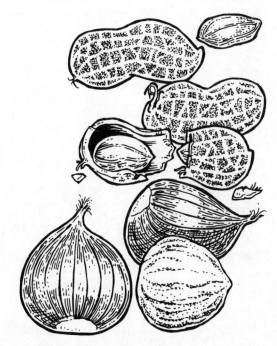

Week 6:
Monday
Potato and Kale Bake with Tofu

1½ lb (680g) potatoes,
  peeled and sliced
½ oz (15g) margarine or
  butter
Seasoning to taste
1 lb (455g) kale, washed
  and trimmed
2 tablespoons vegetable oil
2 medium leeks, finely
  chopped
2 medium carrots, finely
  chopped
10 oz (285g) tofu
1 tablespoon soya sauce
2 oz (55g) sunflower seeds
1 oz (30g) margarine or
  butter

1 Steam the potatoes until tender. Drain and mash with the fat and seasoning.
2 Cook the kale in boiling water for 10 minutes. Drain well and chop finely. Mix with the potatoes.
3 Heat the vegetable oil in a pan and fry the leeks and carrots, stirring frequently, until they begin to soften.
4 Drain and crumble the tofu and add it to the leeks and carrots, mixing well. Add soya sauce and seeds, and cook for a few minutes only.
5 Put the vegetable mixture into a greased ovenproof dish and top with the potato and kale. Smooth the top and add knobs of margarine or butter.
6 Bake at 400°F/200°C (Gas Mark 6) for 20 minutes, or until browned and heated through.

Serve with: A salad of two different lettuces, cucumber and mushrooms, with fresh mint added to the dressing.

Tuesday
Chilli Con 'Carne'

½ lb (225g) cooked kidney
  beans
3 tablespoons vegetable oil
1 large onion, finely
  chopped
1 clove garlic, crushed
½ teaspoon paprika
½ teaspoon ground mixed
  spice
½ teaspoon cayenne
  pepper
14 oz (395g) tin tomatoes,
  coarsely chopped
3 oz (85g) soya 'minced
  meat', hydrated in water
Seasoning to taste
1 bay leaf, crushed

1 Drain the beans, and set aside.
2 Heat the vegetable oil in a pan and fry the onion and garlic for a few minutes. Add the spices and cook a minute more.
3 Add the tomatoes to the pan with their juice. Bring to a boil, then lower the heat and simmer for 15 minutes.
4 Stir in the drained 'meat' and the beans. Season, and add the crushed bay leaf. Continue cooking for 15 minutes more, or until the sauce is thick and all the ingredients are cooked.

Serve with: A traditional accompaniment to chilli is tortillas, small crisp pancakes made by mixing cornmeal and water and dry roasting in a heavy-based pan. Complete the meal with a lettuce, pepper and tomato salad with a creamy avocado dressing.

Wednesday
Lasagne with Soured Cream

½ lb (225g) wholewheat
  lasagne
½ small onion, grated
1 carrot, grated
1 bay leaf
A few peppercorns
1½ pints (850ml) milk
2 oz (55g) margarine or
  butter
2 oz (55g) wholemeal flour
Seasoning to taste
¼ pint (140ml) soured cream
6 oz (170g) grated Edam
  cheese
2 oz (55g) grated
  Parmesan cheese
2 oz (55g) walnuts,
  chopped

1 Cook the lasagne in a large pan of boiling water, dropping them in one at a time, and testing for when they are just beginning to soften. Drain well, rinse in cold water, and lay them out on a clean tea towel.
2 Combine the onion, carrot, bay leaf, peppercorns and milk, and bring to the boil. Remove from the heat and leave covered for at least 15 minutes, then strain off and discard the vegetables.
3 Melt the fat in a clean pan and add the flour. Cook gently for a few minutes, then stir in the milk and continue cooking until the sauce thickens. Season to taste.
4 Off the heat, stir in the soured cream and grated Edam cheese, mixing well until thoroughly blended.
5 In a lightly greased, ovenproof dish arrange alternate layers of the lasagne and sauce until all the ingredients have been used. Sprinkle with the Parmesan cheese and coarsely chopped nuts.
6 Bake at 400°F/200°C (Gas Mark 6) for 30 minutes.

Serve with: A fennel, orange and watercress salad.

Thursday
Nut Meat Salad

10 oz (285g) tin nut meat
1 red pepper, sliced
8 oz (225g) beansprouts
4 tablespoons cooked
  sweetcorn
1 oz (30g) sunflower seeds

For the dressing:
3 tablespoons vegetable oil
1 tablespoon cider vinegar
1 teaspoon mixed herbs, or
  to taste
Seasoning to taste
Endive or lettuce to serve

1 Cut the nutmeat into cubes.
2 Slice the pepper and mix with the beansprouts, sweetcorn, and sunflower seeds.
3 Combine the ingredients for the dressing in a screw-top jar and shake well, then pour over the mixed vegetables and toss lightly.
4 Arrange washed endive around the edges of a salad bowl, spoon the other vegetables into the centre, and top with the nutmeat.

Serve with: French bread or a dark bread such as pumpernickel or rye. Start with hot soup, if liked.

Friday
Yogurt Soufflé with Leeks

2 medium leeks
2 oz (55g) margarine or
  butter
1 oz (30g) wholemeal flour
¼ pint (140ml) milk
Seasoning to taste
4 eggs, separated
¼ pint (140ml) natural
  yogurt
2 tablespoons dry
  wholemeal breadcrumbs

1 Clean the leeks carefully, then trim and cut into very thin slices. Cook in boiling water for literally a minute or two to soften, and drain well.
2 Melt the fat in a pan and add the flour. Cook briefly. Remove from the heat and stir in the milk, then return to the cooker and simmer gently, stirring, to make a thick sauce.
3 Stir the leeks into the sauce with the seasoning and egg yolks. Cool slightly, then stir in the yogurt.
4 Grease a 2-pint soufflé dish and sprinkle with the breadcrumbs, using your fingertips to press them against the base and sides of the dish.
5 Whisk the egg whites until stiff. Use a metal spoon to fold them into the other ingredients, then pour carefully in the soufflé dish. Bake at once in an oven pre-heated to 375°F/190°C (Gas Mark 5) for 35-40 minutes, or until well risen.

Serve with: A cold rice salad with spices, nuts, raisins and celery; plus carrot slices to add colour.

Saturday
Tomato and Pepper Quiche

For the pastry:
8 oz (225g) wholemeal
   flour
⅓ pint (200ml) boiling
   water
3 tablespoons vegetable oil
Pinch of sea salt

For the filling:
1 oz (30g) margarine or
   butter
2 green peppers, sliced
4 large tomatoes
6 oz (170g) curd cheese
3 eggs, beaten
½ oz (15g) wholemeal
   flour
Seasoning to taste
Fresh parsley

1 Sift the flour into a bowl. Whisk together the water, oil and salt, and add to the flour.
2 Knead the dough briefly, then wrap in clingfilm or a polythene bag and chill for at least half an hour.
3 Melt the fat in a pan and lightly sauté the sliced peppers until they soften. Drain well.
4 Roll out the pastry and use to line a medium-sized flan dish. Bake blind at 400°F/200°C (Gas Mark 6) for 10 minutes.
5 Arrange the peppers in the flan case together with 3 of the tomatoes, cut in slices.
6 Beat the curd cheese with a wooden spoon until smooth, then combine with the beaten eggs, flour, seasoning and chopped parsley to taste. Pour over the peppers, and top with a ring of tomato slices.
7 Bake at 375°F/190°C (Gas Mark 5) for 25-30 minutes, or until set.

Serve with: A salad of raw cauliflower florets, avocado, chicory and chopped brazil nuts. Jacket or steamed potatoes could be served for the extra hungry.

Sunday
Spaghetti and Spinach Bake

2 oz (55g) margarine or
   butter
1 onion, sliced
1½ lb (680g) spinach,
   washed and shredded
Seasoning to taste
4 oz (115g) Mozzarella
   cheese, sliced
8 oz (225g) wholemeal
   spaghetti
½ pint (285ml) white
   sauce (see page 153)
3 oz (85g) grated Cheddar
   cheese
1½ oz (45g) margarine or
   butter
2 oz (55g) dry wholemeal
   breadcrumbs

1 Melt the fat in a saucepan and lightly fry the onion. When it begins to colour, add the spinach and cook, stirring frequently, until the spinach is soft. Season to taste.
2 Arrange half the spinach in the base of a greased ovenproof dish and cover with half the Mozzarella cheese slices.
3 Cook the spaghetti in a pan of boiling water for 10 minutes, or until just tender. Drain well. Arrange half of it on top of the spinach and cheese.
4 Heat the sauce and add the Cheddar cheese, stirring until it melts. Pour half of this into the ovenproof dish.
5 Repeat the layers to use up the rest of the ingredients.
6 Melt the remaining fat and stir in the breadcrumbs. Sprinkle over the top. Bake at 375°F/190°C (Gas Mark 5) for 20 minutes, or until crisp on top.

Serve with: A salad including chopped olives, tomatoes, and lots of parsley on a lettuce base.

Week 7:
Monday
Soufflé Jacket Potatoes

4 large potatoes
Vegetable oil
2 large eggs, separated
2 tablespoons cream
1 oz (30g) margarine or
   butter
Seasoning to taste
Paprika
2 oz (55g) grated
   Parmesan cheese
Chopped chives to taste
Watercress to garnish

1 Scrub the potatoes, dry them and prick with a fork. Rub them with a little oil and bake at 400°F/200°C (Gas Mark 6) for about an hour, or until just soft. Cool slightly.
2 Slit the tops and use a spoon to scoop out most of the potato flesh, leaving the skins intact.
3 In a bowl mash the potatoes, and mix with the egg yolks, cream, fat, seasoning, paprika and grated cheese. Add chopped chives to taste.
4 Whisk the egg whites until stiff then mix gently into the other ingredients.
5 Pile some of the mixture back into each of the potato skins. Lower the oven temperature to 350°F/180°C (Gas Mark 4) and bake the soufflé potatoes for about 15 minutes more, or until set. Take to the table at once, garnished with watercress.

Serve with: Brussels sprouts that have been steamed, then lightly fried with peanuts. A mixed salad could also be served.

Tuesday
Tomato Soup with Noodles

½ oz (15g) margarine or
    butter
1 onion, chopped
½-1 clove garlic, crushed
2 carrots, peeled and
    chopped
14 oz (395g) tin tomatoes
Seasoning to taste
1 teaspoon basil
1½ pints (850ml) vegetable
    stock
4 oz (115g) wholemeal
    noodles

1 Melt the fat in a pan and fry the onion with the garlic for a few minutes.
2 Add the carrots, stir, and cook 5 minutes more.
3 Pour in the tomatoes and juice, and mash them coarsely. Add seasoning, basil and vegetable stock. Bring to the boil, then simmer for 15-20 minutes.
4 Sieve or blend the soup. Return to the pan.
5 Drop the noodles into the boiling soup, lower the heat, and cook 5 minutes if they are fresh, 8-10 minutes if from a packet.

Serve with: Garlic bread and a chicory and endive salad with tofu dressing to add protein.

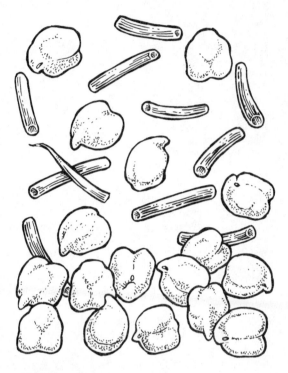

Wednesday
Celeriac and Chick-Pea Bake

1½ lb (680g) celeriac
1 large onion
6 oz (170g) cooked
    chick-peas
¼ pint (140ml) vegetable
    stock
2-3 tablespoons tahini
Seasoning to taste
Chopped chives to garnish

1 Peel the celeriac and slice as thinly as possible; do the same with the onion.
2 Drain the chick-peas. They can be left whole or coarsely chopped.
3 Heat the vegetable stock and stir in the tahini so that it dissolves, adding a generous amount of seasoning.
4 In a shallow, well-greased ovenproof dish arrange layers of the celeriac and onion, sprinkling with chick-peas between layers. Pour on the stock.
5 Bake uncovered at 375°F/190°C (Gas Mark 5) for an hour, or until the celeriac is tender. Garnish with the chopped chives.

Serve with: Brown rice and a tomato and green pepper salad.

Thursday
'Pork' and Apple Casserole

5 oz (140g) soya 'pork'
  chunks, hydrated in
  water
1 oz (30g) wholemeal flour
Seasoning to taste
1 oz (30g) margarine
1 large onion, finely
  chopped
½-1 clove garlic, crushed
1 large apple, chopped
½ pint (285ml) cider
4 tablespoons natural
  yogurt
Pinch of paprika

1 Bring the soya chunks to the boil, then simmer gently for 5 minutes. Drain well and cool slightly.
2 Mix the flour with seasoning. Toss the drained soya chunks in the flour.
3 Melt the fat in a pan and fry the 'pork' together with the onion, garlic and apple, stirring occasionally.
4 When the onion is tender, stir in the cider, and continue simmering until a sauce forms. Cook 10 minutes more, adding a drop more cider if the mixture seems too dry.
5 Stir the yogurt into a little of the sauce, then mix it into the other ingredients. Heat gently for a minute more.
6 Sprinkle with paprika.

Serve with: Wholemeal noodles and a simple green salad.

Friday
Sweetcorn Soufflé Pancakes

For the batter:
4 oz (115g) wholemeal
  flour
Pinch of salt
2 eggs, separated
½ pint (285ml) milk
Seasoning to taste

For the filling:
1½ oz (45g) margarine or
  butter
1 onion, finely chopped
1 green pepper, finely
  chopped
10 oz (285g) sweetcorn
  kernels, fresh or frozen
Seasoning to taste
Vegetable oil for frying
4-5 tablespoons cream or
  tofu mayonnaise
Tomato slices to garnish

1 Sieve the flour into a bowl, and add salt. Stir in the egg yolks, then gradually add the milk, whisking to keep the batter light. Season, and set aside in a cool place.
2 Melt the fat in a pan and sauté the onion and pepper until they begin to soften. Stir in the sweetcorn kernels, season, lower the heat and cook gently for 10 minutes.
3 Meanwhile, whisk the egg whites until they hold their shape, then use a metal spoon to fold them carefully into the batter mixture.
4 Heat a little oil in a heavy-based frying pan and, when hot, spoon in some of the batter, tipping the pan to spread it evenly. When lightly coloured underneath, turn the pancake with a spatula and cook the second side.
5 Keep the cooked pancakes warm whilst using the rest of the batter in the same way.
6 Stir the cream or mayonnaise into the sweetcorn mixture and heat a minute or two longer, taking care not to let it boil.
7 Put a spoonful or two of the vegetables onto each pancake, fold in half, and garnish with slices of tomato.

Serve with: Warm wholemeal baps, and a watercress salad sprinkled with soya 'bacon' bits or dry roasted soya beans.

Saturday
Rice Balls with Sunflower Seeds

1 oz (30g) margarine or
  butter
1 oz (30g) wholemeal flour
⅓ pint (200ml) milk
Seasoning to taste
Pinch of paprika
½ lb (225g) cooked brown
  rice
2 oz (55g) roasted
  sunflower seeds
Dry wholemeal
  breadcrumbs to coat
1 egg, beaten
Vegetable oil for frying
Hot tomato sauce to serve
  (see page 153)
Good pinch of chilli
  powder
Parsley to garnish

1 Melt the fat, add the flour and cook gently for a minute or two. Then pour in the milk and continue cooking, stirring frequently, until the sauce thickens.
2 Add seasoning and paprika to the sauce, with the rice and sunflower seeds. Spread on a plate and leave to cool.
3 Shape the mixture into balls and roll them in the crumbs, the beaten egg, and then the crumbs again.
4 Fry the balls carefully in deep, hot oil until golden. Drain

on paper towels. Transfer to a serving dish. Add chilli powder to the tomato sauce to taste. Pour over the rice balls. Garnish with parsley.

Serve with: A spinach and egg salad sprinkled with olives. If liked, you could also serve potato slices in a white or creamy sauce.

Sunday
Brussels and Butter Bean Crumble

For the base:
1½ lb (680g) Brussels
    sprouts
4 oz (115g) cooked butter
beans
½ pint (285ml) white
    sauce (see page 153)
Seasoning to taste

For the crumble:
3 oz (85g) rolled oats
2 oz (55g) margarine
2 oz (55g) grated Cheddar
    cheese

1 Trim, wash and steam the Brussels sprouts until just tender.
2 Mix together with the butter beans and well-seasoned white sauce, and put into an ovenproof dish.
3 In a bowl mix together the oats, margarine and cheese to make a coarse, crumbly mixture. Spread this over the Brussels sprouts.
4 Bake at 350°F/180°C (Gas Mark 4) for 20-30 minutes, until the crumble is cooked.

Serve with: A grain dish such as wholewheat berries, and a red pepper, beetroot and celery salad sprinkled with nuts.

Week 8:
Monday
Quick 'Chicken' Jardinière

5 oz (140g) soya 'chicken'
    pieces, hydrated in water
½ pint (285ml) brown
    gravy (see page 153)
¾ lb (340g) frozen mixed
    vegetables
Seasoning to taste
Watercress to garnish

1 Cook the soya 'chicken' pieces gently in water for 5-10 minutes, or until just tender. Drain well.
2 Make up the brown gravy; cook the frozen vegetables according to instructions, then drain.
3 Mix the 'chicken' and vegetables into the gravy and cook gently, just long enough to heat through. Season to taste.
4 Garnish with watercress.

Serve with: Hot bulgur, or a bulgur salad, plus sliced tomatoes and cucumber.

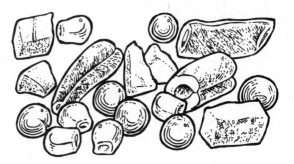

Tuesday
Semolina Gnocchi

1 pint (570ml) milk
4 oz (115g) wholemeal
    semolina
Seasoning to taste
4 oz (115g) grated
    Parmesan cheese
2 oz (55g) margarine or
    butter
1 large egg, lightly beaten
Tomato slices and parsley
    to garnish

1 In a saucepan, bring the milk to a gradual boil, sprinkling in the semolina and stirring continually. Cook for a few minutes to thicken.
2 Remove from the heat and add half the cheese, half the fat and the egg, mixing thoroughly.
3 Turn out onto an oiled or wetted surface, spread evenly to about ¼-inch (mm) thick, and leave to get completely cold.
4 Use a cutter or small glass to cut the mixture into rounds and arrange them, overlapping slightly, in a shallow, greased ovenproof dish.
5 Sprinkle with the remaining cheese, dot with the fat. Bake at 400°F/200°C (Gas Mark 6) for 10 minutes; or put the gnocchi under a medium grill for 5 minutes, then turn to high to brown the top. Garnish with tomato slices and parsley.

Serve with: Whole onions cooked in a tomato sauce, plus a celery salad.

Wednesday
Sweetcorn Filled Tomatoes

8 large tomatoes
2 tablespoons vegetable oil
1 small onion, chopped
½-1 clove garlic, crushed
2 oz (55g) cooked
  sweetcorn
2 oz (55g) wholemeal
  breadcrumbs
2 oz (55g) sunflower seeds
1 egg, lightly beaten
Seasoning to taste
Parsley to garnish
Parsley sauce to serve (see
  recipe for White Sauce,
  page 153)

1 Cut the tops off the tomatoes and scoop out the flesh with a teaspoon. Drain the cups, then arrange side by side in a lightly greased, ovenproof dish.
2 Heat the oil in a pan and fry the onion with the garlic.
3 When soft, stir in the sweetcorn, the breadcrumbs and sunflower seeds, and mix well. Add a little of the tomato flesh.
4 Bind the mixture with the beaten egg, and season to taste. Divide between the tomato cups, piling high if necessary. Sprinkle with grated cheese.
5 Bake at 350°F/180°C (Gas Mark 4) for 20 minutes, or until cooked. Garnish with parsley. Hand round parsley sauce at the table.

Serve with: Hot wholewheat berries and a mixed green salad with a creamy, protein-rich dressing.

Thursday
Tofu Quiche

½ lb (225g) pastry of your
  choice

For the filling:
6 oz (170g) leeks
2 large eggs
6 oz (170g) tofu, mashed
Seasoning to taste
Pinch of tarragon
Pinch of basil
3 tomatoes, sliced

1 Make up the pastry mix and set aside.
2 Trim, wash and finely chop the leeks. Steam for the minimum time, until just tender, then drain well.
3 Beat the eggs together with the mashed tofu to make a

smooth, creamy mixture. (Use a blender if you have one.) Add seasoning and herbs.
4 Roll out the pastry and use to line a medium-sized flan dish. Bake blind at 400°F/200°C (Gas Mark 6) for 10 minutes.
5 Arrange the leeks in the pastry case, top with tomato slices, and pour on the tofu mixture. Reduce oven temperature to 350°F/180°C (Gas Mark 4) and cook for 30 minutes more, or until firm.

Serve with: Hot parsnip fritters and an endive, chicory and lettuce salad, sprinkled with walnuts.

Friday
Curry Omelette with Rice

6 eggs
1 tablespoon curry powder,
  or to taste
3 tablespoons vegetable oil
4 tablespoons left-over
  risotto, heated through
1 oz (30g) peanuts,
  chopped
1-2 tablespoons mango
  chutney

1 Beat together the eggs and curry powder.
2 Heat half the oil in a frying pan and, when hot, pour in half the egg mixture.
3 Cook gently, lifting the sides of the omelette and tilting the pan so that the liquid can run underneath. Continue cooking until it begins to set.
4 Mix together the warmed risotto, nuts and mango chutney, and spread half the mixture over the omelette. Fold and serve cut into two.
5 Use up the remaining ingredients in the same way.

Serve with: A salad of cauliflower florets, red pepper and cucumber in a creamy tofu dressing. Crisp popadums would go well, too.

Sunday
Pasta Roulade

For the pasta:
10 oz (185g) wholemeal
   flour
Seasoning to taste
3 small eggs, lightly
   beaten

For the filling:
3 oz (85g) Ricotta cheese
3 oz (85g) grated
   Parmesan cheese
3 oz (85g) cooked spinach,
   chopped
Seasoning to taste
Pinch of nutmeg
1-2 oz (30-55g) margarine
   or butter
1 oz (30g) walnuts,
   chopped
*Tomato sauce to serve (see
   page 153)*

1 Sift together the flour and seasoning, then add the beaten eggs to make a fairly firm dough. Knead briefly until smooth. then roll out thinly to make a rectangle.
2 Mix together the Ricotta and Parmesan cheeses, the well-drained chopped spinach, seasoning and nutmeg.
3 Spread the mixture evenly over the dough, leaving a small gap around the edges.
4 Roll up carefully like a Swiss roll, and wrap in a piece of muslin. Tie the ends. Lay the roll in a saucepan.
5 Cover with water, bring to the boil, and then simmer for 20 minutes.
6 When cool enough to handle, unwrap the roll and cut into fairly thick slices. Arrange them in a lightly greased, heat-proof dish and dot with butter. Sprinkle with chopped walnuts.
7 Put under the grill for a few mintues to heat through. Hand round hot tomato sauce for those who want it.

Serve with: A salad of chopped fennel, spring onions, watercress and orange segments.

Saturday
Cashew Nut Roast

3 tablespoons vegetable oil
1 large onion, sliced
4 oz (115g) mushrooms,
   sliced
1 oz (30g) wholemeal flour
⅓ pint (200ml) vegetable
   stock
½ lb (225g) cashew nuts,
   coarsely ground
2 eggs, beaten
Approx. 4 oz (115g)
   wholemeal breadcrumbs
Seasoning to taste
1 teaspoon marjoram
Dried wholemeal
   breadcrumbs

1 Heat the oil in a pan and cook the onion for a short time, until it begins to soften. Add the mushrooms and cook a few minutes more.
2 Sprinkle the flour over the vegetables, stir, and leave on the heat to absorb the oil. Stir in the stock, making sure there are no lumps. Cook until the sauce thickens.
3 Remove pan from the heat and stir in the nuts. Cool briefly, then stir in the two beaten eggs and the breadcrumbs to make a mixture with a soft dropping consistency. Add seasoning and herbs.
4 Lightly oil a small loaf tin and coat with breadcrumbs. Spoon in the cashew nut mixture and smooth the top.
5 Bake at 350°F/180°C (Gas Mark 4) for an hour, or until cooked. Turn carefully onto a warmed serving plate and slice.

Serve with: Roast potatoes, and leeks in a tomato sauce.

Week 9:
Monday
Hoppin' John

2 tablespoons vegetable oil
1 onion, chopped
1 clove garlic, crushed
Fresh parsley
6 oz (170g) black-eye peas,
*   soaked overnight*
6 oz (170g) brown rice
1½ pints (850ml) vegetable
*   stock*
Seasoning to taste
Soya 'bacon' bits
Parsley to garnish

1 Heat the oil in a large pan and fry the onion with the garlic to soften.
2 Add the parsley, drained black-eyed peas and rice. Stir and cook briefly.
3 Pour in the stock, bring to the boil, then simmer for 40-50 minutes, or until the black-eyed peas and rice are tender. Add a little more stock if necessary.
4 Season, and stir in a generous amount of soya 'bacon' bits. Garnish with chopped parsley.

Serve with: As Hoppin' John is a traditional dish from the American Deep South, serve it with other foods from that area — hot corn bread or muffins, lightly steamed greens, or maybe a green salad with apple and pecan nuts.

Tuesday
Nutty Oatmeal Croquettes

2 oz (55g) margarine or
*   butter*
1 large onion, chopped
2 large tomatoes, chopped
1 small apple, peeled,
*   cored and chopped*
Approx. 1½ oz (45g)
*   oatmeal*
Seasoning to taste
Parsley
½ lb (225g) mixed nuts,
*   coarsely chopped*
2 eggs, beaten
Vegetable stock to mix
Approx. 1 oz (30g) dry
*   wholemeal breadcrumbs*

1 Heat the fat and sauté the chopped onion, tomatoes, and apple for 5 minutes or until soft.

2 Stir in the oatmeal, seasoning, parsley and nuts, mixing thoroughly.
3 Cool slightly then add half the beaten egg and enough vegetable stock to make the mixture soft but still able to hold its shape.
4 Divide into croquettes. Dip into the remaining beaten egg and then in the crumbs, coating each one as evenly as possible.
5 Arrange on a baking sheet and cook in the oven, temperature 375°F/190°C (Gas Mark 5), for 15-20 minutes, or until cooked.

Serve with: A tomato, pepper, sweetcorn and raw courgette salad, plus steamed potatoes.

Wednesday
Pot Barley Soup

2 pints (1.1 litres) vegetable
*   stock*
6 oz (170g) pot barley,
*   soaked overnight*
4 oz (115g) grated Cheddar
*   cheese*
1-2 teaspoons mixed herbs
Seasoning to taste
Chopped spring onions to
*   garnish*

1 Bring the vegetable stock to the boil and add the drained barley. Cover the pan and simmer gently for 30-45 minutes, stirring often.
2 When the barley is cooked add the cheese, dried herbs and seasoning. Leave the saucepan on the heat a few minutes longer.
3 Serve, sprinkled with chopped spring onions.

Serve with: Wholegrain crispbreads or bread, and a salad of finely sliced green and red cabbage, carrots, a little raw beetroot, and watercress. Roasted peanuts would add protein.

Thursday
Tofu Omelette with Peppers

10 oz (285g) tofu
5 eggs
Seasoning to taste
Approx. 1 oz (30g)
*   margarine or butter*
1 red pepper, sliced
1 green pepper, sliced
Parsley to garnish

1 Drain the tofu and mash. Lightly whisk the eggs and add to the tofu; season to taste.

2 Melt half of the fat in a frying pan and lightly fry the peppers until they begin to colour. Remove half of them from the pan.

3 Pour half the tofu and egg mixture into the pan and cook gently until the eggs begin to set. Fold the omelette over, divide and serve, or keep warm.

4 Add more fat to the pan if necessary. Add reserved peppers. Pour in the rest of the tofu and egg mixture, and cook in the same way to make two more servings. Garnish with parsley.

Serve with: Fried potato balls, and steamed cabbage with caraway seeds.

Friday
Spinach Cannelloni

½ lb (225g) pasta dough
  or 8 cannelloni tubes
2 lb (1.15 kilos) spinach
2 tablespoons vegetable oil
1 onion, sliced
1 oz (30g) wholemeal flour
Approx. ½ pint (285ml)
  milk
2 oz (55g) sesame seeds
Seasoning to taste
Pinch of nutmeg
2 oz (55g) grated
  Parmesan cheese

1 Roll out the pasta to a thin sheet and cut into 8 rectangles about 5×4 inches (13×10cm) in size.

2 Drop the pasta one piece at a time into boiling salted water and cook for 5 minutes, or until just tender. Remove carefully, pat dry, and lay out on a tea towel.

3 Wash, trim and steam the spinach for 10 minutes, or until cooked. Press out as much moisture as possible, then chop finely. Set aside.

4 Heat the oil in a clean pan and fry the onion to soften. Sprinkle in the flour and cook a minute more, then blend in the milk and bring to the boil, stirring, to make a thick sauce.

5 Add the sesame seeds, seasoning and nutmeg.

6 Stir a little of the sauce into the spinach and divide the mixture between the squares of dough, then roll each one up into a tube. (If using ready-made tubes, simply fill them with the mixture.)

7 Place side by side in a shallow, greased ovenproof dish with the join facing downwards, and cover with the sauce, adding a drop more milk if it seems too thick.

8 Sprinkle with the Parmesan cheese. Bake at 400°F/200°C (Gas Mark 6) for about 30 minutes, or until golden on top.

Serve with: Good with a green salad, maybe including a few cooked beans — red beans look good. French bread could be served for the extra hungry.

Note: This dish is much quicker to prepare with ready-made cannelloni tubes, though most of those on the market are made with refined flour. Some need to be cooked before the filling is inserted — check instructions on the packet.

Saturday
Mushroom Curry

*1 pint (570ml) mild curry
  sauce (see page 154)
1 oz (30g) margarine or
  butter
2 sticks celery, chopped
½ lb (225g) mushrooms,
  thickly sliced
1 large apple, finely
  chopped
Approx. ⅛ pint (70ml)
  natural yogurt
2 oz (55g) walnut pieces
Paprika
Watercress to garnish

1 Heat the curry sauce gently.

2 Meanwhile, melt half the fat in a second pan and fry the celery until it begins to colour.

3 Add the rest of the fat and the mushrooms, and cook just a few minutes more. They should be tender but still hold their shape.

4 Stir the mushrooms into the curry sauce with the apple, the yogurt and walnut pieces. Cook very gently for a minute or two to heat through.

5 Serve sprinkled lightly with paprika and garnished with watercress.

Serve with: A grain dish such as bulgur or millet would be a change from rice, and both have delicate flavours more suited to this curry. Add a chicory salad.

*Make a day in advance and leave overnight for the flavour to develop. Reheat gently.

Sunday
Pancake Pie

½ pint (285ml) pancake
  batter (see page 152)
Vegetable oil for frying

For the filling:
½ lb (225g) small Brussels
  sprouts
½ lb (225g) chestnuts
2 oz (55g) margarine
1 small onion, finely
  chopped
1 teaspoon marjoram, or
  to taste
Seasoning to taste
2 tomatoes, sliced
3 oz (85g) grated Cheddar
  cheese

For the sauce:
½ pint (285ml) white
  sauce
1 oz (30g) wholemeal
  breadcrumbs

1 Make up the batter according to instructions. When ready
  to use, pour a drop of oil into a large, heavy-based frying
  pan, and heat. Add a few spoonfuls of batter; cook gently
  until the pancake begins to brown, then turn and cook the
  other side.
2 Use the rest of the batter in the same way. (You need four
  large pancakes for the pie, so if you have extra batter left,
  either keep it for use another day, or make extra pancakes
  and freeze.)
3 Trim and halve the Brussels sprouts. Steam until just tender.
4 Cut a notch in each of the chestnuts and cook in boiling
  water for 10 minutes, then carefully remove shell and inner
  skin. Cook chestnuts a little longer if necessary; when tender,
  halve them.
5 Melt the margarine in a pan and cook the onion for a few
  minutes, then stir in the Brussels sprouts, chestnuts and
  marjoram, and heat gently. Season to taste.
6 Lay a pancake on a lightly greased baking sheet, top with
  half the vegetable and nut mixture, then another pancake.
7 Arrange the sliced tomatoes on top of the pancake; cover
  with grated cheese and the third pancake.
8 Top this one with the rest of the Brussels sprouts and
  chestnuts, and then the final pancake.
9 Pour the white sauce over the top of the pie. Sprinkle with
  breadcrumbs.
10 Bake at 400°F/200°C (Gas Mark 6) for 5-10 minutes, or until
  the breadcrumbs are browned. Serve at once cut into wedges.

Serve with: An endive, lettuce and chicory salad. Hot
buttered carrots would also go well.

Week 10:
Monday
Cottage Cheese and Pasta Bake

½ lb (225g) wholemeal
  macaroni
1 onion, sliced
1 red pepper, sliced
2 tablespoons vegetable oil
½ lb (225g) cottage cheese
¼ pint (140ml) soured
  cream
1 tablespoon fresh parsley
Seasoning to taste
1 oz (30g) wholemeal
  breadcrumbs
1 oz (30g) walnuts,
  coarsely chopped

1 Bring a saucepan of water to the boil and add the pasta. Cook
  for about 10 minutes until tender. Drain, rinse with cold water,
  and drain again.
2 Heat the oil in a pan, and fry the onion and pepper gently
  for 5 minutes until they soften.
3 Mix together the cottage cheese and soured cream, then stir
  into the macaroni. Add the vegetables, parsley and seasoning.
4 Transfer the mixture to a greased ovenproof dish and top with
  the crumbs and nuts. Bake at 350°F/180°C (Gas Mark 4)
  for 20-30 minutes.

Serve with: A crunchy beansprout, tomato and cucumber
salad.

Tuesday
Savoury Waffles

For the waffles:
½ lb (225g) wholemeal
  flour
½ pint (285ml) milk
2 eggs
4 oz (115g) margarine or
  butter, soft
6 oz (170g) grated Cheddar
  cheese
Vegetable oil

For the topping:
1 oz (30g) margarine or
  butter
1 onion, sliced
1 green pepper, sliced
¾ lb (340g) cooked
  sweetcorn
2 oz (55g) pumpkin seeds
Seasoning to taste
Chives to garnish

1 Put the flour in a bowl and whisk in the milk, eggs and softened fat. Blend well to make a creamy mixture — adjust if necessary.
2 Stir in the finely grated cheese. Set aside.
3 Melt the fat in a pan and fry the onion and pepper for a few minutes to soften. Add the sweetcorn, seeds and seasoning, and heat gently.
4 Heat and oil a waffle iron and pour in the batter to fill two thirds of the iron. Close firmly and cook in the usual way.
5 Use up all the batter mixture in the same way. Serve the waffles topped with some of the vegetable mixture and garnished with chopped chives.

Serve with: Fresh wholemeal baps, plus a salad of celery, beetroot, apple and watercress, with a French dressing.

Wednesday
Soya Stuffed Peppers

4 large peppers, red or
  green
6 oz (170g) cooked soya
  beans
2 tablespoons vegetable oil
1 onion, chopped
2 sticks celery, chopped
Good pinch of chilli
  powder
Seasoning to taste
10 stuffed olives, sliced
2 tomatoes, chopped
1 oz (30g) cashews,
  coarsely chopped

1 Cut a lid off the top of each of the peppers and scoop out the seeds and membrane. Bring a pan of water to the boil, drop in the pepper shells, and cook for about 5 minutes.
2 Drain the shells well, and then arrange them close together in a greased ovenproof dish.
3 Heat the oil in a clean saucepan and fry the onion and celery, until they begin to soften. Stir in the chilli powder, seasoning, olives and the tomatoes.
4 Drain the soya beans and chop coarsely or, if you prefer, grind them to a powder. Add to the other ingredients and use the mixture to stuff the peppers. Sprinkle with the nuts.
5 Bake at 350°F/180°C (Gas Mark 4) for 25 minutes, or until peppers are cooked.

Serve with: Creamy mashed potatoes, and a large mixed salad.

Thursday
Baked Parsley Rice

½ lb (225g) brown rice
1 pint (570ml) water
2 oz (55g) margarine or
  butter
2 eggs, lightly beaten
6 oz (170g) grated Edam
  cheese
4-6 tablespoons chopped
  parsley
1 red pepper, finely
  chopped
Seasoning to taste
2 oz (55g) sunflower seeds

1 Rinse the rice, then put into a pan with the water. Bring to the boil. Cover and simmer for 30-40 minutes, or until tender, adding more water if necessary.
2 Drain the rice and put it into a bowl. Mix in the fat, beaten eggs, grated cheese, parsley, pepper and seasoning.
3 Turn the mixture into a lightly greased ovenproof dish, smooth the top and sprinkle with seeds. Bake at 350°F/180°C (Gas Mark 4) for 30 minutes, or until set.

Serve with: A salad of celery, red peppers and lettuce sprinkled with capers.

Friday
Mushroom Soufflé Flan

½ lb (225g) pastry of your
   choice

For the filling:
4 oz (115g) mushrooms,
   chopped
1½ oz (45g) margarine or
   butter
1 oz (30g) wholemeal flour
⅓ pint (200ml) milk
Seasoning to taste
Pinch of cayenne pepper
1½ oz (45g) grated
   Gruyére cheese
1½ oz (45g) grated
   Emmenthal cheese
3 eggs, separated

1 Make up the pastry mix, and set aside in a cool place.
2 Cook the mushrooms in ½ oz (15g) of the fat until they begin to colour. Drain well and set aside.
3 Melt the remaining fat in a clean pan and sprinkle in the flour. Cook briefly, then pour in the milk and continue cooking until the sauce thickens.
4 Still over a low heat, add the seasoning, cayenne, and then the cheeses, continuing to cook and stir until they melt. Set aside to cool.
5 Roll out the pastry and use to line a medium-sized flan dish that is at least 1½-inches (4cm) deep.
6 Beat the egg yolks into the sauce with the mushrooms. Whisk the egg whites until stiff and fold them into the mixture. Spoon into the flan case.
7 Bake in a pre-heated oven at 375°F/190°C (Gas Mark 5) for 30-40 minutes, or until pastry is cooked and the filling set.

Serve with: A crisp green salad with banana slices and a sprinkling of chopped brazil nuts. Hot muffins.

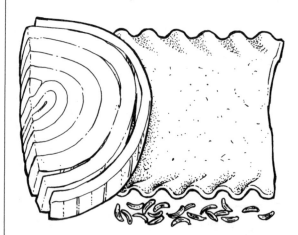

Saturday
Lasagne Lyonnaise

6 oz (170g) wholemeal
   lasagne
2 oz (55g) margarine or
   butter
1½ lb (680g) onions,
   sliced
1 teaspoon caraway seeds,
   crushed
1 oz (30g) wholemeal flour
½ pint (285ml) milk
Seasoning to taste
¼ pint (140ml) single
   cream
4 oz (115g) grated Cheddar
   cheese
2 oz (55g) wholemeal
   breadcrumbs

1 Bring a large pan of water to the boil and add the lasagne sheets one at a time. Cook for 8 minutes, or as long as directed on the packet. Rinse the sheets in cold water, and lay them out on a clean tea towel.
2 Melt the fat in a pan and sauté the onions until they begin to soften. Add the seeds and flour and cook a few minutes more, then stir in the milk and simmer until the sauce thickens. Season to taste.
3 Arrange half the lasagne in the base of a lightly greased, ovenproof dish and cover with the onion sauce. Top with the remaining lasagne.
4 Pour the cream carefully over the dish, then sprinkle with grated cheese and the breadcrumbs.
5 Bake at 375°F/190°C (Gas Mark 5) for 30 minutes.

Serve with: A salad based on raw, finely chopped Brussels sprouts mixed with celery and red pepper, sprinkled with deep-fried soya splits.

Sunday
Sweet and Sour Beans

½ lb (225g) haricot beans,
    soaked overnight
2 tablespoons vegetable oil
1 clove garlic, crushed
1 onion, sliced
1 green pepper, sliced
2 cooking apples, peeled
    and grated
2 oz (55g) sultanas
1 tablespoon red wine
    vinegar
2 tablespoons honey
½ pint (285ml) vegetable
    stock
Seasoning to taste
½ oz (15g) arrowroot
1 tablespoon orange juice

1 Drain the beans, and put in a pan. Cover with fresh water, and boil fast for 10 minutes. Lower the heat and continue cooking gently for 45-60 minutes, or until just tender.
2 Heat the oil in another pan, and fry the garlic with the sliced onion and pepper.
3 Peel and grate the apples and add to the pan with the sultanas, wine vinegar, honey, vegetable stock and seasoning. Stir in the beans.
4 Bring to the boil, then lower the heat and simmer for 10 minutes.
5 Mix the arrowroot into the orange juice and pour into the bean mixture. Bring to the boil, then cook for just a few minutes more. Adjust seasoning if necessary.

Serve with: Brown rice, plus a beansprout and celery salad with a sprinkling of roasted flaked almonds.

Week 11:
Monday
Stuffed Baked Parsnips

4 medium-sized parsnips
2 tablespoons vegetable oil
1 onion, sliced
1 green pepper, sliced
Seasoning to taste
Good squeeze of lemon
    juice
1 teaspoon marjoram
2-3 tablespoons tahini
2 oz (55g) cooked
    chick-peas
1 oz (30g) wholemeal
    breadcrumbs
Parsley to garnish

1 Choose well-shaped parsnips for this recipe. Scrub them, pat dry and prick lightly. Trim off the long ends and stand the parsnips close together in an ovenproof dish.
2 Bake at 375°F/190°C (Gas Mark 5) for about an hour, or until tender.
3 Heat the vegetable oil in a pan and fry the onion and pepper until soft.
4 Halve the parsnips lengthways and scoop out some of the flesh. Chop the flesh coarsely, discarding the woody core, and add to the onion and pepper with seasoning, lemon juice and marjoram.
5 Stir in enough tahini to lightly coat the vegetables, then add the chick-peas (these can be coarsely chopped if you like).
6 Arrange the shell halves in a shallow ovenproof dish. Pile the mixture into the parsnip shells. Sprinkle with breadcrumbs. Return to the oven or pop under the grill until the crumbs are crisp. Garnish with parsley sprigs.

Serve with: A celery, sweetcorn and tomato salad — add cheese dressing or nuts to boost protein, plus a hot grain dish.

Tuesday
Chestnut and Brussels Sprouts Stew

1½ lb (680g) chestnuts
2 onions, sliced
2 sticks celery, sliced
2 tablespoons vegetable oil
1 lb (455g) Brussels
    sprouts
1 lb (455g) tomatoes, or
    tinned equivalent,
    skinned and chopped
Seasoning to taste

1 Make a small notch in the top of each of the chestnuts, then drop them into a saucepan of boiling water. Cook for 10 minutes.
2 Drain the chestnuts and trim the outer shell and inner skin from each one. (As this is easiest to do whilst they are still warm, you may need to use a tea towel to hold them.) If necessary, cook the chestnuts a few minutes longer in fresh water until just soft.
3 Sauté the onions and celery briefly in the vegetable oil.
4 Meanwhile, trim and steam the Brussels sprouts until almost tender. Add them to the onions and celery with the prepared chestnuts. Stir the tomatoes into the other ingredients, seasoning to taste.
5 Simmer gently until the liquid in the tomatoes has thickened to a sauce, and all the ingredients are tender.

Serve with: Mashed or French-fried potatoes. A salad of finely grated raw leeks, tomatoes and mushroom slices, sprinkled with soya 'bacon' bits would make a good accompaniment.

Wednesday
Scone Dough Pizza with Egg Topping

For the dough:
*½ lb (225g) self-raising
wholemeal flour
Salt and pepper
1 teaspoon mixed herbs
2 oz (55g) margarine
Approx. ⅛ pint (70ml)
natural yogurt*

For the topping:
*1 oz (30g) margarine
½ green pepper, finely
chopped
½ onion, finely chopped
4 eggs
2 tablespoons milk
2 tomatoes, chopped
Seasoning to taste*

1 Sift together the flour, seasoning and herbs. Use fingertips to rub the margarine into the flour to make a crumb-like mixture.
2 Add enough yogurt to make a soft dough, kneading it lightly until smooth.
3 Divide the dough into two and roll into circles. Place on greased baking sheets and bake at 400°F/200°C (Gas Mark 6) for about 20 minutes, until cooked.
4 Meanwhile, melt the margarine in a pan and fry the pepper and onion to soften.
5 Whisk together the eggs and milk, and add to the vegetables. Continue cooking over a low heat, stirring continually, until the mixture begins to set. Remove from the heat at once and stir in the tomatoes, seasoning to taste.
6 Spread the egg mixture over the prepared dough. If necessary, return to the oven for literally a few minutes, so that the pizzas are piping hot. Cut in half to serve.

Serve with: A hot vegetable for a change — aubergines with tomato and garlic would go well with this pizza.

Thursday
Brazil Leek Loaf

*3 tablespoons vegetable oil
2 medium-sized leeks,
cleaned and chopped
1 oz (30g) wholemeal flour
¼ pint (140ml) vegetable
stock
6 oz (170g) brazil nuts,
coarsely grated
3 oz (85g) wholemeal
breadcrumbs
1 oz (30g) rolled oats
Seasoning to taste
Good pinch tarragon or
sage
1 egg, lightly beaten
(optional)
2 tomatoes, sliced
Brown gravy to serve (see
page 153)*

1 Heat the vegetable oil in a pan and very lightly sauté the leeks until they begin to soften.
2 Sprinkle in the flour and cook a minute or two more, then add the vegetable stock. Cook gently to thicken, then remove from heat.
3 Add the nuts to the sauce with the breadcrumbs, oats, seasoning and herbs.
4 Stir in the beaten egg, if using, mixing thoroughly. (The loaf will be more crumbly without the egg, but the taste will not be affected.)
5 Turn the mixture into a greased loaf tin and smooth the top. Decorate with slices of tomato.
6 Bake at 350°F/180°C (Gas Mark 4) for 30-40 minutes, or until just set. Hand gravy around at the table.

Serve with: A light grain such as bulgur and maybe a coleslaw of cabbage, carrot and celery, with chopped apricots added.

Friday
'Bacon' Cheese Soufflé

*1 oz (30g) margarine or
butter
1 oz (30g) wholemeal flour
¼ pint (140ml) milk
Seasoning to taste
Good pinch of dry mustard
4 oz (115g) grated mature
Cheddar cheese
4 eggs, separated
1 oz (30g) soya 'bacon' bits*

1 Melt the fat in a saucepan and stir in the flour, cooking briefly.

Off the heat, stir in the milk, then return to heat and cook until the sauce thickens.

2 Add seasoning, mustard, and then the cheese, stirring until it melts. When slightly cooled, add the egg yolks and soya 'bacon' bits.

3 Whisk the egg whites until stiff. Use a metal spoon to fold them into the sauce, then transfer the mixture to a 2-pint soufflé dish.

4 Bake at once in an oven preheated to 375°F/190°C (Gas Mark 5) for 30 minutes if you like a softer centre, 45 minutes for a firmer texture.

Serve with: Crispy potato croquettes, and hot kale in a cream sauce. Fresh watercress would make a good garnish.

Saturday
Fettucine with Tofu

2 tablespoons vegetable oil
1 green pepper, chopped
1 onion, chopped
1 clove garlic, crushed
14 oz (395g) tin tomatoes
6 oz (170g) cooked green
  beans
10 oz (285g) tofu
Seasoning to taste
1 teaspoon basil, or to
  taste
Soya sauce to taste
10 oz (285g) wholemeal
  fettucine
Parsley to garnish

1 Heat the oil in a pan and fry the chopped pepper and onion with the garlic. After 5 minutes, add the tinned tomatoes and cook 5-10 minutes more, until the sauce begins to thicken.

2 Stir in the drained beans; then add the drained and mashed tofu. Season to taste, add basil and soya sauce and continue cooking gently for 10 minutes, stirring occasionally. (Add a drop of cold water if the sauce becomes too thick.)

3 Meanwhile, cook the fettucine in a large pan of boiling water for 10 minutes, or until just tender. Drain well.

4 Tip the fettucine into a warmed serving dish and top with the sauce. Garnish generously with parsley.

Serve with: A salad of red pepper, cucumber, mustard and cress, with roasted sunflower seeds sprinkled on top.

Sunday
Egg and Cheese Pasties

For the pastry:
½ lb (225g) plain
  wholemeal flour
Good pinch of salt
4 oz (115g) margarine
1 egg, beaten
Cold water to mix

For the filling:
1 oz (30g) margarine
2 tablespoons oil
2 onions, sliced
4 oz (115g) grated Cheddar
  cheese
2 hard-boiled eggs, finely
  chopped
Seasoning to taste

1 Sift the flour and salt together into a bowl. Cut the margarine into small pieces with a knife, then use fingertips to rub it into the flour to make a crumb mixture. Stir in the beaten egg.

2 Add enough cold water to make a firm dough and knead it gently for a minute or two. Wrap in clingfilm or a polythene bag and let it stand in the fridge for at least 30 minutes.

3 In a pan, heat together the margarine and oil, then sauté the sliced onions until they soften.

4 Remove the pan from the heat and stir in the grated cheese and finely chopped eggs; season to taste.

5 Roll out the pastry, then cut it into squares about 4-inches (10cm) across. Place one or two teaspoons of the egg and cheese mixture in the centre of each, and fold the pastry to make a triangle. Press the dampened edges together firmly and prick the pastry with a fork.

6 Arrange the pasties on a baking sheet and bake at 400°F/200°C (Gas Mark 6) for 20-30 minutes, or until pastry is cooked. Remove from oven and let the pasties cool slightly before serving.

Serve with: Small potatoes, lightly steamed, plus a chicory and pepper salad sprinkled with cooked peas, walnuts and parsley.

Week 12:
Monday
Lentil and Lemon Soup

½ lb (225g) lentils, soaked
  overnight
1¾ pints (1 litre) vegetable
  stock or water
Grated peel and juice of 1
  lemon
1 large onion, sliced
Chopped parsley
Seasoning to taste
¼ pint (140ml) soured
  cream
Garlic croûtons to garnish

1 Drain the lentils and put into a pan with the vegetable stock, juice and some grated peel of the lemon, the onion and parsley.
2 Bring to the boil, then cover the pan and simmer for 30 minutes, or until the lentils are cooked, adding more liquid if necessary.
3 Purée in a blender, and return to the pan. Season to taste. Add the soured cream. Heat very gently for literally a minute or two. Adjust seasoning.
4 Sprinkle with garlic-flavoured croûtons.

Serve with: Slices of granary bread spread with nut butter, plus a mushroom, endive and lettuce salad with chopped pear.

Tuesday
Brazilian Brussels Sprouts

1 lb (455g) Brussels
  sprouts
3 oz (85g) margarine or
  butter
1 onion, sliced
1 red pepper, sliced
2 sticks celery, chopped
1 large leek, chopped
¼ pint (140ml) vegetable
  stock
Seasoning to taste
1 teaspoon marjoram
½ oz (15g) wholemeal
  flour
4 oz (115g) Brazil nuts,
  chopped
2 oz (55g) wholemeal
  breadcrumbs

1 Trim the Brussels sprouts, cut a cross in the base of each one, and boil or steam for 10 minutes or until tender. Drain well.
2 Meanwhile, melt 2 oz (55g) of the fat in a pan and fry the onion and pepper, celery and leek, stirring frequently. Cook until they all begin to soften. Add the Brussels sprouts.
3 Mix the stock, seasoning and marjoram with the flour. Pour over the vegetables and cook gently to make a thick sauce, adding a drop more liquid if necessary.
4 Melt the remaining fat and fry the Brazil nuts gently, stirring frequently, until they colour. Stir in the crumbs and cook for a minute or two.
5 Transfer the vegetables to a warmed serving dish and top with the nut and crumb mixture.

Serve with: Jacket potatoes, and maybe a carrot purée sprinkled with chives.

Wednesday
Soya Noodles with Chinese-Style Vegetables

For the noodles:
½ lb (225g) soya flour
1 egg, beaten
Cold water to mix

For the sauce:
2 tablespoons vegetable oil
1 large carrot, finely
  chopped
1 onion, finely chopped
2 sticks celery, finely
  chopped
4 oz (115g) beansprouts
½ oz (15g) wholemeal
  flour
Cold water to mix
1 tablespoon soya sauce
Pinch of raw cane sugar
2 oz (55g) almonds

1 Sift the flour into a bowl, add the beaten egg and mix well. Then stir in enough water to make a dough and set aside in a cool place for 30 minutes.
2 Roll out the dough as thin as possible, then shape into a sausage. Use a very sharp knife to cut into fine slices which, when unwrapped, make noodles.
3 To make the sauce, heat the oil in a large pan and lightly fry the carrot, onion and celery.
4 Stir in the beansprouts.
5 Mix the flour with a little cold water, soya sauce and sugar, then pour over the vegetables. Heat gently, stirring until a sauce is formed, adding more water if necessary.
6 Drop the noodles into a pan of boiling water and cook for 5 minutes only. Drain well. Transfer to a warmed serving dish

and top with the sauce. Sprinkle with nuts.

Serve with: A salad of raw or very lightly cooked Brussels sprouts, grated and mixed with celery and tomatoes.

Thursday
'Sausage' Quiche

*½ lb (225g) pastry of your
    choice*

For the filling:
*1 small tin soya 'sausages'
2 oz (55g) Gruyère cheese,
    thinly sliced
2 eggs
¼ pint (140ml) creamy
    milk
Seasoning to taste*

1 Make up the pastry mix and set aside in a cool place.
2 Roll out the pastry to line a medium-sized flan dish.
3 Slice the 'sausages' and arrange them over the base of the flan. Top with the cheese slices.
4 Beat together the eggs, milk and seasoning, and pour over the cheese.
5 Bake at 400°F/200°C (Gas Mark 6) for 30 minutes, or until the pastry is cooked and the filling is well risen.

Serve with: A red cabbage and cucumber coleslaw sprinkled with peanuts. For the extra hungry, serve some steamed parsley potatoes.

Friday
Fried Ravioli with Lentil Filling

*½ lb (225g) wholemeal
    pasta dough (see page
    152)*

For the filling:
*1 tablespoon vegetable oil
½ small onion, sliced
4 oz (115g) split red lentils
¼-½ teaspoon yeast
    extract
1 teaspoon oregano
Seasoning to taste
Vegetable oil for frying
Parsley to garnish*

1 Split the dough into two pieces and roll into oblongs, making the dough as thin as possible. Mark one half into squares about 2-inches (5cm) across.
2 Heat the vegetable oil in a saucepan and fry the onion until it softens. Add the lentils and stir, then just cover with water, bring to the boil, and simmer until very soft. (Check the water and add more if necessary.)
3 Mash to a fairly dry purée and stir in the yeast extract, oregano and seasoning to taste.
4 Drop a little of the filling from a teaspoon into the centre of each of the marked squares. Dampen the lines with water. Place the second sheet over the top and press down lightly.
5 Use a pastry cutter, preferably with serrated edge, to cut into squares, and press the edges to seal. Leave the ravioli on a lightly floured surface, covered with a damp cloth, for 30 minutes.
6 Heat a good quantity of vegetable oil and drop the ravioli, a few at a time, into the pan. Cook steadily for just a few minutes, until crisp and golden. Drain well on paper towels and keep warm whilst cooking the rest in the same way. Garnish with fresh parsley.

Serve with: A salad of leeks, tomatoes and mushrooms. Wholemeal bread could also be served.

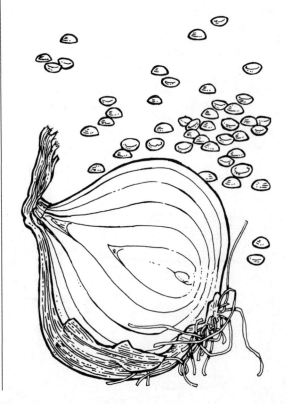

Saturday
Leek and Egg Roulade

For the roulade:
2 oz (55g) margarine or
 butter
2 oz (55g) wholemeal flour
½ pint (285ml) milk
1 teaspoon thyme
2 eggs, separated
Seasoning to taste

For the filling:
2 tablespoons vegetable oil
2 large leeks, trimmed and
 sliced
4 hard-boiled eggs,
 chopped
Seasoning to taste
Tomato slices to garnish

1 Melt the fat in a pan. Sprinkle in the flour and cook gently
 for a few minutes. Remove from the heat and stir in the milk,
 then continue cooking and stirring until the sauce thickens.
2 Add the thyme. Cool slightly, then beat in the egg yolks and
 seasoning.
3 Whisk the egg whites until stiff and fold them carefully into
 the first mixture. Spoon into a greased Swiss-roll tin, level
 the top, and bake at 400°F/200°C (Gas Mark 6) for 20 minutes
 or until firm to touch.
4 Meanwhile, heat the oil in a pan and cook the leeks gently
 until soft, adding a little water if necessary.
5 Drain any excess liquid from the leeks and mix with the
 chopped eggs, seasoning well.
6 Cool the roulade for a few minutes then turn out carefully
 onto a sheet of greaseproof paper. Trim the edges if necessary.
 Spread with the leek and egg mixture and roll up loosely,
 like a Swiss roll. Serve at once or reheat in the oven for 10
 minutes if necessary. Garnish with tomato slices.

Serve with: Jacket potatoes, and a simple green salad with
a tofu or nut dressing.

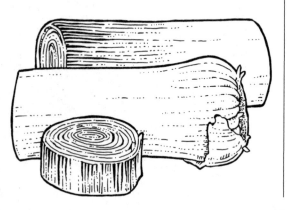

Sunday
Winter Vegetable Casserole

1 large onion
1 large carrot
1 large turnip
1 large swede
1 large potato
2 large leeks
2 sticks celery
2 large tomatoes
Approx. ½ pint (285ml)
 vegetable stock
Seasoning to taste
1-2 teaspoons mixed herbs
2-3 tablespoons tahini
2 oz (55g) cashew pieces
Watercress to garnish

1 Peel, clean and slice all the vegetables. Arrange in alternate
 layers in an ovenproof dish.
2 Heat up the stock and add seasoning, herbs and tahini so
 that it is creamy.
3 Pour the stock over the vegetables, cover, and cook at
 350°F/180°C (Gas mark 4) for about an hour, or until the
 vegetables are cooked but still firm. Add more stock if
 necessary.
4 Sprinkle with the nuts and garnish generously with watercress.

Serve with: Hot wholewheat berries and a green side salad.

Week 13:
Monday
'Meaty' Macaroni Bake

6 oz (170g) wholemeal
 macaroni
2 tablespoons vegetable oil
2 onions, sliced
5 oz (140g) soya 'minced
 meat', hydrated in water
2 large tomatoes, coarsely
 chopped
2 tablespoons tomato
 purée
1 teaspoon oregano
Seasoning to taste
¼ pint (140ml) vegetable
 stock
1 teaspoon yeast extract
3 oz (85g) grated Cheddar
 cheese

1 Cook the pasta in plenty of boiling water for 10 minutes, or until just tender, then rinse through with cold water and set aside.
2 Heat the oil in a frying pan and sauté the onions for 5 minutes. Add the drained 'minced meat' and cook a little longer, stirring frequently.
3 Stir in the tomatoes, the tomato purée, oregano and seasoning. Add the stock in which you have first dissolved the yeast extract. Add the prepared pasta.
4 Transfer the well-mixed ingredients to a casserole and sprinkle with the cheese. Bake at 350°F/180°C (Gas Mark 4) for 15 minutes, or until the cheese has completely melted and begins to brown.

Serve with: Steamed leeks or finely shredded greens.

Tuesday
Creamy Leek Pizza

½ lb (225g) pizza dough
  of your choice

For the topping:
1 lb (455g) leeks
1 oz (30g) margarine
1 oz (30g) wholemeal flour
⅓ pint (200ml) milk
3 oz (85g) curd cheese,
  crumbled
Seasoning to taste
1 oz (30g) walnuts,
  coarsely chopped
Fresh chopped sage to
  garnish

1 Make up dough according to instructions. Divide into two and roll out into circles. Place on baking sheets and bake at 400°F/200°C (Gas Mark 6) for 15 minutes.
2 Meanwhile, trim the leeks, slit lengthways and wash them under running water. Cut into slices and steam until just tender.
3 In a separate pan, melt the margarine and add the flour, cooking until it begins to colour. Pour in the milk and continue cooking, stirring continually, until the sauce thickens.
4 Add the crumbled cheese and stir to make the sauce thick and creamy, then combine with the leeks. Season to taste.
5 Spread the leek mixture over the pizza bases, sprinkle with the nuts, and return to the oven for 5 minutes, or until the dough is cooked.
6 Garnish with sage and slice to serve.

Serve with: A salad of carrot, beansprouts and cress.

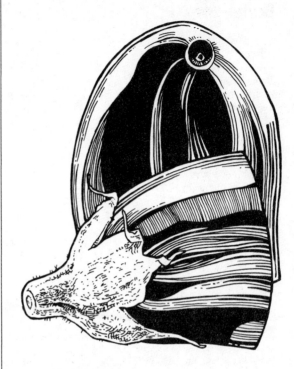

Wednesday
Aubergine Soufflé

1 large aubergine, peeled
  and cubed
1½ oz (45g) wholemeal
  breadcrumbs
½ oz (15g) margarine or
  butter
3 egg yolks
2 oz (55g) grated
  Parmesan cheese
Seasoning to taste
Good pinch of chervil and
  marjoram
4 egg whites

1 Steam the aubergine until just tender, then drain well and mash, push through a sieve or liquidize to make a purée.
2 Add the breadcrumbs, margarine, egg yolks, cheese, seasoning and herbs, mixing well.
3 Whisk the egg whites until stiff, then use a metal spoon to fold them into the aubergine mixture. Spoon into a greased, 2-pint soufflé dish.
4 Bake at once in an oven preheated to 375°F/190°C (Gas Mark 5) for 30-40 minutes, or until puffed up and golden.

Serve with: Hot minted peas, and creamed potatoes.

Thursday
Barley Stew

2 oz (55g) margarine or
   butter
1 onion, chopped
1 stick celery, chopped
1 carrot, diced
1 leek, sliced
14 oz (395g) tin tomatoes
½ small green cabbage,
   shredded
4 oz (115g) pot barley,
   soaked overnight
2 oz (55g) split peas,
   soaked overnight
1 teaspoon yeast extract
1 teaspoon basil
Seasoning to taste
Fresh parsley, chopped

1 Melt the fat in a saucepan and add the onion, celery, carrot
  and leek. Fry the vegetables gently for 10 minutes, stirring
  occasionally.
2 Add the tomatoes and shredded cabbage together with the
  drained barley and split peas. Cover with water. Stir in the
  yeast extract, basil and seasoning.
3 Bring to the boil, then cover the pan and simmer for about
  45 minutes, or until the barley and peas are tender. Add more
  water as necessary.
4 Stir in the chopped parsley.

Serve with: Jacket potatoes, and a crisp green salad with a
protein-rich dressing.

Friday
Two-Rice Risotto

3 tablespoons vegetable oil
1 small onion, finely
   chopped
1 clove garlic, crushed
4 oz (115g) brown rice
4 oz (115g) wild rice
1 pint (570ml) vegetable
   stock
4 oz (115g) spinach, cooked
Seasoning to taste
2 oz (55g) pine nuts

1 Heat half the oil in a pan. Add the onion and crushed garlic,
  and cook gently for 5 minutes.
2 Add the rice, stir, and cook a few minutes more.

3 Pour in the stock, and bring to the boil. Cover the pan and
  simmer for 30 minutes.
4 Add the finely chopped spinach and seasoning and cook for
  10 minutes more, or until the rice is tender.
5 Meanwhile, heat the remaining oil and lightly fry the pine
  nuts until gold in colour.
6 If necessary, drain excess water from the rice mixture. Stir
  in the nuts and any oil left in the pan.

Serve with: A tomato, onion and green bean salad with
crumbled tofu, in a French dressing.

Note: Wild rice is expensive and not always easy to find in
the shops. If you prefer, use white rice, a different grain —
or just double the amount of brown rice.

Saturday
Refried Bean Enchiladas

For the refried beans:
6 oz (170g) kidney beans,
   soaked overnight
2 tablespoons vegetable oil
1 large onion, chopped
1 clove garlic, crushed
2 tablespoons tomato
   purée
½-1 teaspoon chilli powder
1 teaspoon parsley
1 teaspoon oregano
Seasoning to taste

For the tortillas:
½ lb (225g) maize meal
Salt
Approx. ½ pint (285ml)
   warm water
Vegetable oil for frying

For the topping:
¼ pint (140ml) soured
   cream

1 Drain the kidney beans and put into a pan. Cover with fresh
  water and bring to the boil. Continue boiling briskly for 10
  minutes, then lower the heat and simmer until the beans are
  soft enough to mash. When cool, drain and purée with a
  wooden spoon.
2 Make the tortillas. In a bowl sift together the maize meal and
  salt, then gradually add enough water to make a dough. Knead
  lightly, then roll out and cut 8-10 circles of 6-inches (15cm)
  in diameter.
3 Heat a little oil in a heavy-based pan and cook the tortillas
  one at a time for just a minute or two on each side, so that
  they begin to colour. Drain on paper towels and set aside.
4 In another pan heat the 2 tablespoons of oil and fry the onion

with the garlic. When the onion begins to soften, stir in the tomato purée, chilli powder, herbs and seasoning along with the mashed beans. Mix well — if too dry, add a little more tomato purée or some water. Allow to cool slightly.

5 Fill each tortilla with some of the refried bean mixture, roll up like a pancake, and place side by side in a shallow ovenproof dish.

6 Spoon the soured cream over the top and bake at 350°F/180°C (Gas Mark 4) for 15 minutes.

Serve with: A crisp green salad that includes slices of raw avocado.

Sunday
Tofu Spinach Lasagne

1 oz (30g) margarine or
*   butter*
1 tablespoon vegetable oil
1 onion, sliced
1 clove garlic, crushed
3 sticks celery, finely
*   chopped*
1 lb (455g) spinach,
*   washed and shredded*
6 oz (170g) wholemeal
*   lasagne*
10 oz (285g) tofu
2-3 tablespoons water
Seasoning to taste

1 Melt the fat together with the oil in a pan. Add the onion, garlic and celery, and cook for a few minutes, stirring occasionally, to soften.

2 Add the spinach and continue cooking until all the ingredients are tender. Mix well.

3 Meanwhile, bring a large pan of water to the boil and drop in the sheets of lasagne one at a time. Cook for 8 minutes, or as indicated on the packet, then drain and rinse with cold water.

4 Arrange some of the lasagne in the base of a lightly greased ovenproof dish, and top with some of the spinach mixture. Repeat to use up all the ingredients.

5 Mash or blend together the tofu, water and seasoning to make a thick sauce. Pour over the prepared lasagne.

6 Bake at 375°F/190°C (Gas Mark 5) for 30 minutes.

Serve with: A beetroot, onion and cucumber salad sprinkled with soya 'bacon' bits.

Meal for Christmas Day
Chestnut and Brussels Loaf

2 oz (55g) margarine or
*   butter*
1 onion, sliced
4 oz (115g) mushrooms,
*   chopped small*
½ lb (225g) Brussels
*   sprouts*
½ lb (225g) cooked
*   chestnuts*
4 oz (115g) peanuts,
*   chopped*
2 eggs, beaten
Pinch of nutmeg
Seasoning to taste
Parsley to garnish

1 Melt the fat in a pan and lightly sauté the onion until it begins to colour.

2 Add the mushrooms to the pan. Cook for just a few minutes to soften.

3 Meanwhile, trim and steam the Brussels sprouts until cooked but not mushy. Chop coarsely.

4 Peel and mash the chestnuts.

5 Stir together the contents of the pan, the Brussels sprouts, chestnuts and peanuts, mixing well. Add the beaten eggs, a good pinch of nutmeg and seasoning.

6 Spoon the mixture into a small loaf tin, press down and smooth the top. Bake at 350°F/180°C (Gas Mark 4) for 45 minutes, or until set but not too dry.

Serve with: Start the meal with something crisp and fresh such as melon, maybe shaped into balls and mixed with orange segments. Serve the Chestnut and Brussels Loaf with a sauce such as cheese or tomato (cranberry sauce would go well, too). Accompany it with roast or jacket potatoes, buttered carrots and a salad such as one made up of fennel, tomatoes and sweetcorn on an endive base. Honey Ice Cream with Ginger would go well with Christmas Pudding — or make an alternative to the pudding for those who prefer something lighter. Mince tarts, nuts and fresh fruits go without saying.

And finally an extra recipe:

For Leap Year Day
Smoked Tofu with Peppers

2 tablespoons vegetable oil
1 small yellow pepper,
  sliced
1 small red pepper, sliced
1 onion, sliced
4 oz (115g) mushrooms,
  chopped
8 oz (225g) smoked tofu
4 oz (115g) cooked peas
Seasoning to taste

1 Heat the oil in a pan and gently fry the sliced peppers with the onion until just beginning to soften.
2 Add the mushrooms and cook a few minutes more.
3 Drain the tofu, then cut into strips and stir into the other ingredients. Raise the heat slightly so that the tofu browns. Stir the mixture frequently.
4 Add the peas and leave the pan on the heat just long enough to heat them through. Season well before serving.

Serve with: A grain dish such as rice or bulgur. Or combine any left-overs to make a mixed grain base. Add a green salad.

5.

BASIC RECIPES

Shortcrust Pastry

*½ lb (225g) wholemeal
   flour**
Pinch of sea salt
*4 oz (115g) margarine or
   butter*
2-3 tablespoons cold water

1 Sift the flour and salt together into a bowl.
2 Use fingertips to rub in the fat to make a mixture like fine breadcrumbs.
3 Pour in just enough water to bind to a firm dough and knead briefly. If it seems dry, add a drop more water.
4 Wrap in clingfilm or a polythene bag and chill for 30 minutes before rolling out and using as required.

*If preferred, use half plain, wholemeal flour, half self-raising.

Making up extra
The above quantity is sufficient for one large flan. As pastry making takes a little time, it is worth making up extra and keeping it for instant use when next needed. To do this, either rub the fat into the flour and store the mixture in an airtight container in the fridge, or continue to the stage where water is added and then freeze the dough.

Baking blind
A number of recipes call for the pastry to be baked blind before the filling is added. To do this with pastry made from refined white flour it is normal to line the flan case with greaseproof paper or silver foil, fill with beans or rice, then bake. However, although there is no reason why you shouldn't use this method, wholemeal pastry needs only to be pricked with a fork before being put into the oven.

Variations
For savoury pastry add any of the following: fresh or dried herbs to taste; 2 oz (55g) sesame or chopped sunflower seeds;
2-3 oz (55-85g) finely grated Cheddar cheese; 4 oz (115g) cottage cheese (use less liquid); 1 egg yolk (use less liquid).
   For sweet pastry add 1 oz (30g) raw cane sugar. You could also use fruit juice instead of water.

Flaky Pastry

*½ lb (225g) wholemeal
   flour*
Pinch of sea salt
*2 teaspoons baking
   powder*
*6 oz (175g) margarine or
   butter*
Cold water to mix

1 Sift the flour, salt and baking powder together into a bowl.
2 Divide the fat into three portions and rub one of them into the flour, then add enough water to make a soft dough.
3 On a floured board, roll the dough into an oblong shape.
4 Flake another portion of the fat onto two-thirds of the dough, leaving the bottom third without fat.
5 Fold the bottom of the pastry up, and the top down to make an 'envelope' of the dough, then seal the open edges by pressing with a rolling pin.
6 Give the pastry a half-turn, re-roll, then use the last portion of the fat in the same way.
7 Turn, and roll out the pastry again, and if it is still firm to handle, repeat turning, rolling and folding once more. (If it is sticky, leave in the fridge for a while before the final rolling out.)
8 Return the pastry to the fridge again as cold pastry is easier to handle, and will also rise better.
9 Roll out and use as required.

Making up extra
See note re shortcrust pastry.

Basic Recipes

Homemade Pasta

12 oz (340g) wholemeal
flour
Pinch of sea salt
2 eggs
3 tablespoons olive oil
Approx. 2 tablespoons cold
water

1 Sift the flour and salt together into a bowl.
2 Whisk together the eggs and oil and add to the flour with
enough cold water to make a smooth, shiny dough. Knead
briefly.
3 Wrap in clingfilm or a polythene bag, and leave to stand in
the cool for a short time.
4 On a floured board roll out the dough, then cut into required
shapes and use as described in recipe.

Pasta shapes
Ravioli — Roll out into two large, thin, oblong sheets. Mark
one into squares, put some of the filling into the centre of each,
dampen the lines. Cover with the second sheet of dough, and
press down along the lines before cutting into squares. Although
this is the traditional way of making ravioli, pastry made with
wholemeal flour is more crumbly than that made with the more
glutinous refined flour, so it may be easier to use four smaller
sheets, or even to cut into individual squares before adding
the filling.

Cannelloni — Roll the dough into rectangles about 5×4 inches
(13×10cm) and cook in boiling water before adding filling. Then
roll up, place in a greased ovenproof dish, cover with a sauce
and bake briefly in the oven.

Tagliatelle — Roll out the dough into large, very thin rectangles,
flour lightly, roll up loosely into a sausage shape. Cut with a
very sharp knife into ¼-inch (6mm) strips. Unroll and use as
required.

Noodles — These are like tagliatelle, only even thinner!

Lasagne — Roll out the dough and cut into pieces about 2×8
inches (5×20cm). Cook before using layered with the filling
of your choice.

Variations
Green pasta is made by adding approx. 2 oz (55g) puréed and
well-drained spinach to the dough at the same time as the eggs.
Mix very well, then proceed as usual. Make a higher protein
pasta by substituting 2 oz (55g) wheatgerm for flour. Pasta can
also be made without eggs, though it will be heavier and less
easy to handle, so is therefore more suitable for larger shapes
such as lasagne.

Pancake Batter (1)

4 oz (115g) wholemeal
flour
Pinch of sea salt
1-2 eggs
Approx. ½ pint (285ml) (or
half milk, half water)

1 Sift the flour and salt into a bowl.
2 Whisk the egg(s) and stir into the flour with the milk, making
sure the mixture is smooth and free of lumps.
3 Whisk well to make a smooth, creamy batter.
4 Leave in the fridge for half an hour, then whisk again before
using. The batter should be the consistency of thin cream,
so add more milk if it seems too thick.

Pancake Batter (2)

4 oz (115g) wholemeal
flour
2 oz (55g) soya flour
1 teaspoon baking powder
½ pint (285ml) water

1 Sift together all the dry ingredients.
2 Gradually stir in the water, then beat well to lighten.
3 Proceed as above.

Basic Pizza Dough

½ oz (15g) fresh yeast or
¼ oz (7g) dried yeast
⅛ pint (70ml) warm water
½ lb (225g) wholemeal
flour
Pinch of sea salt
2 tablespoons olive oil
Approx. 2 tablespoons
milk

1 Crumble the yeast into a bowl and mix well with the warm
water.
2 Sift together the flour and salt into a warmed bowl. Make
a well in the centre, pour in the yeast and stir.
3 Add the oil and enough milk to make a smooth but firm
dough. Knead for 5 minutes.
4 Place in a clean, floured bowl. Cover with a damp cloth and
leave in a warm spot for about an hour, or until doubled in size.
5 Knead the dough briefly again, then divide into two or four
pieces. Roll out on a floured board to make circles, then
transfer them to a lightly greased baking sheet and proceed
as recipe.

Note: Makes 2 medium-sized or 4 small pizzas.

Crispy Pizza Dough

½ lb (225g) wholemeal
   flour
¼ pint (140ml) warm
   water
½ oz (15g) fresh yeast or
   ¼ oz (7g) dried yeast
1 tablespoon olive oil

1 Sift the flour into a bowl.
2 Add the warm water to the crumbled yeast and mix well, then set aside until the mixture begins to bubble.
3 Add the oil to the yeast, then stir carefully into the flour.
4 Knead for 5 minutes to make a soft, elastic dough.
5 Divide dough into two or four pieces and roll out into circles.
6 Arrange on lightly greased baking sheet and pre-bake for 5 minutes at 400°F/200°C (Gas Mark 6), then add topping and cook approx. 15 minutes more.

Note: Makes 2 medium-sized or 4 small pizzas.

Brown Gravy

2 tablespoons vegetable oil
1 small onion, finely
   chopped
1 oz (30g) wholemeal flour
Good pinch dried thyme or
   1 bay leaf
¾ pint (425ml) vegetable
   stock
Seasoning to taste

1 Heat the vegetable oil in a pan and fry the onion until it begins to colour.
2 Add the flour, stir, and cook briefly.
3 Add the herbs, then the vegetable stock. Bring gently to the boil, stirring frequently, then lower the heat and simmer for 10 minutes.
4 Strain, season to taste, and serve at once.

Variations
For flavouring you can add yeast extract, or soya sauce or try using different herbs. A small glassful of red wine can be added.

White Sauce

1 oz (30g) margarine or
   butter or 2 tablespoons
   vegetable oil
1 oz (30g) wholemeal flour
½ pint (285ml) milk
   (cow's, goat's or soya)
Pinch of ground mace or
   nutmeg
Seasoning to taste

1 Melt the fat or heat the oil in a pan. Sprinkle in the flour, stir, and cook gently for a few minutes.
2 Gradually pour in the milk, stirring continually so that the sauce is smooth.
3 Bring to the boil, lower the heat and simmer for 5-10 minutes.
4 Add spices and seasoning and serve.

Variations
This basic sauce can be adapted to make a number of other sauces. Add 2-3 oz (55-85g) grated Cheddar cheese, or chopped hard-boiled egg. Lightly cooked vegetables such as onion, leeks, and mushrooms go well. Flavour with fresh or dried herbs such as parsley.

Tomato Sauce

2 tablespoons vegetable oil
1 small onion, chopped
1 clove garlic, crushed
¼ oz (7g) wholemeal flour
¼ pint (140ml) water
1 lb (455g) tomatoes,
   peeled and chopped
Chopped parsley
2 tablespoons tomato
   purée
Seasoning to taste

1 Heat the oil in a pan and gently cook the onion and the garlic until they soften and begin to colour.
2 Stir in the flour and cook briefly.
3 Add the water, tomatoes, parsley and tomato purée. Bring the mixture to the boil, then lower the heat and simmer for 20-30 minutes.
4 Sieve or purée to make a smooth sauce, and adjust consistency. Serve at once.

Variations
Any herbs can be used in this sauce. Try finely chopped leeks instead of onion. Tinned tomatoes can replace fresh.

Basic Recipes

Curry Sauce (English)

2 tablespoons vegetable oil
1 onion, finely chopped
1 apple, chopped
1-2 tablespoons curry
powder
2 oz (55g) wholemeal flour
1 pint (570ml) vegetable
stock or water
1-2 tablespoons tomato
purée
1 tablespoon lemon juice
1 teaspoon raw cane sugar
Seasoning to taste

1 Heat the oil in a pan and sauté the finely chopped onion together with the apple.
2 Add the curry powder and flour, stir and cook a few minutes more.
3 Pour in the liquid, add the tomato purée, lemon juice and sugar.
4 Bring to the boil, then lower the heat and simmer, stirring occasionally, for 20-30 minutes.

Note: Curry sauce improves in flavour if made a day in advance.

Curry Sauce (Indian)

3 tablespoons ghee
1 clove garlic, finely
chopped
1 large onion, finely
chopped
2 teaspoons ground
coriander
2 teaspoons ground cumin
1 teaspoon turmeric
powder
Pinch of clove powder
2 bay leaves
⅓ pint (200ml) water
4 tablespoons coconut milk
Garam masala
Seasoning to taste

1 Melt the ghee in a pan. Sauté the garlic and onion for 5 minutes.
2 Add the spices and cook for a few minutes more, stirring continually.
3 Add the bay leaves, water and coconut milk. Bring to the boil, then lower the heat, cover the pan, and simmer for 30 minutes. The resulting sauce should be quite thick, so if it is too watery, cook a little longer without the lid. Remove the bay leaves.
4 Adjust flavouring with garam masala and seasoning. Add chosen ingredients and follow the recipe.

Note: Curry sauce improves in flavour if made a day in advance.

All the above sauces can be thinned or thickened to suit a particular recipe.

INDEX

Index

Index

Of further interest . . .

The Very Best of Vegetarian Cooking

Edited by
Janet Hunt

Enjoy the delights of vegetarian cooking with this lavishly illustrated compilation of recipes edited by Janet Hunt. Here are ideas for eating out of doors in the summer, treats to warm you up in the winter, and delicious desserts for all year round.

It is a book for every day as well as special occasions. Whether you want a new look for family favourites, need some quick and easy recipe ideas, or want something with a more international flavour, you will find it in this imaginative collection. The easy-to-follow style is ideal whether you are new to the kitchen or an experienced cook.